Internet Child Abuse

Current Research and Policy

Edited by
Julia Davidson and Petter Gottschalk

Routledge
Taylor & Francis Group

a GlassHouse book

First published 2011
by Routledge
2 Park Square, Milton Park, Abingdon, Oxfordshire OX14 4RN

Simultaneously published in the USA and Canada
by Routledge
711 Third Avenue, New York, NY 10017

A GlassHouse book

Routledge is an imprint of the Taylor & Francis Group, an informa business

First issued in paperback 2011

Typeset in Times New Roman by
Taylor & Francis Books

British Library Cataloguing in Publication Data
A catalogue record for this book is available from the British Library
Library of Congress Cataloguing in Publication Data
  Internet child abuse : current research and policy /
  edited by Julia Davidson and Petter Gottschalk.
    p. cm.
  ISBN 978-0-415-55980-5
  1. Child sexual abuse–Prevention. 2. Child sexual abuse–Psychological
aspects. 3. Online sexual predators–Psychology. 4. Child molesters–
Psychology. 5. Child pornography–Law and legislation. 6. Internet and children.
I. Davidson, Julia C. II. Gottschalk, Petter, 1950-
  K5189.I59 2010
  364.15'36–dc22
                                                              2010002180

ISBN13: 978-0-415-55980-5 (hbk)
ISBN13: 978-0-415-69780-4 (pbk)
ISBN13: 978-0-203-84743-5 (ebk)

Contents

Editors' Note

This book has sought to avoid the use of the word 'paedophile'; the term 'sex offender' is used as an alternative. The term paedophile refers to those who have a sexual attraction to only pre-pubescent children; the term has become a popular label that includes all types of child sexual abuse.

Contributors

John Carr is one of the world's leading authorities on young people's use of the new online digital technologies. He is Secretary of the UK's Children's Charities' Coalition on Internet Safety and, among others, has acted as an adviser to the UK Government, the European Union (EU) and the International Telecommunication Union.

Julia Davidson is Professor of Criminology and is Director of Research in Criminology at Kingston University. She is also Co-Director of the newly formed Centre for Abuse & Trauma Studies (with Royal Holloway University of London). Professor Davidson has conducted a considerable amount of research in the criminal justice area and has a PhD in Social Policy from the London School of Economics and Political Science. She has extensive experience of applied policy and practice research and has directed work with young victims, serious violent and sexual offenders, criminal justice practitioners and sentencers. Professor Davidson has published widely in the abuse area and has recently focused upon Internet abuse. Professor Davidson provides regular expert advice on criminal justice issues to the media and has worked extensively with the BBC and ITN News in the UK.

Petter Gottschalk is Professor of Information Systems and Knowledge Management in the Norwegian School of Management. He teaches Knowledge Management in Law Enforcement and Organized Crime in the Norwegian Police University College. Oxford University Press published the book *Knowledge Management in Policing and Law Enforcement* by Dr Dean and Dr Gottschalk in 2007. Professor Gottschalk's book *Entrepreneurship and Organized Crime – Entrepreneurs in Illegal Business* was published by Edward Elgar Publishing in 2009, and his book *Policing Organized Crime: Intelligence Strategy Implementation* was published by Taylor & Francis in 2010. Dr Gottschalk has been managing director of several business enterprises including ABB Data Cables and the Norwegian Computing Centre.

Zoe Hilton has worked in a range of roles in the voluntary sector including working on child participation projects and with vulnerable and excluded children. Zoe was the National Society for the Prevention of Cruelty to Children's (NSPCC's) National Policy Adviser for Child Protection with responsibility for sexual abuse and exploitation (including the Internet and trafficking), before recently moving to the Child Exploitation and Online Protection Centre (CEOP) to take up the post of Head of Safeguarding and Child Protection.

Elena Martellozzo is a Lecturer in Criminology at Middlesex University. Elena's primary research interests lie at the intersection between cybercrime, child abuse and internet safety. Elena has extensive experience of applied research within the Criminal Justice System arena and has presented her research findings at a range of international conferences.

Matt O'Brien has worked with sexual offenders for 13 years. He has been an invited speaker at a Combating Paedophile Information Networks in Europe (COPINE) conference and has authored a number of chapters and has a journal article that relate to Internet offending. Matt is currently delivering programmes for offenders in Canadian prisons, many of whom have Internet offences.

Jon Taylor has been an active online undercover police officer working with the Metropolitan Police High Technology Crime Unit since 2005. He interacts every day with online groomers and has just completed research exploring Internet offender behaviour. Jon's work featured recently on the ITN documentary *To Catch a Paedophile*.

Stephen Webster is Acting Director of the Qualitative Research Unit at the National Centre for Social Research. He has vast experience of research with sexual offenders and has published widely in the peer-review literature. He is co-author of the Internet Attitudes and Behaviour Questionnaire and is currently examining online grooming behaviours.

Introduction

Julia Davidson and Petter Gottschalk

This book provides a timely overview of international policy, legislation and offender treatment practice in the area of Internet child abuse. The book is based upon the most recent and current research (some of which is unpublished) in the area. Contributors are key experts, police practitioners and researchers working in the Internet abuse field. The book will appeal to an international audience of academics, researchers, criminal justice agencies, policy makers and criminal justice practitioners. The Editors and one of the chapter contributors (Webster) are involved in the largest European study of Internet abusers' victim-targeting practices, funded by the European Commission Safer Internet Programme (2009–11).

Context and relevance

Internet use has grown considerably in the last decade. Information technology now forms a core part of the formal education system in many countries, ensuring that each new generation of Internet users is more adept than the last. Recent comparative work (EUKids Online) on Internet use across 27 European countries reveals that there were substantial changes in Internet use between 2005 and 2008. In 2005 70% of 6–17-year-olds in the European Union (EU) used the Internet. By 2008, this had risen to 75 per cent on average. The most striking rise was among younger children – by 2008, 60 per cent of 6–10-year-olds were online. There was also a substantial difference between 2005 and 2008 concerning location of use. In 2005 use of the Internet at school was as common as home use. By 2008, 6–17-year-olds in all European Community (EC) countries were much more likely to use the Internet at home (65 per cent) than school (57 per cent), and 34 per cent are now going online using their own computer. (Livingstone and Haddon, 2009). In Russia recent research in large urban centres on children and teenagers' attitudes and perceptions of the Internet reveals that it is the primary information source ahead of television, books and printed mass media for both 14–15-year-olds and 16–17-year-olds. Approximately 65 per cent of 16–17-year-olds say that parents allow them free use of the Internet and do so without imposing any time-limit. This was less the case with the younger 14–15-year-olds (58 per cent claiming the same). In terms of perceived risks and dangers, it is clear that the 16–17-year-olds are currently more aware of pornography (80 per cent) than the 14–15-year-olds (45 per cent) although as many of the older group placed viruses as an equal risk to pornography.

The Russian data on risk-taking behaviour revealed that more than half from each age group gave out personal data without thinking. The difference between the two age groups in terms of the type of personal data was that a larger proportion of 16–17-year-olds (23 per cent) appeared to be providing both personal photos and photos of relatives as compared with 11 per cent of 14–15-year-olds doing so (The Russian Foundation for Internet Development Research, 2009).

Research studies in the UK suggest that the majority of young people aged 9–19 access the Internet at least once a day. The Internet provides the opportunity to interact with friends on Social Networking Sites (SNSs) such as MySpace and Bebo and enables young people to access information in a way that previous generations would not have thought possible. The medium also allows users to post detailed personal information, which may be accessed by any site visitor and provides a platform for peer communication previously unknown (Davidson and Martellozzo, 2008).

Research, carried out by Ipsos Mori on behalf of Ofcom in the UK, comprised 797 face-to-face interviews with children aged 7–16 and their parent or carer. Just over 10 per cent of the children claimed that they use their mobile phone to go online. When online they most frequently say they are downloading or playing music (80 per cent), visiting social networks (45 per cent) and making use of instant messaging (38 per cent). The EUKids Online research also looked at risks for children online. Giving out personal information is the most common risk – approximately half of online teenagers seeing pornography as the second most common risk. Mobile phone use is widespread among children and young people and an increasing number access the Internet via a mobile phone. They make extensive use of the Internet using interactive services such as games, SNSs and instant messages, increasingly to be found as mobile phone applications.

In a study of Internet use among young people conducted in Belgium (2008) by the *Centre de Recherche et d'Information des Organisations de Consommation* (CRIOC; Belgian centre for consumer group information and research), it emerged that 88 per cent of the sample ($N = 2336$) surfed the Web regularly. The general average was 9.5 times a week, that is, more than once a day. All the age groups surveyed engaged in surfing. Indeed, it was already customary practice for 72 per cent of respondents 10 years of age. The pre-adolescents surveyed (11–12 years old) declared requiring no help to connect to and use the Internet. Their favourite online activities were (a) viewing cartoons or music videos, (b) playing games, and (c) communicating via the Microsoft Service Network (MSN) or email. Young adolescents

(13–14 years old), too, required no help using the Internet and their favourite activities included (1) creating and managing a personal blog to showcase themselves, (2) communicating, and (3) downloading music, games and videos. As for adolescents over 15 years of age, they reported for the most part possessing their own personal computer and using the Internet to (1) communicate with others, (2) comment on specific topics in discussion forums and (3) download music, games and videos. As we can see, although the points of interest vary across age groups, 'communicating' is nevertheless a constant. When asked what activity they most engaged in, 'chatting' came out on top (82 per cent of respondents). Surprisingly, 74 per cent of the children still in elementary school already chatted on a daily basis.

Recent research suggests that young people associate the term 'online' strictly with the computer. They do not associate the term 'online' with using a mobile phone to, for example, check their Facebook page or to chat on MSN. The connectivity now offered on mobile phones increases risk by isolating potential victims for online grooming. Research also suggests that adult perceptions of online risk-taking behaviour such as providing personal information to strangers or agreeing to meet with strangers or 'virtual friends' (Davidson and Martellozzo, 2008:56) are perceived by young people as acceptable Social Networking Site behaviour (Davidson et al., 2009).

Book structure

In Chapter 1 Davidson describes and critically evaluates legislation designed to protect children and young people from Internet abuse. One of the key problems in policing this global crime is the variation in legislation between countries. This new offence category was included in the Sexual Offences Act 2003 in England and Wales (with application also to Northern Ireland[1]): section 15 makes 'meeting a child following sexual grooming' an offence, with application to the Internet, other technologies such as mobile phones and the 'real world'. 'Grooming' involves a process of socialisation during which an offender seeks to interact with a child (a young person under 18 in Scotland, England or Wales), possibly sharing their hobbies and interests in an attempt to gain trust in order to prepare them for sexual abuse. The process may also involve an attempt to normalise sexual relations between adults and children. The Protection of Children and Prevention of Sexual Offences (Scotland) Act 2005 includes 'meeting a child following certain preliminary contact' (s1) meaning where a person arranges to meet a child who is under 16, having communicated with them on at least one previous occasion (in person, via the Internet or via other technologies), with the intention of performing sexual activity on the child.

Several countries are beginning to follow the UK lead in legislating against 'grooming' behaviour. Sexual grooming has also recently been added to the legislation in Norway (2007-Crimes Civil Penal Code ('straffeloven'),

S201)[2] Section 201a is the new grooming section in Norwegian criminal law. This section was included in The General Civil Penal Code in April 2007. The grooming section is different from other sections about sexual activity in that it does not concern a completed offence, but rather the *intention* of committing an act. However, the perpetrator must actually appear for a meeting (sometimes a police trap); intention itself is not sufficient. Possibly it should be, but it is difficult to prove beyond doubt. Therefore, the legal phrase is: 'has arrived at the meeting place or a place where the meeting place can be observed', meaning that the offender has arrived at, or is in view of, the place where the offence was intended to take place. In the United States it is an offence to electronically transmit information about a child aged 16 or under for the purpose of committing a sexual offence (US Code Title 18, Part 1, Chapter 117, AS 2425). Davidson (2009) argues that differences in legislation across jurisdictions, such as variations in the age of consent to sexual relations, make international consensus and agreements such as the EU Framework Decision (2009) difficult to enforce.

In Chapter 2 Gottschalk provides a definition of Internet child abuse. Internet use has grown considerably over the last five years. Information technology now forms a core part of the formal education system in many countries, ensuring that each new generation of Internet users is more adept than the last. Research conducted in the UK by Livingstone and Bober in 2004 suggested that the majority of young people aged 9–19 accessed the Internet at least once a day. The Internet provides the opportunity to interact with friends on Social Networking Sites such as MySpace and Bebo and enables young people to access information in a way that previous genera-tions would not have thought possible. It also allows users to post detailed personal information, which may be accessed by any site visitor and which provides a platform for peer communication hitherto unknown. There is, however, increasing evidence that the Internet is used by some adults to access children and young people in order to 'groom' them for the purposes of sexual abuse; MySpace have recently expelled 29,000 suspected sex offen-ders and is being sued in the United States by parents who claim that their children were contacted by sex offenders on the site and consequently abused (http://news.bbc.co.uk/1/hi/business/6277633.stm 19/7/2007 'MySpace is sued over child safety'). The Internet also plays a role in facilitating the production and distribution of indecent illegal images of children.

In Chapter 3 Carr and Hilton describe international moves to protect children online. There have already been considerable efforts to increase online child protection internationally. The G8 countries have agreed a strategy to protect children from sexual abuse on the Internet. Key aims include the development of an international database of offenders and victims to aid victim identification, offender monitoring, and the targeting of those profiting from the sale of indecent images of children. Internet service pro-viders and credit card companies, such as the UK's Association For Payment

Clearing Services, have also joined the international movement against the production and distribution of sexually abusive images of children online. Their efforts have focused primarily on attempting to trace individuals who use credit cards to access illegal sites containing indecent images of children. There has also been an attempt to put mechanisms into place which would prevent online payment for illegal sites hosted outside of the UK. Organisations such as the Virtual Global Taskforce (VGT) and the Internet Watch Foundation (IWF) are making some headway in attempting to protect children online. VGT is an organisation that comprises several international law enforcement agencies from Australia, Canada, the United States, the United Kingdom and Interpol. Through the provision of advice and support to children, VGT aims to protect children online and has recently set up a bogus website to attract online groomers. A report to VGT by a child has recently led to the conviction of a sex offender for online grooming and the possession of indecent images (VGT, 2006). The Internet Watch Foundation is one of the main government watchdogs in this area. Although based in the UK the IWF is a part of the *EU's Safer Internet Plus Programme.* Carr and Hilton argue that much more needs to be done to centralise international efforts to protect children online.

Chapter 4 provides the context for the following two chapters. Gottschalk presents the idea of a staged approach to online grooming, suggesting possible stages through which an offender might move in progressing from indecent image use to contact abuse.

In Chapter 5 Martellozzo explores perpetrators' online behaviour. Very little is known about Internet offenders and there is little research in this area. The author has just completed a doctorate with the Metropolitan Police High Technology Crime Unit (one of the foremost online Internet abuse policing units in Europe) exploring online offender behaviour. Her research provides a current and unique perspective – applicable across the international community. It is clear that the Internet is more than just a medium of communication: it constitutes a new virtual reality, or a cyberworld, with its own rules and its own language. The Internet provides a supportive context within which the child sexual abuser is no longer a lonely figure but rather forms part of a larger community that shares the same interests. The Internet gives new meaning to the term 'sex offender ring', as the potential for offenders to organise to abuse children is so considerable. The chapter also explores the concept of denial in Internet sex offenders.

In Chapter 6 Taylor builds upon the preceding chapters by exploring online grooming behaviour in the context of Internet policing. Jon Taylor is an undercover officer working at the Metropolitan Police High Technology Crime Unit who interacts every day with adult men seeking sexual relations with young people. The chapter offers a unique, first hand insight into both offender behaviour and policing response. The aim of Taylor's research was to explore how Internet Social Networking Groups have influenced sex offenders' modus operandi, in an attempt to enhance the understanding of grooming techniques amongst researchers, law enforcement agencies and practitioners working in this arena.

In Chapter 7 O'Brien and Webster explore the treatment of Internet sex offenders. This is a very new area and there are few programmes that focus specifically on this issue. The chapter will provide an overview of current treatment practice in the Europe, the US and Canada. Stephen Webster is a researcher at the forefront of this area of work: he designed one of the first assessment tools (Internet Behavioural Attitudes Questionnaire (IBAQ)) for Internet sex offenders which is currently used in the UK Prison Service. Treatment approaches with sex offenders whose offending is Internet-related tend to be based on the cognitive behavioural treatment (CBT) model. However the structure and delivery of such programmes differs. In England and Wales there has been a recent attempt to centrally develop and organise a CBT programme for Internet sex offenders that is now in use by the National Probation Service (July 2006) and will possibly be introduced to prisons. The Internet Sex Offender Treatment Programme (i-SOTP) runs alongside the existing sex offender treatment programme. Another CBT treatment programme is currently operational at a local level at the Forensic Department, University Hospital, Basel, Switzerland. This inpatient and outpatient clinic for sex offenders includes those remanded in custody; those on probation; those post-release from prison and some self-referring (approximately 15–20 per cent of all Internet offenders are self-referring). Forty men have attended the programme so far; therapy lasts for 1 year (weekly sessions of 1.5 hours) and is based upon relapse prevention models adapted for use with Internet sex offenders.

Notes

1 The Sexual Offences Act 2003 (England and Wales) is currently under review in Northern Ireland. Some concerns have been raised regarding a lack of clarity around the age of consent and informed consent. Currently the age of consent is 17 in Northern Ireland (it was raised from 16 to 17 under the Children and Young Persons Act 1950). NI Office, July 2006.

2 Section 201a:

> With fines or imprisonment of not more than 1 year is any person liable, who has agreed a meeting with a child who is under 16 years of age, and who with intention of committing an act as mentioned in sections 195, 196 or 200 second section has arrived at the meeting place or a place where the meeting place can be observed.

References

Centre de Recherche et d'Information des Organisations de Consommation (CRIOC; Belgian centre for consumer group information and research) 2008.

Davidson, J. and Martellozzo, E. (2008) 'Protecting vulnerable young people in cyberspace from sexual abuse: raising awareness and responding globally', *Police Practice & Research*, an International Journal.

Davidson, J., Lorenz, M., Martellozzo, E. and Grove-Hills, J. (2009) 'Evaluation of CEOP ThinkUKnow Internet Safety Programme and Exploration of Young People's Internet Safety Knowledge', 2010 in press; full report will be available from 1/4/2010 on www.cats-rp.org.uk

Livingstone, S. and Haddon, L. (2009) 'EU Kids Online Report', Conference, June 2009, LSE, London.

Livingstone, S. and Bober, M. (2004) 'Taking up Opportunities? Children's uses of the internet for education, communication and participation', *E-Learning*, 1(3), 395–419. Available at http://www.wwwords.co.uk/ELEA/.

Ofcom 'Digital Lifestyles: Young adults aged 16–24' May 2009. Available at: http://www.ofcom.org.uk/advice/media_literacy/medlitpub/medlitpubrss/digital_young/.

Russian Federation of Internet Research (2009) 'Young people's use of the Internet in Russia' (unpublished).

Chapter 1

Legislation and policy

Protecting young people, sentencing and managing Internet sex offenders

Julia Davidson

Introduction: young people's online behaviour

Young people's use of the Internet, perceptions of 'risk-taking behaviour' and online experience have become the subject of an increasing amount of research. A national random sample of young Internet users in the United States (ages 10–17) found that 13 per cent had experienced an unwanted sexual solicitation on the Internet in the past year (Mitchell *et al.*, 2008). Many of these incidents were confined to the Internet and were relatively mild in nature. However, the potential for online sexual solicitation and harassment has raised obvious concerns among parents, teachers, and mental health professionals. What risks are children taking when using the Internet? Recent research led by Livingstone (2009) and funded by the European Commission Safer Internet Programme (EC SIP) suggests a rank for young people's online risk-taking behaviour. The work draws upon findings from research studies exploring young people's Internet behaviour across Europe and includes the views of thousands of young people.

The ranking of risk incidence is as follows:

1. Providing personal information to strangers (50 per cent).
2. Seeing adult pornography online (40 per cent).
3. Seeing violent or hateful content (30 per cent).
4. Meeting an online contact (10 per cent).

(Livingstone, 2009)

There is some variation in behaviour between European countries

Recent research conducted by Ofcom (2009) exploring young people's (aged 16–24) online behaviour suggests that the younger age range (16–19) were much less aware of potential risks in accessing and entering personal information on websites than were the older age range in the sample: 'Young adults are less likely to make any kind of judgment about a website before entering personal details, less likely to have any concerns about entering personal details online – within the young adult population, it is the attitudes and behaviours of the youngest adults – those aged 16–19 – which are the most striking. These adults are the most likely to share information and download content from the Internet, at the same time as being less likely to make any checks or judgments, and more likely to believe that the Internet is regulated' (2009: 2). This suggests that older children are more likely to engage in risk-taking behaviour online and appear less likely to act on advice regarding Internet safety. This finding is supported by research undertaken in the UK by Davidson, Lorenz, Martellozzo and Grove-Hills (2009) on behalf of the National Audit Office. The research included an online survey of 11–16 year olds (n = 1,808) and focus groups (n = 83) of young people. A substantial proportion of children reported having engaged in high-risk behaviour online (defined by the degree to which they share information with strangers): 37 per cent had shared an email address; 34 per cent provided information about the school they attended; 23 per cent provided a mobile number; and 26 per cent a personal photograph. A significant proportion said that they will continue with such behaviour following Internet safety training (particularly 13+); only 36 per cent said that Internet safety training would make them more careful online. Focus group findings indicated that interacting with strangers (that is, adding them as Instant Messaging (ISM) or Facebook friends and exchanging messages) is becoming an accepted behaviour not perceived as 'risk-taking'.

In terms of contact, sexual abuse, not necessarily related to initial Internet contact, the UK children's charity Childline report that of the 13,237 children counselled for sexual abuse in 2007/2008 alone, 8457 were girls (64 per cent) but 4780 were boys (36 per cent) (NSPCC Press Release, Feb 2009). Boys are no less susceptible to risk of abuse than girls. There is evidence to suggest that this sort of finding is similar in terms of risk of abuse through the Internet. A recent evaluation of a safety Internet awareness training initiative in schools revealed that girls appear to be at higher risk than boys because they use social aspects of the Internet more (notably instant messaging and Social Networking Sites), and are slightly more willing to share some types of personal information with, and interact with, strangers. Girls are far more likely to have had a 'threatening' experience online. However, boys are twice as likely to do nothing in reaction to a 'threatening' experience (Davidson et al., 2009).

Legislation: online grooming

Offenders using the Internet to perpetrate sexual offences against children fall into two principal categories: those who use the Internet to target and 'groom' children for the purposes of sexual abuse (Finkelhor et al., 2000); and those who produce and/or download indecent illegal images of children from the Internet and distribute them (Quayle and Taylor, 2002; Davidson and Martellozzo, 2005). This chapter explores the online grooming

use of children and the legislative and institutional measures
ped to prevent it both in the UK and internationally.
gislation has sought to protect young people from Internet abuse
he introduction of a 'grooming' clause. This new offence category
oduced in the Sexual Offences Act (2003) in England and Wales (the
s̖   . of the Act having application also to Northern Ireland[1]). Section 15
makes 'meeting a child following sexual grooming' an offence; this applies
to the Internet, to other technologies such as mobile phones and to the
'real world'.

'Grooming' involves a process of socialisation through which an offender
seeks to interact with a child under the age of 16, possibly sharing their hobbies
and interests in an attempt to gain trust in order to prepare them for sexual
abuse. The concept of 'grooming' is now also recognised in legislation in the
UK. The Sexual Offences Act (2003) in England and Wales, and Northern
Ireland and the Protection of Children and Prevention of Sexual Offences
Act (2005) in Scotland includes the offence of 'meeting a child
following certain preliminary contact' (section 1). 'Preliminary contact' refers
to occasions where a person arranges to meet a child who is under 16, having
communicated with them on at least one previous occasion (in person, via
the Internet or via other technologies), with the intention of performing
sexual activity on the child. The definition of 'grooming' in UK legislation is
provided by the Crown Prosecution Service (CPS) (England and Wales):

> The offence only applies to adults; there must be communication
> (a meeting or any other form of communication) on at least two pre-
> vious occasions; it is not necessary for the communications to be of a
> sexual nature; the communication can take place anywhere in the world;
> the offender must either meet the child or travel to the pre-arranged
> meeting; the meeting or at least part of the journey must take place
> within the jurisdiction; the person must have an intention to commit any
> offence within or outside of the UK (which would be an offence in the
> jurisdiction) under Part 1 of the 2003 Act. This may be evident from the
> previous communications or other circumstances e.g. an offender travels
> in possession of ropes, condoms or lubricants etc; the child is under 16
> and the adult does not reasonably believe that the child is over 16.
>
> (CPS, 2007).

Several countries are beginning to follow the UK in legislating against
'grooming' behaviour. Sexual grooming has, for example, recently been
added to the Crimes Amendment Act (2005) in New Zealand. In the US it is
an offence to transmit information electronically about a child aged 16 or
under, for the purpose of committing a sexual offence.[2] The Australian
Criminal Code[3] makes similar restrictions, as does the Canadian Criminal
Code.[4] The legislation in the UK differs in that the sexual grooming offence

applies both to the new technologies including the Internet and mobile phones, and also to the 'real world'; legislation in other countries addresses only electronic grooming via the Internet and mobile phones. The concept of sexual grooming is well documented in the sex offender literature (Finkelhor, 1984), and is now filtering into legislation policy, crime detection and prevention initiatives. A recent report in the *Guardian* newspaper suggested that the Child Exploitation and Online Protection Centre in the UK receive an average of four phone calls per day from young people planning to meet people with whom they have developed an online, sexual relationship (25/02/2009).

Norway is the only other European country to adopt the grooming legislation. The relevant sections in the General Civil Penal Code ('straffeloven') concerned with sexual offenders in Norway are: 'Section 195: Any person who engages in sexual activity with a child who is under 14 years of age shall be liable to imprisonment for a term not exceeding 10 years. If the said activity was sexual intercourse the penalty shall be imprisonment for not less than 2 years. Section 196: Any person who engages in sexual activity with a child who is under 16 years of age shall be liable to imprisonment for a term not exceeding 5 years.' Section 201a is the new grooming section in Norwegian criminal law. This section was included in The General Civil Penal Code in April 2007: 'With fines or imprisonment of not more than 1 year is any person liable, who has agreed a meeting with a child who is under 16 years of age, and who with intention of committing an act as mentioned in sections 195, 196 or 200 second section has arrived at the meeting place or a place where the meeting place can be observed.' In Norwegian law the grooming section refers to the *intention* of committing an act. However, the perpetrator must actually appear for a meeting (sometimes a police trap); 'intention' itself is not sufficient. Possibly it should be, but it is difficult to prove beyond doubt. Therefore, the legislation is phrased as follows: ' ... has arrived at the meeting place can be observed', meaning that the offender has arrived at, or is in view of, the place where the offence was intended to take place.

The crime description is such that it is technology neutral. It is therefore not important how the adult and the child came in contact or agreed to meet. The important thing is that there is an agreement to meet physically. Agreement is to be understood in a wide sense. There is no requirement that this agreement to meet was made explicitly; it is sufficient that the offender had a reasonable expectation to meet the child at a specific location within a specific time frame. It is also irrelevant who initiated the meeting. Where an adult communicates with a child and agrees to meet with the intention of committing a sexual offence, the adult can be sentenced for the grooming crime. It is the intention, the goal and the purpose of the appointment that is a crime. Before the grooming section was introduced in Norwegian criminal law in 2007, a preparation for the criminal act of committing a sexual offence on a child less than 16 years of age did not make the offender liable to imprisonment. The grooming section was introduced in an attempt to protect children at an earlier stage.

Contact itself is not a crime. There may be good reasons for adults and children to have contact using media such as the Internet. Adult and child may share the same interest in sports or games, and may exchange experiences and compete in pastimes on the Internet. An appointment is defined as a place and time where an adult and child have agreed to meet. It may be at the adult's location, the child's location, or another location to which both have to travel.

Indecent images of children

The Internet Watch Foundation is the IT industry watchdog in the UK. The IWF reported a rise in the number of websites containing indecent images of children from 3,438 in 2004 to 6,000 in 2006. The IWF claimed that over 90 per cent of the websites are hosted outside of the UK (many being hosted in the US and Russia), and are therefore extremely difficult to police and control and there is currently no international agreement on regulation of the Internet in respect of online grooming and indecent child images.[5] The IWF 2008 Annual Report suggests a 10 per cent reduction in websites hosting indecent child images; however the report also suggests 'a continuing trend in the severity and commercialisation of the images:

- *58 per cent of child sexual abuse domains traced contain graphic images involving penetration or torture (47 per cent of domains in 2007);*
- *69 per cent of the children appear to be 10 years old or younger; 24 per cent 6 or under, and 4 per cent 2 or under (80 per cent appeared to be 10 or under in 2007);*
- *74 per cent of child sexual abuse domains traced are commercial operations, selling images (80 per cent commercial in 2007);*
- *it is still rare to trace child sexual abuse content to hosts in the UK (under 1per cent).'*

(IWF, 29/04/2009 http://www.iwf.org.uk/media/news.archive-2009.258.htm [26/10/09])

Many indecent images depict the sexual abuse of children who are victimised both in the creation of the image and in its distribution. It could be argued that a child is re-victimised each time their image is accessed, and images on the Internet can form a permanent record of abuse. The ACLU has undoubtedly formed a powerful lobby in the United States. No such objections have been voiced in the UK in such an organised manner; it could be argued that groups such as the IWF and key individuals such as John Carr (see Chapter 3), have campaigned more successfully in the UK for the rights of child victims of Internet abuse. In the United States under COPA (Child Online Protection Act 1998) the making available of material that is harmful to children for commercial purposes on the web is also illegal, unless child access has been restricted. It was argued by the ACLU that more effective, less restrictive mechanisms exist to protect children and that educating children and their parents about Internet awareness would be a more effective approach (Supreme Court Transcripts, *Ashcroft v ACLU* 2/3/04).

The scale of the problem is considerable; the National Society for the Prevention of Cruelty to Children estimate that approximately 20,000 indecent images of children are placed on the Internet each week (NSPCC, 2009). Many of these child victims are amongst the most vulnerable, from poor countries and are repeat victims. The police are attempting to identify victims from the images produced on the Internet but the process is slow and time consuming and yields little identification (Davidson, 2007). There is no doubt that such abuse has a damaging and negative impact upon child victims. It has been claimed that in many instances children are abused and the abuse recorded by members of their own family or people known to them (Klain, Davies and Hicks, 2001). Many indecent images depict the sexual abuse of children who are victimised both in the creation of the image and in the distribution of the image. It could be argued that a child is re-victimised each time their image is accessed, and images on the Internet can form a permanent record of abuse. Images tend to depict white female children. Recent unpublished research conducted by Quayle and Jones (2009) included an analysis of 25,000 indecent images of children and found that 91 per cent of the victims were white and 81 per cent were female. Recent research conducted by Lee (2008) on behalf of the National Centre for Missing and Exploited Children in the United States suggests that victims appearing in images are predominantly female and that the majority of the images are taken by the child's family or someone known to them and not by strangers.

Legislation has been introduced in the UK in an attempt to curb the production and distribution of indecent images of children. The legislation in England and Wales (Sexual Offences Act 2003 [England and Wales], sections 45–46)[6] and Scotland (the Protection of Children and Prevention of Sexual Offences [Scotland] Act 2005, section 16) attempts to protect children from abuse in the creation of such images in order to curb circulation. The age of consent is raised from 16 to 18 in both Acts with certain provisions.[7] Legislation in most EU Member States is similar but the age of consent to sexual relations (the legal definition of childhood) varies widely across Europe; the age of consent is 13 in Spain and 18 in Malta for example. Legislation to curb the possession and distribution of indecent child images should shortly be introduced in Russia (Dr Borisovna Mizulina, Duma Committee on Children, Women & Families, 11/2009) where the age of consent is currently 16.

In the US the law is similar (Child Online Protection Act 2000 [COPA]); indecent images of children do not have to be overtly sexual, and the possession of suggestive images of children may be prosecuted under the legislation. It is also an offence to simply access images, that is without saving them on a computer. There has been considerable debate in the US regarding the introduction of COPA; the Act has been returned to the Supreme Court several times on the basis of representations made by the American Civil Liberties Union (ACLU) regarding its restrictiveness. The ACLU has argued consistently and fairly effectively that the Act infringes upon civil liberties and individual autonomy, as it is possible accidentally to encounter such images online. In the US under COPA, the making available for commercial purposes on the web of material that is harmful to children is also illegal, unless child access has been restricted. It was argued by the ACLU that more effective, less restrictive mechanisms exist to protect children and that educating children and their parents about Internet awareness would be the better approach to safeguarding (Supreme Court Transcripts, *Ashcroft v ACLU* 2/3/04).

Legislation in other countries places greater emphasis upon the production of indecent images of children. In Switzerland, Articles 135 and 197 of the Penal Code (The Production and Distribution of Illegal Pornography [Child]), imply that if the indecent material is only to be used for personal viewing, possession is not punishable. But recent research indicates that some federal courts are arguing that the downloading of such material from the Internet constitutes *computer storage* rather than possession, which is illegal and therefore contravenes the Articles (Davidson, 2007). Other EU countries have organisations that play a similar role to the Internet Watch Foundation in the UK. Belgium, for example, has an organisation called Child Focus, which is a civilian contact point for reporting images of child sexual abuse online and provides complete anonymity. Upon receipt of reports, Child Focus follows procedures by forwarding the report to the Human Trafficking Unit and the Federal Computer Crime Unit (FCCU) of the federal police who, in turn, keep Child Focus informed on the follow-up. Child Focus also manages a prevention site (clicksafe.be) tailored to younger children, adolescents, parents, teachers and all other persons looking for tips on how to use new technologies more safely. It is also possible for victims to report offences committed online, through the 'eCops' website created by the federal police. A hotline (110) is available as well for reporting any information regarding wrongful sexual behaviours or prostitution.

The European Union has introduced a Framework Decision in this area and suggests that: 'to combat child pornography, especially where the original materials are not located within the EU, mechanisms should be put in place to block access from the Union's territory to Internet pages identified as containing or disseminating child pornography' (EU Council Framework Decision 2009: 5).

A recently published EU (2009) document entitled 'Combating the Sexual Abuse: Sexual Exploitation of Children and Child Pornography' sets out the shortcomings and vision in protecting young people from sexual abuse. The framework decision outlines the difficulty in protecting young people when there is such widespread variation in national criminal law and law enforcement practice in Europe. The situation is seen as exacerbated by the hidden nature of the offending and compounding issues such as victims' reluctance to report abuse.

The role of information technology in facilitating global abuse and sex offender networks is discussed. The EU suggest that:

> developments in information technology have made these problems more acute by making it easier to produce and distribute child sexual abuse images while offering offenders anonymity and spreading responsibility across jurisdictions. Ease of travel and income differences fuel so-called child sex tourism, resulting often in child sex offenders committing offences abroad with impunity. Beyond difficulties of prosecution, organised crime can make considerable profits with little risk
>
> (EU Council Framework Decision 2009: 2)

Following this Framework decision it is likely that other European countries will introduce grooming legislation and the 'viewing' of indecent child images will become an offence:

> New forms of sexual abuse and exploitation facilitated by the use of IT would be criminalised. This includes knowingly obtaining access to child pornography, to cover cases where viewing child pornography from websites without downloading or storing the images does not amount to "possession of" or "procuring" child pornography. Also the new offence of "grooming" is incorporated closely following the wording agreed in the COE [Council of Europe Convention (on cybercrime)] Convention.
>
> (EU Council Framework Decision 2009: 2)

Article 5 refers to online grooming as the 'solicitation of children for sexual purposes' (EU Council Framework Decision 2009: 5) and asks that each Member State ensure that such conduct is punishable in law. This refers to cases involving children under the age of consent under national law, where an adult arranges to meet for the purposes of sexual abuse via the means of 'an information system' (EU Council Framework Decision 2009: 5).

UK and other national law provides a distinction between the regulation of adult material and that depicting children, in recognition of the vulnerability of minors. However the task of legally defining when childhood ends is complicated and varies across jurisdictions. The UN Convention on the Rights of the Child defines a child as a person under the age of 18[8] but given wide variation in the age of consent to sexual relations across Europe there is clearly legal disagreement regarding the age at which childhood ends. Even for these purposes there is no consensus in international law. The *Optional Protocol to the UNCRC on the sale of children, child prostitution and child pornography* does not state what age a child is but as a protocol to the UNCRC itself it would mean 18. The EU Framework Decision states that a child is someone under the age of 18. The Council of Europe Convention on Cybercrime also states that a child is someone under the age of 18 but that a State has the right to lower this threshold: 'The age of 18 is an agreed international definition of the age of majority and so there is logic in using this already-agreed age. The difficulty this brings is where this is higher than the age of consent and so it appears to create something of a paradox' (Gillespie, 2009).

In summary, UK and US legislation seeks to curb the production, supply of, and demand for, indecent images of children and the EU directive (2009) seeks to support this position through the blocking of websites containing indecent child images.

The relationship between indecent image collection and contact offending

The extent to which those offenders who collect indecent images of children are likely to have perpetrated contact sexual offences is unknown. This is a key question for both legislation and risk approaches with Internet sex offenders. There is some emerging research in this area but it is in its infancy. The Butner Redux Study (Bourke and Hernandez, 2009) of indecent image offenders revealed that many who had no known history of contact sexual offences subsequently admitted to such crimes after participating in treatment. This is true for some other crimes but the critical issue is what impact that information about self-reported crimes has in the realm of risk assessment and intervention. A number of other studies have reported a co-occurrence of contact sexual offences among indecent image collectors entering the criminal justice system or in clinical settings (Wolak, Finkelhor and Mitchell, 2005; Seto and Eke, 2005; Hernandez, 2009). A particular analysis path conducted in the Butner Redux Study was to look at the age of onset for online and offline (contact) sexual crimes on a subset of $n = 42$ ($N = 155$). The rationale for this was to shed light upon the developmental pathway of indecent child image offences. Although caution is needed in terms of the small sample, the majority reported that they committed acts of hands-on abuse prior to seeking child pornography via the Internet.

However, work on comparisons on variables that have been identified as risk factors among contact sex offenders suggest that child pornography offenders are, on average, at lower risk for contact sexual offending than already identified sex offenders. Elliott et al. (2008) examined these findings with a large comparison of 505 indecent image offenders and 526 contact sex offenders. It was found that there were many similarities on some risk variables such as impulsivity, but contact sex offenders had more needs on measures of victim empathy and offence-supportive attitudes and beliefs.

Hernandez (2009) suggests that 'There is a complex interaction between child pornography and contact sexual offences worthy of empirical investigation.' Clearly more research is needed in this area.

Sentencing of Internet sex offenders

The use of custody for sex offenders as a group has fluctuated little over recent years in the UK. It rose by 5 per cent over a ten-year period between 1995 and 2005; 55 per cent were given immediate custodial sentences in 1995 compared with 60 per cent in 2005. The average prison sentence length for all sex offenders increased from 36.8 months in 1995 to 41.5 months in 2005 (Home Office, 2007). It is, however, too early to comment upon sentencing practice with Internet sex offenders as only a small number of cases have been prosecuted under the Sexual Offences Act (2003).[9] In recent research undertaken by one of the authors (Davidson, 2007), police practitioners expressed concern regarding variance in sentencing practice and particularly the ways in which courts view the possession of indecent images of children. It was suggested that sentencers have different views regarding the seriousness of possession of indecent images, on the basis that no *direct* victimisation appears to occur. This view was echoed by a psychiatrist working with sex offenders in Switzerland:

> 'The problem is that federal areas treat the offence differently in that some will remand these offenders into treatment and some will not. Some view this as an offence and some do not. There is no equity and sentencing varies by federal area.'
>
> (Graf, 2006, cited in Davidson, 2007: 10)

More research is needed into sentencing practice in this area. Punishment of sex offenders does not and should not always involve a custodial sentence. In England and Wales the National Probation Service runs a community treatment programme for sex offenders (Sex Offender Treatment Programme) that allows for diversion from custody for more minor offences. The current legislative framework introduces a range of sentences, including a community order (formally a probation order), which may include a number of requirements (including treatment). Offenders given a community order must agree to comply with any measures imposed; these usually include attending the probation sex offender treatment programme (for those charged with online grooming and other non-Internet related sexual offences) or the recently introduced Internet Sex Offender Treatment Programme (i-SOTP) for those convicted of indecent image-related offences (discussed in greater detail in Chapter 7). Other measures may include the use of electronic tagging and, in future, hormone-suppressing drugs (Home Office, 2007a).

The management of all sex offenders in the community is supported by the present legislative framework in the UK.[10] All newly convicted sex offenders are required to register under the Sex Offenders Act 1997 (strengthened by Part Two of the Sexual Offences Act [2003], which introduces a number of new orders), including offenders supervised in the community, those cautioned and those released from prison. The duration of the registration requirement depends on sentence length, type of offence, age of the offender and age of the victim. The minimum period of registration is five years and the maximum an 'indefinite period', for sentences of 30 months or more in custody. These arrangements follow automatically on conviction and are not, as such, a part of the sentencing process, but sentencers have a duty to inform offenders about the requirement at the point of sentence. Sentencers may consider extended periods on licence for sex offenders where risk to the public is considered high (Criminal Justice Act 2003, sections 225–29). There are currently 32,336 (2008–9) registered sex offenders in the community in England and Wales compared to 28,994 in 2004/05 (Probation MAPPA statistics, 2009. http://www.probation.justice.gov.uk/files/pdf/MAPPA%20National%20Figures%202009 26/10/09).

Some countries have passed legislation that allows for the detention and supervision of all sex offenders beyond sentence completion. In the UK, the Crime and Disorder Act (1998) allowed courts to extend periods of supervision beyond custodial sentences where a person was considered to be at risk of further offending. The Sexual Offences Act (2003) now allows sentencers to pass indeterminate sentences on completion of a custodial sentence for sexual and violent offenders considered to be high risk. In Australia, the High Court, in *Fardon v Attorney-General For The State of Queensland* (2004), upheld the Queensland Dangerous Prisoners (Sexual Offences) Act (2003), which allows for the detention of sex offenders beyond sentence where offenders are considered to be at high risk of re-offending. In the US, sentencers also have the power to detain sex offenders indefinitely; the system differs from the UK in that the decision to detain indefinitely is made at the end of the period of imprisonment and no minimum term for parole review is set, as the detention takes the form of a civil commitment on mental health grounds. This could lead to incarceration for life with no opportunity to appeal. A US Supreme Court ruling (by a 5 to 4 majority) in June 1997 held that sex offenders could be subject to indefinite civil commitment in a psychiatric institution if, due to a 'personality disorder' or 'mental abnormality', they are deemed to be at a high risk of perpetrating further sexual offences.

Internet sex offenders: assessing and managing the risk – the UK example

In the UK, all sex offenders are subject to the restrictions placed upon them by Multi-Agency Panel Protection Arrangements (MAPPA).[11] These arrangements require criminal justice, housing, health, local authority, social work and probation services to put into place arrangements for establishing and monitoring risk from sex offenders and violent offenders. The Criminal Justice and Court Services Act (2000) formalised MAPPA arrangements by placing a statutory duty on police and probation services, working jointly as the 'responsible authority' in each area, to establish arrangements for the assessment and management of the risk posed by such offenders. The Criminal Justice Act (2003) (sections 325–27) extends the definition of 'responsible authority' to include the Prison Service; establishes a reciprocal 'duty to co-operate' between the responsible authority and a range of other authorities and social care agencies; and requires the Secretary of State to appoint two lay advisers to assist with the strategic review of arrangements in each area. In Scotland, MAPPAs were introduced in September 2006, and legislation which amends the Sexual Offences Act (2003) has now come into force (Police, Public Order and Criminal Justice [Scotland] Act 2006).[12] MAPPAs address several areas of good practice: ongoing risk assessment; the development of risk management plans that focus upon public protection; and service performance evaluation. There are several core functions: identifying MAPPA offenders; sharing relevant information across agencies involved in the assessment of risk; and assessing and managing risk of serious harm. A responsibility is placed upon the Prison Service, the police and local authorities jointly to establish arrangements for the risk assessment and management of sex offenders subject to the notification requirements of Part Two of the Sexual Offences Act (2003).

This collaborative multi-agency response to the monitoring of sex offenders in the community is unusual and has not been adopted as a model by other countries. The advantages of this system are that the responsibility for monitoring is a shared one and that decisions regarding offenders will be taken by a range of agencies represented under the arrangements.

In England and Wales and in Scotland violent and sex offenders are divided into three distinct categories under MAPPAs: Category One includes all registered sex offenders; Category Two includes violent offenders; and Category Three includes offenders with previous convictions whose behaviour suggests that they pose a continuing risk. Level 1 offenders (considered to be the least serious group) are overseen by one agency, usually the police or National Probation Service; whilst level 2 offenders are subject to multi-agency oversight; and level 3, high-risk offenders, may be subject to intensive measures, such as monitoring on a daily basis by a private care firm or police surveillance.[13] The Home Office has recently conducted a review of measures to control all sex offenders in the community and plans to legislate to strengthen MAPPAs. Measures include: the use of medication to control offending (chemical castration);[14] compulsory use of polygraph testing; enhanced use of satellite tracking; provision of early treatment for self-referring sex offenders who have not been convicted; expansion of treatment;

and a review of the continuity between prison and probation treatment (which currently does not exist) (Home Office, 2007b).

The majority of Internet sex offenders using indecent images of children are categorised as low risk (level 1). At present there are no specific MAPPAs for Internet sex offenders but measures are planned, which may include: the screening of all sex offenders for Internet use in offending; regular inspection of home computers; and the installation on home computers of the kind of software currently employed in the US to monitor the Internet use of registered sex offenders (Davidson, 2007). In theory it may be easier to control the behaviour of this group as it may soon be possible to monitor their computer use electronically and remotely – this may initially prove costly, but such a move will provide a more cost-effective alternative in the long term than MAPPA officer visits. There is no evidence to suggest that these methods will prevent further offending, however, and it is probable that computers will be used outside of the home environment in order to escape detection.

In terms of judging seriousness and risk when sentencing, the Court of Appeal accepted the advice of the Sentencing Advisory Panel (2002) in sentencing Internet sex offenders using indecent images of children, following *R v Oliver, Hartrey and Baldwin* (2003).[15] The offence of possession of indecent images of children is triable either way under the Sexual Offences Act (2003) in England and Wales, and carries a maximum penalty of five years' custody for possession and up to 10 years' custody for production and distribution. Aggravating circumstances include: distribution; evidence of systematic collection; use of drugs or alcohol; collection stored so that others may view it accidentally; intimidation or coercion; and financial gain. Mitigating factors include: a small number of images held for personal use and images viewed but not stored.[16]

The effectiveness of UK multi-agency public protection arrangements in monitoring Internet sex offenders

In the UK the Home Office suggests that strengthening MAPPA is essential in supporting notification requirements and the proposed legislation, but how effective is the current system?

As we have seen, MAPPA should include: ongoing risk assessment; the development of risk management plans that focus upon public protection; and performance evaluation. There are four core functions: identifying MAPPA offenders; sharing relevant information across agencies involved in the assessment of risk; assessing risk of serious harm; and managing that risk.

The Home Office Review (2007) suggests that the MAPPA currently operate effectively. However recent research raises doubts over this claim. Research conducted by the author for the Risk Management Authority (RMA) Scotland (2007) invited practitioners to comment on the effectiveness of MAPPA. The RMA commissioned the research to explore current international policy, legislation and practice with Internet sex offenders and as part of this research police officers, probation officers and criminal justice social workers who work with sex offenders in the UK were interviewed regarding their experiences of MAPPA.

International respondents commented generally upon the positive aspects of the MAPPA system, which it would seem is fairly unique, particularly in Europe where communication between agencies is usually more informal. All respondents supported the principle of multi-agency working and MAPPA arrangements but some questioned the adequacy of the system in assessing and managing risk with sex offenders (including those convicted of Internet-related offences). One police respondent questioned how far agencies are currently committed to enforcing MAPPA arrangements: 'It's (MAPPA) certainly a step in the right direction, but is this really a priority for the agencies involved? It's not really and resourcing is an issue' (Davidson, 2007: 25). Respondents identified some useful steps that might be taken in ensuring more effective management of Internet sex offenders:

1. There should be unlimited access to registered sex offenders' home computers (all sex offenders not just Internet) (aided in Scotland by the Police, Public Order and Criminal Justice [Scotland] Bill, 2006).
2. MAPPA officers should be making regular unannounced visits to sex offenders in order to view home environments and computers.
3. There should be regular and effective collaboration between police officers from specialist sex offender units and social workers/probation officers regarding risk assessment and management at social enquiry/ pre-sentence report stage and throughout the sentence.

(Davidson, 2007: 47)

Police officers commenting in the author's study pointed to the probable link between offending and the use of the Internet, suggesting that computer searches and gathering information about computer use should be routine for all sex offenders.

> MAPPA Officers should be regularly 'dip-sampling' from the register to check all sex offenders and should be checking out their lifestyles regularly. They should be checking Internet sex offenders' computers on a regular basis – in fact they should be checking all sex offenders' computers. I would be suspicious of an offender using an evidence eliminator. Consideration should be given to obtaining a condition placed on the offender's licence, to gain regular access to their computer. Resourcing is however a big issue here.
> (Davidson, 2007: 36).

Research was originally conducted by Kemshall *et al.* in 2005 (Home Office) to explore the effectiveness of MAPPA for sex offenders. A similar Home Office study was undertaken by Wood and Kemshall in 2007(a), the key findings from which support some of the issues raised by the RMA work:

1. The importance (and sometimes lack of) of effective communication between police, probation and prisons – particularly upon release from custody.
2. The lack of systematic exchange of information between agencies.
3. Uneven access to specialist supervised accommodation and difficulty finding accommodation post-release.
4. Varied response in cases of escalating risk.
5. MAPPA resources are considered to be very overstretched and practitioners were very concerned about increases in workload due to any public notification requirements and the consequences of notification.

(Wood and Kemshall, 2007a)

It is clear that MAPPA arrangements provide a useful framework for the management of Internet sex offenders in the UK, but it also seems that a more proactive approach should be taken by agencies in monitoring sex offenders, particularly via regular access to homes and home computers in order to assess risk, and that a greater degree of collaboration between agencies would aid this process.

Conclusion

Criminal justice agencies in the UK and internationally are attempting to build upon existing good practice in terms of assessment of and treatment for sex offenders and to adapt this practice for use with sex offenders whose offences are Internet related. Although practitioners are dedicated and much of the work is innovative, it is essential that good quality research underpins practice; there is a scarcity of such research regarding the behaviour of different types of Internet sex offender (Quayle and Taylor's [2003] and Krone's [2004] work is the exception). Research has focused upon those who produce and collect indecent images of children, whilst very little is known about those who groom children online and the boundary between online abuse and contact abuse. The police have suggested that a greater number of such cases are now being prosecuted under the legislation in the UK. It is therefore of concern that so little is known about this potentially high risk group. There is an urgent need for research to explore the behaviour of online groomers who target children; the link/boundary between non-contact online sexual abuse of children; and Internet offenders' propensity for contact abuse.

Grooming legislation has been introduced in several countries but is now recognised in the EU Framework Decision (Article 5). The difficulty of course is that the framework is not in any way enforceable and countries may simply chose to 'opt out', particularly if their current legislative framework, especially in respect of the age of consent, does not easily accommodate the recommended legislation.

Notes

1 The Sexual Offences Act 2003 (England and Wales) is currently under review in Northern Ireland. Some concerns have been raised regarding a lack of clarity around the age of consent and informed consent. Currently the age of consent is 17 in Northern Ireland (it was raised from 16 to 17 under the Children and Young Persons Act 1950) (Northern Ireland Office, 2006).

2 US Code Title 18, Part 1, Chapter 117, AS 2425.

3 Australian Criminal Code, s 218A.

4 Canadian Criminal Code, s 172.1.

5 A breakdown of countries where websites containing child abuse images appear to have been hosted during the period 1996–2006 is provided by the Internet Watch Foundation (IWF): US 51%; Russia 20%; Japan 5%; Spain 7% and the UK 1.6% (IWF, 2006).

6 The Sexual Offences Act 2003 does not create any new offences in this category but raises the age from 16 to 18 by making amendments to the Criminal Justice Act 1991 and the Protection of Children Act 1978.

7 The provisions allow a defence to the charge if: the picture is of a 16-or 17-year-old; the 16-/17-year-old 'consents'; the pictures of 16-/17-year-olds are not distributed; and the perpetrator and the 16-/17-year-old are in a long-term sexual relationship/ married/cohabiting: S. 8H 2005.

8 Article 1.

9 The Metropolitan Police estimate, for example, that approximately 70 convictions for grooming have been secured since the Act came into force in May 2004, but no national figures are currently available.

10 The Sex Offenders Act (1997); the Crime (Sentences) Act (1997); the introduction of Sex Offender Orders under the Crime and Disorder Act (1998) and later under the Sexual Offences Act (2003); the Risk of Sexual Harm Order introduced under the Sexual Offences Act (2003).

11 Established by the Criminal Justice and Court Services Act 2000 and re-enacted and strengthened by the Criminal Justice Act 2003 in England and Wales, and by the Management of Offenders (Scotland) Act 2005 in Scotland.

12 Section 80 of the Police, Public Order and Criminal Justice (Scotland) Act (2006) amends the Sexual Offences Act (2003) by inserting s 96A. Police can apply to a sheriff to obtain a warrant to enter and search a known (registered) sex offender's home address for risk assessment purposes or following failure to gain entry on more than one occasion.

13 Categories and levels of offending are not mutually exclusive: someone in category 1 on the sex offenders register, for example, could be classed as level 1, 2 or 3.

14 Drugs have been used in an attempt to control sex offender behaviour, in the UK, other European countries such as France and the Netherlands, the US and Canada for some time. This procedure is often referred to as 'chemical castration' and involves the use of testosterone-reducing anti-androgen drugs, administered to control sexual desire. The drugs are synthetic progestins which inhibit hormone development and limit the development of testosterone.

15 Here the two determining factors of seriousness were taken to be the nature of the material and the degree of the offender's engagement with the material. In considering the custody threshold, the fact that the material upon which the convictions were based constituted a small part of the collection and that the potential for others to access and view the collection was great was taken into account. The defendants all received a custodial sentence.

16 The sentencing guidelines may be viewed at http://www.sentencing-guidelines. gov.uk/docs/advice-sexual-offences.pdf (Sentencing Advisory Panel, 2004), p. 99.

References

Borisovna Mizulina, E. (2009) Welcome speech from Duma Committee on Children, Women & Families, Child Safety on the Internet Conference, November 12–13 2009, Moscow.

Bourke, M.L. and Hernandez, A.E. (2009). 'The "Butner Study" redux: A report of the incidence of hands-on child victimization by child pornography offenders,' *Journal of Family Violence*, 24, 183–191.

Clarke, G. (2007) 'They Measured my Fingers to See if I was Fat'. *Daily Mail*, 29 May.

CPS (Crown Prosecution Service) (2007) Legal Guidance on Sexual Offences Act 2003 – Grooming, http://www.cps.gov.uk/legal/s_to_u/sentencing_manual/s15_grooming/index.html.

Craissati, J. (2004) *Managing High Risk Sex Offenders in the Community: A Psychological Approach*. New York: Routledge.

Davidson, J. (2006) 'Victims Speak: Comparing Child Sexual Abusers' and Child Victims' Accounts'. *Perceptions and Interpretations of Sexual Abuse Victims and Offenders*, 1(2), 159–74.

Davidson, J. (2007) Current Practice and Research into Internet Sex Offending, Risk Management Authority (Scotland), http://www.rmascotland.gov.uk/ViewFile.aspx?id=235.

Davidson, J. and Martellozzo, E. (2005) Policing the Internet and Protecting Children from Sex Offenders Online: When Strangers Become Virtual Friends. Available at www.oii.ox.ac.uk./research/cybersafety/extension.pdfs/papers/julia-davidson.pdf.

Davidson, J., Lorenz, M., Martellozzo, E. and Grove-Hills, J. (2009) 'Evaluation of CEOP ThinkUKnow Internet Safety Programme and Exploration of Young People's Internet Safety Knowledge', 2010, in press, full report will be available from 1/4/2010 on www.cats-rp.org.uk.

Elliot, I. A., Beech, A. R, Mandeville-Norden, T., and Hayes, E. (2008) 'Psychological Profiles of Internet Sexual Offenders' *Sexual Abuse: A Journal of Research and Treatment*, 21, 76–92.

EU Council Framework Decision (2009) 'Combating the Sexual Abuse, Sexual Exploitation of Children and Child Pornography', http://eur-lex.europa.eu/LexUriServ/LexUriServ.do?uri=COM:2009:0135:FIN:EN:PDF.

Finkelhor, D. (1984) *Child Sexual Abuse: New Theory and Research*. New York: The Free Press.

Finkelhor, D., Mitchell, K.J. & Wolak, J. (2000) Online Victimization: A report on the nations youth. National Centre for Missing and Exploited Children. www.missingkids.com/missingkids/servlet/PublicHomeServlet?LanguageCountry=en_US.

Guardian (2009) '100 children a month alert police to internet predators: Officers fear social networking sites have triggered a surge in complaints of online child abuse', Robert Booth, guardian.co.uk, 25 Feb.

Gillespie, A. (2009). 'Defining Child Pornography: Challenges for the Law,' Global Symposium on Internet Abuse, North Carolina, April, 21–14.

Hernandez, A. E. (2009) 'Psychological and Behavioural Characteristics of Child Pornography Offenders in Treatment,' Global Symposium: Examining the retationship between online and offline offenses and preventing the sexual exploitation of children. April 5–7.

Home Office (2007) Regulatory Impact Assessment: Making Provision in the Management of Offenders and Sentencing Bill for the Mandatory Polygraph Testing of Certain Sexual Offenders, http://66.102.9.104/search?q=cache:yaX1mUmiqOQJ:www.home office.gov.uk/documents/ria-manage-offenders-bill-060105/ria-offender-polygraphy-06 01053Fview3DBinary+Home+Office+polygraph+testing+of+sex+offenders&hl=en& ct=clnk&cd=1&gl=uk.

——(2007a) Statistical Bulletin Sentencing Statistics 2005, England and Wales RDS NOMS.

——(2007b) National Offender Management Service website, http://noms.homeoffice. gov.uk/protecting-the-public/risk-assessment.

——(2007c) Review of the Protection of Children from Sex Offenders 6/2007, http:// www.homeoffice.gov.uk/documents/CSOR/chid-sex-offender-review-130607.

——(6/2007) 'Review of the protection of children from sex offenders', http://www. homeoffice.gov.uk/documents/CSOR/chid-sex-offender-review-130607.

IWF Annual Report (2006) Available at: http://www.iwf.org.uk/documents/ 20060803_2006_biannual_report_v7_final4.pdf.

Johnson, B. and Connolly, K. (2007) 'Briton under investigation in global Internet paedophile ring'. *The Guardian*, 8 February.

Kemshall, H., Mackenzie, G., Wood, J., Bailey, R. and Yates, J. (2005) Strengthening Multi-Agency Public Protection Arrangements, London: Home Office.

Kemshall, H. and Wood, J. (2007b) 'Beyond Public Protection: An Examination of the Community Protection and Public Health Approaches to Public Protection'. *Criminology and Criminal Justice.*

Klain, E. J., Davies, H. J., and Hicks, M. A. (2001) *Beyond tolerance: Child pornography on the Internet.* New York: New York University Press.

Krone, T. (2004) 'A typology of online child pornography offending,' Trends and Issues in Crime and Criminal Justice, No 279. Canberra: Australian Institute of Criminology.

Lee, J. (2008) 'Child indecent images', National Center for Missing and Exploited Children (NCMEC) Publication.

Livingstone, S. (2009) *Children and the Internet: Great Expectations and Challenging Realities.*

Livingstone, S. and Bober, M. (2004) *UK Children Go Online: Surveying the experiences of young people and their parents* (LSE).

Mitchell, K. J., Wolak, J. and Finkelhor, D. (2008) 'Are blogs putting youth at risk for online sexual solicitation or harassment?' *Child Abuse & Neglect*, 32: 277–294.

Net Family News (2007) 'Sex offenders on MySpace', 3 August, http://www.netfamily news.org/letterindex4.html.

Northern Ireland Office (2006) Reforming the Law on Sexual Offences in Northern Ireland: A Consultation Document, Vol 2, Northern Ireland Sex Crime Unit.

NSPCC Press Release (2009) Available at www.nspcc.org.uk/whatwedo/mediacentre/ pressreleases/2009_09_february.

NSPCC (2009) NSPCC launches campaign to keep children safe online. Available at http://www.nspcc.org.uk/whatwedo/mediacentre/pressreleases/2009_15_june_nspcc_ launches_campaign_to_keep_children_safe_online_wdn66078.html.

Ofcom (2009) 'Digital Lifestyles: Young adults aged 16–24', May, http://www.ofcom. org.uk/advice/media_literacy/medlitpub/medlitpubrss/digital_young/.

Quayle, E. and Jones, T. (2009) 'Children in the abusive image', Child Safety on the Internet Conference, November 12–13, Moscow.

ylor, M. (2002) 'Paedophiles, Pornography and the Internet: Assess-
ritish Journal of Social Work, 32: 863–875.

ylor, M. (2003) 'Model of Problematic Internet Use in People with
t in Children,' Cyberpsychology and behaviour, 6, 1, 93–106.

.uvisory Panel (2004) Sexual Offences Act 2003: The Panel's Advice to
the Sentencing Guidelines Council, http://www.sentencing–guidelines.gov.uk/docs/
advice-sexual-offences.pdf.

Seto, M. C. and Eke, A. W. (2005) 'The future offending of child pornography
offenders,' Sexual Abuse: A Journal of Research & Treatment, 17, 201–210.

Winick, B. J. (1998) Sex Offender Law in the 1990s: A Therapeutic Jurisprudence
Analysis. Psychology, Public Policy, and Law, 4(1/2), 505–70.

Wolak, J., Finkelhor, D. and Mitchell, K.J. (2005) 'Child Pornography Possessors arrested
in Internet-related Crimes' National Centre for Missing and Exploited Children.

Wood, J. and Kemshall, H. (2007a) The Operation and Experience of MAPPA:
Findings, London: Home Office Research Findings 285.

——(2007b) 'Beyond Public Protection: An examination of the community protection and public health approaches to public protection,' Criminology and Criminal
Jusice, 7, 3.

Legislation

Child Online Protection Act 2000 (COPA) (US)
Crime and Disorder Act 1998 (UK)
Crimes Amendment Act 2005 (NZ)
Criminal Code (Australia)
Criminal Code (Canada)
Criminal Justice Act 2003 (UK)
Criminal Justice and Court Services Act 2000 (UK)
Dangerous Prisoners (Sexual Offences) Act 2003 (Queensland, Australia)
Jacob Wetterling Crimes Against Children Law 1996 (US)
Management of Offenders Act (Scotland) 2005
Obscene Publications Act 1959 (England and Wales)
Obscene Publications Act 1964 (England and Wales)
Penal Code (The Production and Distribution of Illegal Pornography [Child])
(Switzerland)
Police, Public Order and Criminal Justice (Scotland) Act 2006
Protection of Children and Prevention of Sexual Offences (Scotland) Act 2005
Sex Offenders Act 1997 (England and Wales)
Sexual Offences Act 2003 (England and Wales)
US Bill of Rights 2007

Cases

Ashcroft v ACLU 2/3/04, US Supreme Court, transcript available at http://www.
supremecourtus.gov/oral_arguments/argument_transcripts/03–218.pdf.
Fardon v Attorney General For The State Of Queensland (2004) Deakin Law
Review, http://www.austlii.edu.au/au/journals/DeakinLRev/2005/13.html (Australia)
R v Oliver, Hartrey and Baldwin [2003] 2 Cr App R28: (2003) Crim LR 127 (UK).

Chapter 2

Characteristics of the Internet and child abuse

Petter Gottschalk

Introduction: understanding the Internet

The Internet is an international network of networks that connects people all over the world. Any computer can communicate with almost any other computer linked to the Internet. The Internet has created a universal technology platform on which to build all sorts of new products, services, communities and solutions. It is reshaping the way information technology is used by individuals and organisations. The Internet has provided an expedient mode of communication and access to a wealth of information (Dombrowski *et al.*, 2007).

In less than two decades, the Internet has moved from being a communications medium used by some to an everyday tool used in our homes, schools, workplaces and travels. It enables us to search for information, perform routine tasks and communicate with others. The technological aspects of the Internet are developing at the same high speed as the number of users globally. The Internet provides a social context for us to meet with others and to exchange information on a scale we would never have thought possible in the past (Quayle *et al.*, 2006).

The World Wide Web is a system with universally accepted standards for storing, retrieving, formatting, changing and displaying information in a networked environment. Information is stored and displayed as electronic pages that can contain numbers, text, pictures, graphics, sound and video. These web pages can be linked electronically to other web pages, independent of where they are located. Web pages can be viewed by any type of computer.

In a survey of young people in Norway between the ages of 8 and 18, 78 per cent of the respondents said that they are involved in chatting. The use of chatting for communication is more common than the use of email in this age group. In the age group 17–18, all respondents said that they take part in chatting. The percentage reporting that they have been plagued while chatting was 9 per cent. Among chatters about one-third have met persons in reality that they first met while chatting (Medietilsynet, 2008).

The Internet is a valuable tool; however, it can also be detrimental to the well-being of children due to numerous online hazards (Dombrowski *et al.*, 2007: 153):

> There is the potential for children to be abused via cyberspace through online sexual solicitation and access to pornography. Indeed, the Internet is replete with inappropriate material, including pornography, chat rooms with adult themes and access to instant messaging wherein others could misrepresent themselves. Because children are actively utilizing the Internet where unknown others can have access to them or where they can be exposed to inappropriate sexual materials, they require safeguarding and education in safe Internet use.

Online grooming might be compared to online learning and other forms of online activity. The purpose of such analogies is to identify both similarities and differences. Learning on the Internet, for example, is structured as a formal and non-anonymous activity. To some it is scary rather than safe, because students are asked to reveal personal information on the Internet and to share it with others.

Generally, going online enables individuals to play a personality role, which might be more or less different from their real personality. There will always be a difference between your role in virtual reality and in the real world. We play roles as adults and parents, or children and students, both in the real world and in virtual realities. However, in the virtual world we may find it easier to live our dreams and fantasies. In the type of 'Second Life'[1] environments on the Internet, players can be unfaithful and can build their dream existence alone or with others.

What is so appealing about being online? One answer to this question is that you can be in a different, informal and anonymous setting where you can live out dreams and fantasies.

Seventeen Internet characteristics

We are all familiar with online services on the Internet. A typical example is online banking, where we complete our payments of bills at home. Most Norwegians have many years of personal experience using online services on the Internet. According to the United Nations (2008), Norway is ranked third in the world in terms of online services provided by the government. Sweden and Denmark are on the top of the list, and Norway is followed by the United States and the Netherlands. The United Kingdom is ranked tenth.

A number of characteristics of the Internet for online services have been observed and are described in the following, which may shed light on the methods that offenders use to groom children:

1. *Disconnected personal communication.* While communication on the Internet might be personal in content, it is not perceived as inter-personal in meaning. A typical example is email, where the sender might feel completely disconnected from the time and place the recei-ver reads the email message. Even when chatting in real time, sender and receiver may perceive both involvement and disconnectedness at the same time. Some may unconsciously change their personality when moving from face-to-face communication to email communication (Weber, 2004). Internet grooming can be and often is different from 'real world' grooming in that offenders spend little time chatting and will come straight to the point, sometimes instantly, for example, 'Would you like to meet for sex?' This would suggest that the Internet might act to remove inhibitions associated with face-to-face contact, which can be explained by the disconnected nature of personal com-munication on the Internet, thereby avoiding unpleasant emotional states (Quayle *et al.*, 2006). There are however some offenders who will still spend a considerable amount of time grooming a child online, particularly in peer-to-peer networks, in order to prepare them for abuse (Davidson, 2008).

2. *Mediating technology.* The Internet is a mediating technology that interconnects parties that are independent (Afuah and Tucci, 2003). The interconnections can be business-to-business (B2B), business-to-consumer (B2C), government-to-business (G2B), person-to-person (P2P) or any other link between individuals and organisations. In the case of grooming, the Internet serves as a mediating technology mainly for person-to-person (P2P) communication, but person-to-group (P2G) and group-to-person (G2P) do also occur.

3. *Universality.* The universality of the Internet refers to the Internet's ability to both enlarge and shrink the world. It enlarges the world because anyone anywhere can potentially make his or her services, messages and requests available to anyone anywhere else at anytime. It shrinks the world in that distance is reduced on electronic highways (Afuah and Tucci, 2003). In the case of grooming, the Internet enables each grooming individual to potentially contact anyone, anywhere and anytime. Contact is established without the groomer having to travel physically, all he needs to do is travel electronically. The Internet combines global communications with an incredible range of resources (Calder, 2004). The global reach enabled by the Internet permits grooming to cross-cultural and national boundaries far more con-veniently and cost-effectively than is true in traditional grooming (Laudon and Laudon, 2010).

4. *Network externalities.* A technology or product exhibits network externalities when it becomes more valuable to users as more people take advantage of it. A classic example is the first person in Norway

who got himself a telephone. Until a second person got a telephone, there was nobody in Norway to talk to on the phone. The value of the telephone for each subscriber increases with the number of subscribers. Similarly, the value of the Internet increases with the number of Internet users. The more people who are connected to a network within the Internet, the more valuable the network is to each user (Afuah and Tucci, 2003). The more children who are connected to a network, the more valuable the network is to each groomer, since he is able to reach and get in contact with more potential victims. Since Internet access is found in more and more homes all over the world (Livingstone, 2009), the number of potential victims rises accordingly.

5. *Distribution channel.* The Internet acts as a distribution channel for products that are information bits, such as software, music, video, news, tickets and money. There is a replacement effect if the Internet is used to serve the same deliveries, which were serviced by the old physical distribution channel. There is an extension effect if the Internet is used by more people and for new services (Afuah and Tucci, 2003). When grooming children, the offender may use the Internet not only for communications. He may use it also to send gifts and other digital items that the child might be interested in. He may also send digital items that the child is not always interested in, such as pornographic pictures and videos, in order to test children's reactions.

6. *Time moderator.* The Internet has an ability to shrink and enlarge time. It shrinks time for people who want information when information sources are closed. It enlarges time when related work can be done at different points in time (Afuah and Tucci, 2003). Both dimensions of the Internet as a time moderator can be important in online victimisation of children. When a child is offline, the groomer can leave messages and gifts for the child to pick up next time the child logs on.

7. *Low cost standard.* Individuals could not exploit the properties of the Internet if they didn't understand it. Internet usage has been easy for two reasons. First and foremost, the Internet and web application are standards open to everyone and are very easy to use. Second, the cost of the Internet is a lot lower than that of earlier means of electronic communication (Afuah and Tucci, 2003). Given the low cost standard, access to the Internet is not limited to affluent or well-educated people; both adults and children have access independent of social class in most countries. For a groomer, this enables access not only to a large number of children but also to a large variety of children. Universal technical standards of the Internet enables any computer to link with any other computer regardless of the technology platform each is using (Laudon and Laudon, 2010).

8. *Electronic double.* It is not the real person who is present on the Internet. It is a digital copy of the person who is present. The digital information about the person creates an image of the person, which we call the electronic double. The way in which a groomer is perceived by a child on the Internet is thus dependent both on the information the person provides and the image this information creates in the child's mind. Even if the groomer is completely honest in all communication with the child, the child may perceive the person as very different from what they are actually like in reality and possibly as similar to someone the child already knows. In a similar vein, the groomer may perceive the child and create in their head as electronic double which can be far removed from reality, but which may serve their fantasy.

9. *Electronic double manipulation.* The electronic double created on the Internet represents an image of the real person. The real person can change his or her electronic double and make it more or less similar to the real self. The most obvious change is age, where a groomer may claim to be younger than they actually are. This requires consistency in all other information, so that the presented age matches other information about the person. Similarly, children may claim to be older than they actually are.

10. *Information asymmetry.* Information asymmetry is often reduced on the Internet. Information asymmetry exists when one party to a transaction has information that another party does not – information that is important to the transaction. The World Wide Web reduces such information asymmetries, as the other party can find the same information on the web (Afuah and Tucci, 2003). Neither the person nor the child has information monopoly in areas where information is available on the World Wide Web.

11. *Infinite virtual capacity.* Access to the Internet is perceived as unlimited; you do not have to wait on hold or in a long line. For example, virtual communities such as chatting houses have infinite capacity for members who can talk anytime of the day for as long as they want (Afuah and Tucci, 2003).

12. *Independence in time and space.* While a traditional meeting requires that participants are present at the same place at the same time, meeting on the Internet is possible even if different participants are present at different places at different times. The online environment enables access to a wealth of information and communication across both distance and time (Kierkegaard, 2008). The independence in time and space is typically the case when using email. When participating in a chat room, participants are required to respond within a short time frame, eliminating independence in time, but still keeping independence in space. On the mobile phone, SMS (simple message service) messages have the same characteristic of independence in time and space. Calder (2004) has

suggested that the Internet promotes better social relationships as people will be freed from the constraints of time and place; however it could also limit social relationships to the virtual world and reinforce isolation.

13. *Cyberspace.* Using the Internet is not just a supplement to or add-on to real life. It is also an enabler of an alternative life style in cyberspace with its own cyber culture. Cyberspace is an abstract space, rather than a physical space, where a culture has emerged from the use of computer networks for communication, entertainment and business. Cyber culture can, for example, be found in virtual communities, which is a group of people who primarily interact via communication media such as newsletters, telephone, email or instant messages rather than face-to-face for social and other purposes (Whittaker, 2004). In terms of online grooming, both adults and children are sometimes members of virtual communities. Calder (2004) argues that there are many benefits that can be derived from the development of online relationships including online relationships that become sexual in cyberspace. Cyberspace can facilitate the formation of romantic relationships, improve the chances of finding an 'optimal' partner, highlight that relationships can develop from attachments, and improve one's skills in interpersonal, yet virtual, communication.

14. *Dynamic social network.* The emergence of social network services has radically challenged our understanding of traditional, territorial social networks. An average Westerner's social network comprises about 150 individuals. Once a physical social network is established, this number of members tends to change little over time, and the members themselves do not change very much. In contrast, the Internet enables individuals to expand and reduce their social network and replace members in the network (CEOP, 2006). The Internet provides a social context for more and more people to meet more and more people. There is a dynamic social network rather than a stable one. When both offenders and potential victims dynamically change their social networks, the likelihood of contact increases.

15. *Ubiquity.* In traditional grooming, a place for grooming is a physical place, such as a bar, club or other public place. Online grooming is ubiquitous, meaning that it is possible just about everywhere, at all times. It makes it possible to groom from a laptop, at home, at work, or even from a car, using mobile technology. The result is called a grooming space – a grooming place extended beyond traditional boundaries and removed from a temporal and geographic location. From a groomer's point of view, ubiquity reduces transaction costs – the costs of grooming children. To transact with children online in the virtual world, it is no longer necessary that the sex offender spends time or money travelling to a grooming place, and much less mental effort is required to make contact (Laudon and Laudon, 2010).

16. *Richness.* Information richness refers to the complexity and content of a message. Traditional communication channels have great richness; they are able to provide personal, face-to-face communication using aural and visual cues when making contact. The web makes it possible to deliver rich messages with text, audio, and video simultaneously to large numbers of people (Laudon and Laudon, 2010).

17. *Interactivity.* Systems used on the Internet are interactive, meaning they allow for two-way communication between adult and child. Interactivity allows an online groomer to engage a child in ways similar to face-to-face experience but on a massive, global scale (Laudon and Laudon, 2010).

The Internet is a special artefact system that has enormous technical and social positive impacts on modern society (Kierkegaard, 2008: 41):

> The online environment enables access to a wealth of information and communication across both distance and time. There is a vast amount of data available on virtually every subject, making it an effective learning tool.

However, the Internet is also a double-edged sword with negative and positive consequences (Kierkegaard, 2008: 41):

> It has a potential for misuse and has generated societal concerns. Today, the danger for children is even greater because the Internet provides anonymity to predators.

Recent advances in computer technology have been aiding sexual predators, stalkers, child pornographers, child traffickers, and others with the intent of exploiting children. While they have existed prior to the Internet, the advent of the new technology two decades ago has allowed for easier and faster distribution of pornographic materials and communication across national and international boundaries (Kierkegaard, 2008).

On the other hand, the Internet is not all negative concerning sexual communication (Calder, 2004: 3):

> It can be used for healthy sexual expression. For example, the Internet offers the opportunity for the formulation of online or virtual communities where isolated or disenfranchised individuals e.g. gay males and lesbians can communicate with each other around sexual topics of shared interest; it offers educational potential; and it may allow for sexual experimentation in a safer forum, thus facilitating identity exploration and development.

The Internet allows sex offenders instant access to other sex offenders worldwide; forums facilitate open discussion of their sexual desires, shared ideas about ways to lure victims, mutual support of their adult–child sex philosophies, instant access to potential child victims worldwide, and disguised identities for approaching children, even to the point of presenting as a member of teen groups. Furthermore, the Internet allows sexual offenders ready access to chat areas and Social Networking Sites reserved for teenagers and children to discover how to approach and who to target as potential victims. The Internet provides a means to identify and track down home contact information, and the Internet enables adults to build long-term virtual relationships with potential victims, prior to attempting to engage the child in physical contact.

Relationships are built using social software. Through the Internet, people are discovering and inventing new ways to share knowledge and interests. People communicate on the Internet with each other in a human voice. These conversations using social software are collectively referred to as social media, a wide-ranging term that encompasses the practice and resulting output of all kinds of information created online by those who were previously consumers of that media (Cook, 2008: 7):

> Philosophically, social media describes the way in which content (particularly news and opinion) has become democratized by the Internet and the role people now play not only in consuming information and conveying it to others, but also in creating and sharing content with them, be it textual, aural or visual.

For this reason, social media are interchangeably referred to as consumer- or user-generated content. Social media are often defined by the categories of software tools that people use to undertake this consuming, conveying, creating and sharing content with each other, including blogs, podcasts, wikis and social networking that have found their place on the Internet (Cook, 2008).

Blogs in terms of online personal journals are one of the examples mentioned by Cook (2008), and Mitchell *et al.* (2008) phrased the following question: 'Are blogs putting youth at risk of online sexual solicitation or harassment?' They conducted a telephone survey of 1,500 youth Internet users, ages 10–17, in the USA. They found that 16 per cent of youth Internet users reported blogging in the past year. Teenagers and girls were the most common bloggers, and bloggers were more likely than other youth to post personal information online.

However, Mitchell *et al.* (2008) found that bloggers were not more likely to interact with people they met online and did not know in person. Youth who interacted with people they met online, regardless of whether or not they blogged, had higher odds of receiving online sexual solicitations.

Bloggers who did not interact with people they met online were at no increased risk for sexual solicitation. Moreover, posting personal information did not add to risk. The only difference found was related to harassment, since youthful bloggers were found to be at increased risk of online harassment, regardless of whether they also interacted with others online.

The role of web cams

Before web cams became common on most children's personal computers and laptop computers, offenders were able to present themselves as someone else. With the advent of web cams, children can check the identity of online friends. However, where groomers adopt a more direct approach to children and are honest about their intentions, web cams can serve as useful devices allowing groomers to request that the child takes off their clothes and performs sex acts. Perpetrators may also ask the child to view sex acts.

Web cams are video capture devices connected to computers or computer networks, often using a stick into the personal computer. Their most popular use is for video telephony, enabling a computer to act as a videophone or videoconferencing station. Web cams are inexpensive and can easily be connected to a computer. Combined with the Internet, web cams are changing the way people communicate as it is adding video support to chatting (Lindgreen et al., 2004).

Web cams have become part of the social media used by children in their social and learning activities. The Internet and web cams as part of the information technology infrastructure used by children offer a platform for a diversity of political discourse, unique opportunities for cultural development, and myriad avenues of intellectual activity (Broek et al., 2009).

Technology behind MySpace

An example of a social networking Internet site where grooming takes place is provided by Laudon and Laudon (2010: 260). MySpace is a Social Networking Site that has experienced substantial growth in recent years. The site was launched in 2003. Four years later, it had 175 million member accounts. The challenge for MySpace in terms of technology has been to avoid technological letdowns that degrade website performance and frustrate its rapidly expanding network of users.

The technical requirements of a site such as MySpace are very different from other heavily trafficked websites. On a normal website, a small number of people are active in changing the contents on the site over time. The site may retrieve thousands of read-only requests from its underlying database without having to update the database. On MySpace, however, tens of millions of users are constantly updating their contents, resulting in an enormous number of database interactions that require updates to the underlying database (Laudon and Laudon, 2010: 260):

> Each time a user views a profile on MySpace, the resulting page is stitched together from database lookups that organize information from multiple tables stored in multiple databases residing on multiple servers.

In its initial phases, MySpace operated with two web servers communicating with one database server and a Microsoft SQL (Structured Query Language) server database. As the popular Social Networking Site approached 2 million accounts, the database servers approached their input–output capacity, which refers to the speed at which they could read and write data. This caused the site to lag behind in contents updating. MySpace switched to a vertical partitioning model in which separate databases supported distinct functions of the website, such as the log-in screen, user profiles, and blogs (Laudon and Laudon, 2010).

A web server is software locating and managing stored web pages. It locates the web pages requested by a user on the computer where they are stored and delivers the web pages to the user's computer. Web servers run on the World Wide Web (WWW), which is a system with universally accepted standards for storing, retrieving, formatting, and displaying information using a client-server architecture. Client-server computing is a distributed computing model in which some of the processing power is located within small, inexpensive client computers, and resides mainly on desktops, laptops, or in handheld devices (Laudon and Laudon, 2010).

Web pages are formatted using hypertext with embedded links that connect documents to one another and that also link pages to other objects, such as sound, video, or animation files. Web server applications usually run on dedicated computers, although they can all reside on a single computer in small organisations (Laudon and Laudon, 2010).

In 2005, MySpace had to fortify its technology infrastructure by installing a layer of servers between the database servers and the web servers to store and serve copies of frequently accessed data objects so that the site's web servers would not have to query the database servers with lookups as frequently. Despite all these measures, MySpace still tends to overload more frequently than other major websites (Laudon and Laudon, 2010). In 2007 MySpace was sued by parents of teenage girls in the United States who had been groomed by adult men on the site (http://news.bbc.co.uk/1/hi/uk/6275611.stm). In response to this, MySpace introduced a safety section listing safety tips (http://www.myspace.com/index.cfm?fuseaction=cms.viewpage& placement=safety_pageteens&sspage=4) and links to Internet safety organisations such as the Child Exploitation and Online Protection Centre in the UK.

Virtual communities

A number of individuals join virtual communities where they meet other persons who have the same or similar interests. A virtual community provides an online meeting place where people with similar interests can communicate and find useful information. Communication between members may be via email, bulletin boards, online chat, web-based conferencing, or other computer-based media. As a business model, a virtual community can make money from membership fees, direct sales of goods and services, advertising, click-through, and sales commissions (Gottschalk, 2006).

Vidnes and Jacobsen (2008) surveyed 772 persons from 16 to 29 years of age. One of the key findings was that especially the youngest ones are active users of web cameras, and that young people who use web cameras have certain characteristics: they are more socially active on the Net than others, and more interested in getting to know new people. Fifty-three per cent of youngsters between 16 and 19 years that use web cameras have come in contact with people on the Net that they later on have met outside the Net. Only 25 per cent of those who do not use web cameras report the same. This shows that web camera users to a greater extent than others expand their social network on and outside the Net. At the same time it is evident that web camera users to a far greater extent are involved in activities that are perceived as potentially dangerous.

However, most young web camera users communicate mainly with persons that they already know. When getting to know a new person, they seldom start by using their web cameras. Rather, they start using sites such as Facebook or Nettby (Net village), which are characterised by openness in the sense that individuals present themselves through real pictures, name, interests and friends. These net societies function as cocktail parties, where one can be introduced to others and move on, get contacts and continually expand networks (Vidnes and Jacobsen, 2008).

Thorgrimsen (2008) emphasises the following findings from the Vidnes and Jacobsen study:

- Seven out of 10 youngsters between 16 and 19 years old have access to a web camera on their computer; 48 per cent of them use it at least once a month.
- Almost all youngsters are using MSN (Microsoft Service Network) on a daily basis, but very few use their camera daily.
- First and foremost the camera is used with persons that one seldom meets.
- Web cameras are far less used than other communication tools such as net community and MSN.
- Young people are careful in providing identifiable information before feeling safe in new Net relationships.

- The web camera also works as a control mechanism, as one cannot be sure who is on the line before the camera is turned on. Resistance to turn it on is interpreted as the other person having something to hide.

If young people want to get to know each other better, then they may move into more private areas such as MSN, which intensifies the communication. If the relationship is developed further, then the use of the private arena of web cameras emerges. By choosing different tools for different relationships and for different phases in a relationship, Vidnes and Jacobsen (2008) thus found that young people are able to regulate the degree of intimacy in the relationship.

MySpace and other Social Networking Sites like it offer thriving communities where young people engage in countless hours of photo sharing. In addition to MySpace, other social networking and blogging sites such as Friendster.com, FaceBook.com and MyYearbook.com allow users to post pictures, videos, and blogs, and they support email and instant messaging. Initially, MySpace and Facebook did differ in that MySpace was open to anyone, and had loose age restrictions (set at 13 plus but not enforced or monitored: http://www.myspace.com, 22/10/09),[2] while Facebook users were encouraged and often required to register using their real name (Kierkegaard, 2008). However, Facebook is now open to anyone and has no age restrictions, leading to an enormous growth in use over the recent years.

The most prevalent examples of social network sites are Facebook, which started as a college site and is still dominated by college users, and MySpace, which has always been open to the public. Somewhere between 80 and 90 per cent of all college students have a profile on a social network site. All social network sites allow users to articulate their social network via links between their profile page and other profiles (Tufekci, 2008: 546, emphasis in original):

> Profiles linked to each other in this manner are called *friends*. Profile owners also express an online persona through pictures, words and page composition, as well as through data fields where information ranging from favourite books and movies to sexual orientation and relationship status (single, in a relationship, etc.) is indicated.

Kierkegaard (2008) argues that the anonymity and availability of extremely sensitive personal information and ease of contacting people make Social Networking Sites a useful tool for online child predators. While many of the sites have age restrictions, it is possible for offenders to misrepresent their age (how far the MySpace threat to remove those believed to be over 18 but posing as under 18 is carried out in practice for example is questionable). To hide their IP (internet protocol) addresses and locations, many offenders piggyback on Wi-Fi (wireless fidelity) connections or use proxy servers. Decentralised peer-to-peer networks prevent material from being tracked to a specific server, and encryption lets them keep online chats private from those policing the web.

Social Networking Sites have been studied in different contexts. For example, Tufekci (2008) explored the rapid adoption of online social network sites by students on a US college campus. Using quantitative and qualitative data based on a diverse sample of college students, demographic and other characteristics of Social Networking Site users and non-users were compared. A distinction was made between social grooming and presentation of self. In the study, non-users displayed an attitude towards social grooming (gossip, small-talk and generalised, non-functional people-curiosity) that ranged from incredulous to hostile. Contrary to expectations in the study, non-users did not report a smaller number of close friends compared with users, but they did keep in touch with fewer people. Users were also heavier users of the expressive Internet, which is the practice and performance of technologically mediated sociality.

Thus, while social grooming through language may well be an important human activity, there seems to be no reason to presuppose that everyone will be equally disposed to such activity. Interest in exchange and browsing social information about friends and acquaintances, and curiosity about people, is likely to be related to interest in how an application specifically facilitates such activity (Tufekci, 2008).

When we apply Tufekci's (2008) terminology to online grooming, online groomers are likely to be heavier users of the expressive Internet than paedophilic non-users of Social Networking Sites. As users of the expressive Internet, online groomers use the Internet as an instrument to express opinions and communicate information. 'Expressive Internet' is the practice and performance of technologically mediated sociality. It is the use of the Internet to perform and realise interactions, self-presentations, public performance, social capital management, social monitoring, and the production, maintenance and furthering of social ties. The expressive Internet might be recognised as a social ecology involving other people, values, norms and social contexts.

'Instrumental Internet', on the other hand, refers to information seeking, knowledge gathering and commercial transactions on the Internet, and the non-social communication involved in such transactions. This is typically the Internet of online banking, shopping and checking the weather. Tufekci (2008) found no difference in the use of instrumental Internet for users versus non-users of Social Networking Sites.

The expressive Internet has been expanding rapidly, a process often described in the popular press as the rise of social computing. These tools have been assimilated as a means of social interaction and social integration for increasing numbers of people and communities. People are increasingly using the expressive Internet in ways that complement or further their offline sociality (Tufekci, 2008).

The distinction between the two groups of users is a point also raised by some of the probation officers interviewed by Davidson (2008) in the UK.

The probation officers were working with groomers in treatment programmes. They spoke about offenders for whom the Internet played a significant role in their lives and who had many online relationships. Using the Internet to offend was almost a natural progression for these offenders as it played such a big part in other areas of their lives.

Because the sample of college students studied by Tufekci (2008) tended to have a high level of offline–online integration, students typically used their real names and engaged in high levels of self-disclosure, especially on Facebook. Facebook allows users to tag individuals on photographs uploaded to the site, which means identifying the person in the photograph and thereby linking the picture to that person's profile, and thus creating a searchable digital trail of a person's social activities. Since online groomers and their potential victims initially have no offline–online integration, we expect the behaviours of online paedophilic grooming to differ from campus social grooming.

According to the encyclopaedia Wikipedia (www.wikipedia.org), 'online chat' can refer to any kind of communication over the Internet, but is primarily meant to refer to direct one-on-one chat or text-based group chat, formally also known as synchronous conferencing. Online chat uses tools such as instant messaging, Internet relay chat, talkers and other means. The expression 'online chat' comes from the word 'chat', which means informal conversation.

The term 'chatiquette' is a variation of 'netiquette' (chat netiquette) and describes basic rules of online communication. To avoid misunderstandings and to simplify the communication between users in a chat, these conventions or guidelines have been created. An interesting issue is whether, how and why online groomers violate the chatiquette. Chatiquette varies from community to community, generally describing basic courtesy; it introduces a new user into the community and the associated network culture. As an example, it is considered rude to write only in UPPER CASE, because it looks as if the user is shouting (www.wikipedia.org).

The Internet has afforded sex offenders the opportunity to create their own virtual communities by allowing instant access to other offenders' worldwide, an open discussion of their sexual desires, shared ideas about ways to lure victims, and mutual support of their adult–child sex philosophies. Computer technology and the Internet enable sex offenders to locate and interact with other offenders more readily than before. The organisational aspects of a common gathering place and the resultant support child predators are providing each other is probably their most significant advantage – and the most troublesome for a concerned public.

Child predators are forming online communities and bonds using the Internet. They are openly uniting against legal authorities and discussing ways to influence public thinking and legislation on child exploitation. While sex offender websites are being tracked down and removed from Internet servers in countries all over the world, they are popping up again at a higher pace in most parts of the world, many sites are hosted in major countries such as the United States and Russia.

An example of a website representing a virtual community for sex offenders is 'Boylove', currently one of the largest sex offender networks on the Internet. On the website, The Boylove Manifesto could be found, which argued the case for intergenerational relationships (www.prevent-abuse-now.com):

> As boy lovers we distance ourselves from the current discussion about 'child sexual abuse'. Human sexuality plays the same part in a boy love relationship as it undoubtedly does in any relationship between human beings. A boy lover desires a friendly and close relationship with a boy.

Similar text can be found on Boylovers.net:

> Over the years, paedophilia, or boy love as it is sometimes known, has come under heavy criticism from those who are opposed to it in the media, government and general society. Often, this can be very one-sided and extremely vitriolic in nature.
>
> Here at BoyLover.net, we believe that people deserve the chance to hear both sides of the argument. Doubtless, by now you will have read or heard many opinions against paedophilia. With this in mind, we have taken the opportunity to present different views so that people can make an informed decision regarding the subject.

Boylover.net seems important to mention here, as sex offender research in countries such as Norway, Sweden and the UK tends to focus on girls more than boys. As listed in Norwegian court sentences, almost all cases are concerned with the victimisation of girls. Lillywhite and Skidmore (2006) argue that the view that boys are not sexually exploited is very common among many professionals working with vulnerable young men. Do sex offenders interested in boys perform online grooming in a different way from sex offenders who are interested in girls? Different grooming behaviours may be employed with different genders.

Male children have traditionally been exploited in hidden locations such as public toilets, parks, bus and train stations, cruising areas, shopping areas and arcades. Because of the Internet, a shift in the sites for abuse is occurring. Young men are sexually exploited via the Internet in a range of ways. These include: a young man who was stripped, shaved and photographed by a friend of his so-called older 'boyfriend'; a 15-year-old client who was groomed over the Internet by a man in his thirties; and a young man whose photograph was placed on a website where men sell sex.

Giving mobile phones is a common grooming technique when men are grooming boys (Lillywhite and Skidmore, 2006: 356):

One young man we worked with was given ten mobile phones over a one-year period. Giving mobiles is now a common grooming technique experienced by the young men we work with. It means that a young man can be contacted at any time and place by a child sex offender.

Do sex offenders who are grooming girls online operate differently from sex offenders who are grooming boys online? This is absolutely a key question for the future study of online grooming and for the policing of online groomers. From the existing literature on contact offending it seems clear that offenders' grooming behaviour is tailored to the victim's style / characteristics. It is hard to see any reason why it would be different online, but future research will be needed.

A 'sex offender ring' is a group of persons working together across the Internet in different countries and jurisdictions to collect and distribute child pornography for their own gratification. This can also involve sharing expertise and experiences on avoiding detection and planning criminal activities against children. There is a strong perception that the Internet has become a major factor in the development of child sex offender rings worldwide. For example, the Metropolitan Police High Tech Crime Unit (HTCU) in the UK has suggested that large international abuser rings are commonplace. These rings share images, but how far they are contact abusing is another question, and one that needs to be explored in future research. The HTCU also suggest that every day many hundreds of men approach their undercover police officers (who pose as children online) on Social Networking Sites for sex.

Understanding online groomers

The Internet represents an attractive medium for grooming and soliciting youth for sexual encounters (Dombrowski *et al.*, 2007: 155):

> It provides access to countless children in a relatively anonymous environment. An online predator can masquerade as a young person with similar background, age and interests. Further, the cyber predator can join with the young person in the disinhibition process and encourage discussion of sexual fantasies at too early an age. The purpose of this dialogue might be to play out sexual deviant fantasies. However, the purpose might also be to desensitize the young person to child–adult sexual activity, with the ultimate goal of perpetrating offline.

Unwanted sexual solicitations are defined as requests to engage in sexual activities or sexual talk or provide personal sexual information that are unwanted or, when made by an adult to a young person, the same but without regard to whether they were wanted or not. Online harassment episodes are defined as threats or other offensive behaviour (not sexual solicitation), sent online to the youth or posted online about the youth for others to see (Mitchell *et al.*, 2008).

Sex offenders are using the Internet to solicit sexually explicit images of young people. Internet bulletin boards, chat rooms, private websites, and peer-to-peer networks are being used daily by sex offenders to meet unsuspecting children (Kierkegaard, 2008: 41):

> The misuse of the Internet for pornography, cyber bullying, grooming and paedophilia has become a major issue of international concern. Because of the freedom and the anonymous environment offered by the Internet, child molesters and pornographers are increasingly using the Internet to further their criminal activity.

The tactic of grooming, where sex offender criminals contact children and gain their trust for the purpose of meeting them and engaging in sexual behaviour, consists of a spectre of approaches. The Internet enables sex offenders to entice multiple victims at once. Aside from chat rooms, grooming is facilitated through mobiles, email exchange, blogs and other types of Social Networking Sites where offenders can create their own social contents and make it accessible to potential victims (Kierkegaard, 2008).

According to Quayle *et al.* (2006: 1), there is increasing evidence that people use the Internet to avoid negative emotional states, such as boredom, anxiety, or depression:

> This may be of increasing relevance for sex offenders. While the primary function of accessing the Internet for sex offenders is to obtain material that aids sexual arousal, the Internet functions to help people address some of the more immediate feelings of distress or dissatisfaction in their lives. For those with a sexual interest in children, once online offenders can then download child pornography and masturbate to such images, providing a highly rewarding or reinforcing context for further avoidance [of negative emotional states]. The intensity of such behaviour often has properties that offenders call 'addictive', with high levels of activity associated with the avoidance of unpleasant emotional states.

An online groomer is someone who has initiated online contact with a child with the intention of establishing a sexual relationship involving cyber sex or physical sex. A groomer is a kind of traveller, in that he uses the Internet to gain access to a child whom he coerces into meeting him for sexual purposes. Quayle *et al.* (2008: 27) phrased the question 'Who are these people?' in relation to child pornography:

> We have no idea of the numbers of people who offend on the Internet. We can examine conviction rates, but these reflect only the countries

where possession and distribution of child pornography is both illegal and where there are either the resources or inclination to act upon detection.

It has been estimated that there are between 50,000 and 100,000 sex offenders involved in organised pornography rings around the world, and that one-third of these operate from the United States. In the US, law enforcement made 3,000 arrests in one year for Internet sex crimes against minors. These crimes were categorised into three mutually exclusive types: Internet crimes against identified victims (39 per cent); Internet solicitations to undercover law enforcement (25 per cent); and possession, distribution or trading of child pornography with no identified victim (36 per cent). Two-thirds of offenders who committed any of the types of Internet sex crimes against minors possessed child pornography (Quayle *et al.*, 2008).

There are a number of grooming practices on the Internet. Some may directly and quickly approach victims for sex (see Chapters 6 and 7 in this volume by Martellozzo and Taylor). However, victim selection methods vary, and the groomer may go through the following grooming phases (O'Connell, 2004):

1. *Friendship-forming phase* involves the sex offender getting to know the child. The length of time spent at this phase varies from one sex offender to another and the number of times this stage of the relationship is re-enacted depends upon the level of contact the sex offender maintains with a child.
2. *Relationship-forming phase* is an extension of the friendship-forming phase, and during this phase the adult may engage with the child in discussing, for example, school and/or home life. Not all adults engage in this phase but generally those who are going to maintain contact with a child will endeavour to create an illusion of being the child's best friend.
3. *Risk assessment phase* refers to the part of the conversation when a sex offender will ask the child about, for example, the location of the computer the child is using and the number of other people who use the computer. By gathering this kind of information it seems reasonable to suppose that the sex offender is trying to assess the likelihood of his activities being detected by, for example, the child's parents, guardians, or older siblings.
4. *Exclusivity phase* typically follows the risk assessment phase where the content of the conversation changes so that the child is invited to reveal personal problems in the context of a private conversation. The interactions take on the characteristics of a strong sense of mutuality, where secrets are shared.
5. *Sexual phase* is introduced after the adult has positioned the conversation so that a deep sense of shared trust seems to have been

established. It is during this phase that the most distinctive differences in conversational patterns occur. For those adults who intend to maintain a relationship with a child and for whom it seems to be important to maintain the child's perception of a sense of trust and love having been created between child and adult, the sexual phase will be entered gently. The relational framing orchestrated by the adult is for the child to perceive the adult as a mentor and possible future lover.

Dombrowski *et al.* (2007) argue that the full extent of technology used by predators remains largely unknown. There is a wide range of Internet technologies that are reasonably accessible to online predators. Website portals and Internet-worked synchronous chat are two examples of technological resources that sexual predators have access to and employ in online grooming.

Like many criminals, sex offenders try to decriminalise or normalise their crimes. They say that they are misunderstood. Sex offenders are trying to eliminate the term 'sex offender' and replace it with the more positive 'boy lover', 'girl lover' or 'child lover'. Rather than use the word 'victims', sex offenders refer to 'young friends', which is what they call the children that they are either grooming for sexual abuse or actually molesting. Suggesting that they are 'friends' with the child places the abusive relationship on an even footing, establishing an equality between the sexual abuser and the child that does not exist.

Sex offenders want to have sex with children, but that is illegal, so they seek to promote a child's right to have sex with them. One point of most sex offender agendas is a belief that there are children who want to have sex with adults.

Understanding children's online behaviour

Children use the Internet a great deal, and this has been well documented in other research. More than 30 million in the USA alone used the Internet in 2000. It has been suggested that 1 in 4 children on the Internet have an unwanted exposure to sexually explicit pictures that were inappropriate for children to view. Approximately 1 in 5 receive a sexual solicitation or approach, 1 in 17 are threatened or harassed, and 1 in 33 receive an aggressive sexual solicitation from someone who asked to meet them somewhere, called them on the telephone, sent them regular mail, money or gifts (Davidson and Martellozzo, 2008).

The children interviewed in Davidson and Martellozzo's (2008) research were enthusiastic Internet users and enjoyed discussing the topic. Older children in the sample (12+) tended to use chat rooms and interactive games and chat facilities such as MySpace and MSN Messenger. Younger children (10–11) tended to play secure games on websites such as Disney's Toontown and were much less familiar with peer-to-peer networks. All of the children used the Internet for research and homework and were actively encouraged to do so at school.

Given that some of the younger children (10–11) had no experience of chat rooms and did not understand how they function, Davidson and Martellozzo (2008) argue that it may be better to target educational programmes addressing Internet safety at the 12 plus age group, who are actively involved in chatting online, or to adapt such programmes to make them more suitable for younger children. Maybe older children retain such information more effectively and are more able to act upon it.

The majority of children (65 per cent) in Davidson and Martellozzo's (2008) study had access to at least one computer at home; 49 per cent had computers in their bedrooms. Other children did not have a computer at home, but had access to a computer at relatives' or friends' houses. Fifteen per cent used Internet cafés on a regular basis (more than once a week). The findings suggest that almost all of the children had access to the Internet outside school. Sixty per cent accessed the Internet more than four times per week, this being particularly the case for the 12–14 age group. Of those children accessing the Internet, 76 per cent were largely unsupervised and spent long periods of time on their computer particularly during school holidays and at weekends. Generally, the children had a great deal of knowledge about computing, and the majority of 12–14-year-olds were extremely confident Internet users.

Children were questioned about their interactions in chat rooms, and 13 per cent reported occasions where they believed themselves or a friend/relative had been talking to an adult posing as a child. On several occasions this was clear as the person's Internet profile revealed their real age. Eleven per cent of the children had been approached in a chat room regarding sex and had told their parents. They reported feeling uncomfortable and uncertain about the identity of the person they were talking to. The majority of children claimed that they would always know if they were talking to a child as children use a unique computer slang online that adults would not be able to understand and would not use (Davidson and Martellozzo, 2008).

Seventy per cent of the children believed that girls were much more at risk of sexual abuse. The children seemed to use gender stereotypes in explaining why girls are more at risk. Girls were described as weaker and boys as stronger and more able to defend themselves. The children often noted that men seem to perpetrate this type of offence and would therefore target girls. Several children also noted that most cases covered by the media involve the sexual abuse of girls. Whilst it is the case that males perpetrate the vast majority of sexual abuse against female victims, Davidson and Martellozzo (2008) find it important to reinforce the point with children that boys are also at risk.

Perspectives on child sexual abuse

In the United States, an estimated one million children a year live in an environment of abuse or maltreatment (Conrad, 2006). Child abuse creates long-lived problems for those affected. Child abuse is defined as death, serious physical or emotional harm, sexual abuse or exploitation. Abuse is a non-accidental injury to a child, which, regardless of motive, is inflicted by an adult. It includes any injury, which is at variance with the history given and maltreatment such as, but not limited to, malnutrition, sexual molestation, deprivation of necessities, emotional maltreatment or cruel punishment.

Children are particularly vulnerable to different kinds of victimisation because of developmental immaturity in key areas such as physical, cognitive and emotional capabilities. A range of different maltreatment types exist to which children are subjected that are defined either by perpetrator behaviour or by the resulting type of harm to the child (Higgins, 2004).

According to Higgins (2004), child maltreatment can be both a one-dimensional and a multidimensional construct. She argues that it may be more meaningful to talk about the degree of negative adult behaviour (high, medium, low) rather than about the type (for example, sexual, physical). It is not maltreatment type per se but the extent of maltreatment that is important to understand. Victims of maltreatment are children who have experienced substantiated or indicated maltreatment or are found to be at risk of experiencing maltreatment.

In her book on child sexual abuse, Davidson (2008) argues that there is a need to define what is meant by childhood. Perceptions of childhood vary over time and across cultures. As sexual activity is associated with adulthood and maturity in Western societies, the age at which a person can give consent to sexual relations implies the end of childhood.

The global encyclopaedia Wikipedia (wikipedia.org) describes child sexual abuse as a form of child abuse in which a child is abused for the sexual gratification of an adult or older adolescent. In addition to direct sexual contact, child sexual abuse also occurs when an adult indecently exposes their own genitalia to a child, asks or pressures a child to engage in sexual activities, displays pornography to a child, or uses a child to produce child pornography. Child sexual abuse is the engagement of a child in sexual activities for which the child is developmentally unprepared and cannot give informed consent. Child sexual abuse is characterised by deception, force or coercion. Child sexual abuse can include fondling, genital exposure, intimate kissing, forced masturbation, oral, penile or digital penetration of the mouth, vagina, or anus. A central characteristic of any abuse is the dominant position of an adult that allows the adult to force or coerce a child into sexual activity.

Effects of child sexual abuse include depression, post-traumatic stress disorder, anxiety, propensity to re-victimisation in adulthood, and physical injury to the child. Children who experience the most serious types of abuse exhibit behaviour problems ranging from separation anxiety to post-traumatic stress disorder.

Internet crime

Online grooming of children for sexual abuse by sex offenders is a serious crime on the Internet. But it is not the only kind of Internet crime. A variety of crime types occur online every day. To put online grooming into a crime perspective, another kind of Internet crime is to be mentioned here for comparison. The example is advance fee fraud on the Internet, where victims can be found all over the world.

Victims of advance fee fraud have traditionally been approached by letter, faxes or email without prior contact. Victims' addresses are obtained from telephone and email directories, business journals, magazines, and newspapers. A typical advance fraud letter describes the need to move funds out of Nigeria or some other sub-Saharan African country, usually the recovery of contractual funds, crude oil shipments or inheritance from late kings or governors (Ampratwum, 2009).

Victims are often naïve and greedy, or at worst prepared to abet serious criminal offences such as looting public money from a poor African state. The advance fee fraud has been around for centuries, most famously in the form of the Spanish prisoner scam (Ampratwum, 2009: 68):

> In this, a wealthy merchant would be contacted by a stranger who was seeking help in smuggling a fictitious family member out of a Spanish jail. In exchange for funding the 'rescue' the merchant was promised a reward, which of course, never materialized.

Advance fee fraud is expanding quickly on the Internet. Chang (2008) finds that this kind of fraud is a current epidemic that rakes in hundreds of millions of dollars per year. The advent of the Internet and proliferation of its use in the last decades makes it an attractive medium for communicating the fraud, enabling a worldwide reach. Advance fee fraudsters tend to employ specific methods that exploit the bounded rationality and automatic behaviour of victims. Methods include assertion of authority and expert power, referencing respected persons and organisations, providing partial proof of legitimacy, creating urgency, and implying scarcity and privilege.

Generally, the Internet is a 'double-edged sword' providing many opportunities for individuals and organisations to develop but, at the same time, bringing with it new opportunities to commit crime. The Internet presents new challenges to law enforcement as the technology and its use develop. Internet crime has become a global issue that requires the full participation and cooperation of both developed and developing countries at the international level, as Internet crime investigations often require that evidence be traced and collected in more than one country (Salifu, 2008).

Conclusion

Online grooming of children on the Internet for sexual abuse by sex offenders is a serious crime. Most sexual abuse offenders are acquainted with their victims, and sexual abuse by a family member is called incest. However, in our discussion of Internet groomers, we focus on adults who did not know their victims before they met on the Internet. Online groomers use the Internet to identify and groom children with the goal of sexual abuse.

In this chapter, various characteristics of the Internet have been described and related to child abuse. Important characteristics include disconnected personal communication, mediating technology, universality, network externalities, distribution channel, time moderator, low cost standard, electronic double, electronic double manipulation, information asymmetry, infinite virtual capacity, independence in time and space, cyberspace, and dynamic social network.

Notes

1 Second Life is a 2D virtual community where players can adopt fantasy personas and can interact with others in fantasy worlds.
2 The MySpace site makes some attempt at age verification: 'Your profile may be deleted and your Membership may be terminated without warning, if we believe that you are under 13 years of age, if we believe that you are under 18 years of age and you represent yourself as 18 or older, or if we believe you are over 18 and represent yourself as under 18.' http://www.myspace.com/index.cfm?fuseaction= misc.terms 22/10/09

References

Afuah, A. and Tucci, C.L. (2003). *Internet Business Models and Strategies*, 2nd edn, New York: McGraw-Hill.

Ampratwum, E.F. (2009). 'Advance Fee Fraud 419 and Investor Confidence in the Economies of Sub-Saharan African (SSA)', *Journal of Financial Crime*, 16 (1), 67–79.

Broek, K.S.V., Puiszis, S.M. and Brown, E.D. (2009). 'Schools and Social Media: First Amendment Issues Arising From Student Use of the Internet', *Intellectual Property & Technology Law Journal*, 21 (4), 11–27.

Calder, M.C. (2004). 'The Internet: Potential, Problems and Pathways to Hands-on Sexual Offending', in: Calder, M.C. (editor), *Child Sexual Abuse and the Internet: Tackling the New Frontier*, Russell House Publishing, Dorset, UK, 1–23.

CEOP (2006). Understanding Online Social Network Services and Risks to Youth, Child Exploitation and Online Protection Centre, London, UK, www.ceop.gov.uk.

Chang, J.J.S. (2008). 'An Analysis of Advance Fee Fraud on the Internet', *Journal of Financial Crime*, 15 (1), 71–81.

Conrad, C. (2006). 'Measuring Costs of Child Abuse and Neglect: A Mathematical Model of Specific Cost Estimations', *Journal of Health & Human Services Administration*, Summer, 103–23.

Cook, N. (2008). *Enterprise 2.0: How Social Software Will Change the Future of Work*, Gower Publishing Limited, Aldershot, UK.

Davidson, J. (2008). *Child Sexual Abuse – Media representations and government reactions*, Routledge, Abingdon, UK.

Davidson, J. and Martellozzo, E. (2008). 'Protecting Vulnerable Young People in Cyberspace from Sexual Abuse: Raising Awareness and Responding Globally', *Police Practice and Research*, 9 (4), 277–89.

Dombrowski, S.C., Gischlar, K.L. and Durst, T. (2007). 'Safeguarding Young People from Cyber Pornography and Cyber Sexual Predation: A Major Dilemma of the Internet', *Child Abuse Review*, 16, 153–70.

Gottschalk, P. (2006). *E-Business Strategy, Sourcing and Governance*, Idea Group Publishing, Hershey, PA, USA.

Higgins, D.J. (2004). 'The Importance of Degree Versus Type of Maltreatment: A Cluster Analysis of Child Abuse Types', *The Journal of Psychology*, 138 (4), 303–24.

Kierkegaard, S. (2008). 'Cybering, Online Grooming and Ageplay', *Computer Law & Security Report*, 24, 41–55.

Laudon, K.C. and Laudon, J.P. (2010). *Management Information Systems: Managing the Digital Firm*, 11th edn, Pearson Education, London, UK.

Lillywhite, R. and Skidmore, P. (2006). 'Boys Are Not Sexually Exploited? A Challenge to Practitioners', *Child Abuse Review*, 15, 351–61.

Lindgreen, A., Antioco, M. and Wetzels, M. (2004). 'Bla-bla-ba: Video Chat Service on the Internet – A Market Feasibility Study', *Qualitative Market Research: An International Journal*, 7 (1), 20–33.

Livingstone, S. (2009). 'Eu Kids Online Report', (Conference June 2009, LSE, London).

Medietilsynet (2008). Trygg Bruk Undersøkelsen 2008 (Safe use survey 2008), Medietilsynet (Norwegian Media Authority, Fredrikstad, Norway.

Mitchell, K.J., Wolak, J. and Finkelhor, D. (2008). 'Are Blogs Putting Youth at Risk for Online Sexual Solicitation or Harassment?' *Child Abuse & Neglect*, 32, 277–94.

O'Connell, R. (2004). 'From Fixed to Mobile Internet: The Morphing of Criminal Activity On-line', in: Calder, M.C. (editor), *Child sexual abuse and the Internet: Tackling the new frontier*, Russell House Publishing, Dorset, UK, 37–55.

Quayle, E., Vaughan, M. and Taylor, M. (2006). 'Sex offenders, Internet Child Abuse Images and Emotional Avoidance: The Importance of Values', *Aggression and Violent Behaviour*, 11, 1–11.

Quayle, E., Loof, L. and Palmer, T. (2008). Child Pornography and Sexual Exploitation of Children Online, World Congress III against Sexual Exploitation of Children and Adolescents, ECPAT International, Rio de Janeiro, Brazil, 25–28 November.

Salifu, A. (2008). 'The Impact of Internet Crime on Development', *Journal of Financial Crime*, 15 (4), 432–43.

Thorgrimsen, T.C.S. (2008). Forsiktige Med Webkamera (Careful with web camera), Aftenposten (daily newspaper Aftenposten), www.aftenposten.no, published 07.11.08.

Tufekci, Z. (2008). 'Grooming, Gossip, FaceBook and MySpace: What can we Learn About These Sites from Those Who won't Assimilate?' *Information, Communication & Society*, 11 (4), 544–64.

United Nations (2008). United Nations e-Government Survey 2008, Department of Economics and Social Affairs, Division for Public Administration and Development Management, United Nations, New York.

Vidnes, A.K. and Jacobsen, H. (2008). 'Strengt på nett (Strict on the Net)'. *Aftenposten* (daily newspaper Aftenposten), Friday 7th November, culture section, page 4.

Weber, R. (2004). 'The Grim Reaper: The Curse of E-mail, Editor's Comments', *MIS Quarterly*, iii–xiii.

Whittaker, J. (2004). *The Cyberspace Handbook*, Routledge, Taylor & Francis Group, London, UK.

Chapter 3

Combating child abuse images on the Internet
International perspectives

John Carr and Zoe Hilton

Introduction and context

This chapter will explore issues relating to the collection and distribution of child abuse images, acknowledging the considerable level of overlap between this and other forms of online exploitation. It will look in detail at the changing nature of the problem and some of the key political and practical moves being taken to tackle the production and distribution of such images. Examples are given where genuine progress is being made in reducing access to child abuse images over the Internet and it is argued that these concrete examples need to be taken up and acted upon more widely. The chapter concludes by suggesting that the true nature and scale of this problem lies largely hidden and argues that a more concerted and collaborative international effort from governments and industry is urgently needed. In order to bring this about it is further suggested that new ways need to be found to focus public attention on the issues. Lessons need to be learnt from the environmental and other successful civil society global movements.

Child abuse images are visual representations of a child being sexually abused.[1] The abuse usually takes place in the offline world, although some forms of sexual abuse which involve the capture of images can take place remotely, for example, through the use of web cams. The Internet facilitates the mass distribution of the images, often for profit.[2] This, in turn, creates an incentive for abusers to harm yet more children in order to create new images for sale.

Within our definition of child abuse images we also include realistic simulated representations of sexually abusive activity or representations of the sexual parts of a child for sexual purposes. Such images can be created either by editing or 'morphing' a genuine image of an actual child to make it appear as if they are being sexually abused. Alternatively the image might have been generated entirely by a computer, but nonetheless is for all practical purposes indistinguishable from a genuine image. In some jurisdictions, for example, in the USA, in principle the image is illegal precisely and only because it depicts actual harm being done to a real child. In other jurisdictions, for example, the UK, it is not necessary to establish or prove that an actual child was harmed. The image is illegal if it is sufficiently realistic to convince a jury, as a finding of fact, that it looks like a real child is being sexually abused. This change in the law was introduced in the UK and several other countries in order to keep pace with technological changes which made it possible to edit existing videos or photographs or create new ones which are indistinguishable from genuine images of real events.[3] It is hard to know with any great precision how much 'pseudo' child pornography of this kind is in existence but it is thought that it is only a very small part of the total, that is, the great majority of child abuse images in circulation on the Internet are of real children being criminally assaulted or abused for sexual purposes.[4]

Child abuse images on the Internet have massively increased in prevalence over the last ten years. This growth maps directly to the emergence of the Internet as a mass consumer technology. For example in the UK, in the first quarter of 1999, only 3.2 million UK households had an Internet connection. This then represented 13 per cent of all households. By the end of 2000, this had gone up to 8.6 million, or about 33 per cent.[5] Today it stands at 16.5 million households, of which approximately 13.5 million have a broadband connection.[6] The growth in arrests and prosecutions for offences related to child abuse images in England and Wales has followed a similar trajectory. In 1999 403 persons were cautioned or proceeded against for offences related to child abuse images. In 2007 it was 1,402.[7] In 1996 the Internet Watch Foundation (IWF) processed 615 complaints relating to online abuse images compared with 34,871 in 2007 (Internet Watch Foundation Annual Report, 2008[8]).

The Internet has enabled a shift from small-scale, 'amateur' production of images, exchanged by and between collectors, to the distribution of images on a huge scale by members of organised crime for financial benefits. There does remain a sizeable and still very significant non-monetary online trade in child abuse images, often between highly organised groups of collectors, but it is thought that the bulk (74 per cent) of the images available online are still provided through sites which sell the images.[9] However, images which might initially have been produced for the commercial market will quickly find their way into the 'amateur' environment, and vice versa.

The link between possession and contact offending

Downloading child abuse images is a serious offence against the children depicted and it deserves police attention entirely in its own right, but there is also evidence to suggest that people who become involved in downloading such images may find themselves on a path that ultimately leads them to commit new offences, this time against children either in the real world or online.

Various studies have been carried out that explore the link between the possession of child abuse images and contact offending. The studies have produced significantly different results; however with some either the methodology is problematic or they have been carried out on a very small scale, and many have been carried out in North America where the laws and approaches to sentencing can sometimes be very different.[10] Work carried out in the UK by Middleton (2006) suggests that with UK-based perpetrators there are similarities between the psychological profiles of convicted child sex offenders and those convicted of offences relating to child abuse images.[11]

Middleton's study ought to be contrasted with one from Switzerland published in July, 2009,[12] which claimed that ' … consuming child pornography per se is not a risk factor for people who have not … molested children before'. In the Swiss study the researchers only had access to the offenders' official criminal records. By contrast Middleton had access to a much richer data set about the individuals who had been convicted of possession offences.

Large-scale research is needed to determine whether or to what extent there is a link between the offence of possessing child abuse images and committing other types of sexual offences against children. Research should also seek to establish if the possession of different types or levels of seriousness of child abuse images is a significant aspect in predicting likely future risk. Currently there is ongoing debate and considerable discrepancy in the analysis of the future risks posed by those known to have viewed child abuse images of any kind.[13] Without more conclusive research it is a struggle to predict the likelihood of future risks to children and be confident about the appropriateness and impact of different criminal justice and treatment interventions.

Step change in the scale of production and distribution

The Internet has completely transformed the scale and nature of the production and distribution of Child Abuse Images. In 1997, in *People Like Us*, Sir William Utting described 'child pornography' as being a 'cottage industry'.[14] That was probably the last moment in history when such a claim could be made. Today it is global. In 1995 the police in Greater Manchester in the UK seized a grand total of 12 images.[15] In 2004 the same Manchester police force arrested one man who was found to be in possession of almost 1,000,000 images (including very many duplicates). In typical arrests today, the number of images found can usually be counted in the thousands or the tens of thousands. This is partly because modern computers can facilitate the automated downloading of large volumes of images in ways that previously were simply not possible, but it is also a reflection of the fact that larger numbers of images are now available and can be exchanged and accessed via the Internet.

It is clearly very difficult to determine the size or shape of what is essentially a clandestine and illegal business.[16] All kinds of estimates have been made at different points about the number of websites involved,[17] and the total monetary value of the market in the images. No one familiar with the terrain doubts that the 'business' is worth many millions of dollars, certainly sufficient to attract the interest of organised crime.[18] Equally, there can be no doubt at all that the number of illegal images now in circulation on the Internet runs into the millions and the number of individual children depicted in those images runs into the tens of thousands.[19]

Originally one of the main ways of distributing child abuse images over the Internet was from within Usenet Newsgroups. That remains an important source but today several other Internet technologies are also being used. Of these perhaps the World Wide Web is the most important, because it is the most accessible and easiest to use. However, as more and more countries are making it difficult to use the web to distribute child abuse images, other Internet technologies are also being used. Of these Peer2Peer (P2P) or file sharing software is the most significant. According to Interpol, P2P is technically quite easy to police but it is highly labour intensive in relation to police time and resources. When linked to the very large numbers of perpetrators this makes it very difficult, in practical terms, to tackle this crime at a global level.

A child's legal right to protection

Under the UN Convention on the Rights of the Child (UNCRC) children have a right to protection from all forms of violence. Article 34 of the UNCRC commits states to 'protect the child from all forms of sexual exploitation and sexual abuse … ' and to take all appropriate national, bilateral and multilateral measures to that end. Article 19 commits states to protect children from all forms of 'violence, injury or abuse, neglect or negligent treatment, maltreatment or exploitation, including sexual abuse'.

The UNCRC also contains important general principles which should be taken into account throughout all relevant legislation and measures, including the principle that the child's best interests should be taken into account in actions which affect them. There is also an Optional Protocol to the CRC on the Sale of Children, Child Prostitution and Child Pornography which is the only universal treaty specifically addressing this topic. The Optional Protocol explicitly criminalises 'child pornography' offences and provides a significant focus on the welfare and protection of the child, for example laying down minimum standards on the protection of a child victim in the criminal justice process.

Whilst the commitments outlined under the UNCRC and Optional Protocol are a significant step in indicating a commitment by member states to tackle online forms of sexual exploitation from a children's rights perspective there have nonetheless been criticisms of the willingness of individual states to engage with a wider agenda around children's welfare. In particular, it has been argued that despite the additional protections outlined in the Optional Protocol and its focus on the welfare protection of the child through the criminal justice process, the reservations and declarations of states', parties demonstrated little commitment to the welfare or rehabilitation of child victims.[20] Indeed Quayle *et al.* argue that 'The Optional Protocol has emerged more as an instrument of international criminalisation as its central tenet rather than a comprehensive package of welfare protection' (2008: 91).[21]

The most obvious and enduring problem with the UNCRC as an instrument of international child protection is of course that the provisions it contains are not applicable in domestic courtrooms, nor are there mechanisms to ensure that signatories are compliant with the Convention nor for parties to take up complaints for failures under the UNCRC. The UNCRC is internationally monitored in relation to progress but little detailed consideration is given to the ways in which children may be exploited through the new technologies. It would be helpful if international monitoring of the UNCRC, as well as other relevant international treaties, paid greater attention to monitoring this aspect.

Political initiatives at EU level and beyond

There has in recent years been a concerted attempt to enhance the protection of children through political initiatives at EU level. In 2003 the EU adopted a Council Framework Decision 'on combating the sexual exploitation of children and child pornography' committing EU member states to bringing their national laws in line with the standards it contains, including criminalising child pornography and other child sexual exploitation offences.[22] In addition there has recently been a European Commission proposal[23] for a revised EU Framework Decision 'on combating the sexual abuse, sexual exploitation of children and child pornography' which provides a renewed opportunity to focus the debate on sexual exploitation, improve, share and update our understandings of sexual abuse, and strive for a more consistent implementation process.

As discussed in Chapter 1 (Davidson) the new proposal for a Framework Decision would replace the existing 2003 Framework Decision and as it stands would provide a useful basis for improved cross-border cooperation around protecting children from sexual abuse and exploitation. The new Framework Decision builds on the 2007 Council of Europe Convention on the protection of children against sexual exploitation and sexual abuse – which asks member states to introduce specific legislation on grooming. At the time of writing the new revised Framework decision enhances the protection of children in a number of ways including introducing anti-grooming legislation, expanding the definition of child pornography to include 'realistic images of a non-existent child' (Article 1b), and criminalising any intentional viewing of child abuse images whether or not the material is downloaded (Article 4). The proposed framework decision also includes provisions to ensure that local forces have the resources to undertake victim identification work (Article 12) and to ensure that all Internet Service Providers (ISPs) are blocking access to websites containing 'child pornography' (Article 18).

As Davidson argues (Chapter 1) it will be important that in the EU member states support the proposed EU Framework Decision 'on combating the sexual abuse, sexual exploitation of children and child pornography', and strive to ensure that it is fully implemented. There will be considerable work to do to ensure that these provisions remain within the EU legislation even as it goes through the council and that provisions contained in the decision are embraced by member states and are adopted in national strategies to address the sexual exploitation of children. In the current EU treaty these matters remain a reserved area with the status of a Framework Decision. A Framework Decision of this kind has the potential to carry considerable moral and political influence but has far lesser powers than a Framework Directive which can ensure direct translation into law of the provisions it outlines.

Other key international treaties include the 2001 Council of Europe Convention on Cybercrime which was one of the first attempts to harmonise national and international definitions of 'child pornography', and has a specific provision criminalising it (Article 9). The Convention is useful insofar as it contains important procedural and international cooperation measures in dealing with this offence as well as other criminal offences committed by means of a computer. However, this Convention contains a number of optional aspects – for example in relation to age – which render it problematic. The more recent 2007 Council of Europe Convention on the Protection of Children Against Sexual Exploitation and Sexual Abuse goes much further and gives a clearer definition of age as well as strengthening a number of provisions in relation to online abuse and exploitation. Although at the time of writing the Convention has had 37 signatories, it has only been ratified by two countries (Greece and Albania) and has therefore not yet entered into force.

In July 2009, the Committee of Ministers of the Council of Europe formulated Recommendation CM/Rec (2009)5 on 'measures to protect children against harmful content and behaviour (and to promote their active participation in the new information and communications environment)'[24]. While again lacking legal force it is yet another indication of a growing momentum at political level within the international community to mobilise against online child abuse images.

Other important international commitments include Article 3 of the International Labour Organisation Convention concerning the Prohibition and Immediate Action for the Elimination of the Worst Forms of Child Labour (1999) which includes the use of a child in the production of child pornography in the definition of the worst forms of labour. Other important international activity in this area includes the three World Congresses on the Sexual Exploitation of Children, held in Stockholm in 1996, in Yokohama in 2001 and in Rio in 2008. Most recently, at the 3rd World Congress the 'Call for Action' gave special attention to the issue of sexual exploitation via the use of the Internet, mobiles and other new technology, including calling for the criminalisation of all aspects of 'child pornography' including virtual images as well as the call for ISPs and mobiles to develop codes of conduct in relation to child protection.[25] These high profile international meetings have also resulted in stated commitments to criminalise forms of sexual exploitation and to provide access to protection for victims as well as standards for child-friendly judicial procedures, a strengthening of victims' rights to legal aid, the development and implementation of national plans of action, and focal points to tackle sexual exploitation.

Overall, despite the fact that there have been and still are a growing number of international initiatives to tackle these issues and a number of different international instruments have been developed, it is fair to say that there is still a lack of concerted and sustained international political action that comprehensively spans all of the relevant areas. What we have seen hitherto, whilst most welcome, nonetheless is quite piecemeal or is very focused on a narrow range of nations, principally in Europe and North America.

The Child Online Protection (COP) initiative, started in 2008 by the International Telecommunication Union (ITU), represents the first major attempt by a well-established intergovernmental global body to focus on a range of online child protection issues, of which child abuse images is a key part.[26] The ITU has no formal powers in these areas but it is an important part of the United Nations 'family' of organisations, connecting directly with 191 member states.

The need for more concerted action at an international level could hardly be any clearer. Whilst it is true that in a number of countries it is getting harder to access child abuse images, and child abuse images are universally reviled and denounced, overall the volume of images becoming available online shows no obvious signs of reducing. On the contrary, it appears to be continuing to increase.

There remain a number of issues both about how child abuse images should be defined as well as the methods most appropriate for disruption. This leaves open substantial questions about how a joint approach to crime control can actually translate into meaningful, ongoing protection for victims. Many countries appear reluctant to transform agreements and sentiments made in international arenas into legislative reality, much less operational reality on the ground.[27]

Report of the International Center for Missing and Exploited Children

In 2008 the US-based International Center for Missing and Exploited Children (ICMEC) produced the 5th Edition of 'Child Pornography: model legislation & global review'[28]. The primary purpose of this series of ICMEC reports is to gain an understanding of existing legislation relating to child abuse images legislation and to ascertain the importance of the issue with regard to national political agendas. Via this report ICMEC also seeks support for its model laws, as part of an ongoing attempt to introduce greater coherence internationally.

The ICMEC studies focus on a number of key areas: legislation specific to child abuse images; laws that provide a definition of child abuse images; laws that criminalise possession, regardless of intent to distribute; laws that address computer-facilitated crimes related to child abuse images; and reporting of child abuse images by ISPs. It is evident from the report that there are considerable and very important variations in the legislative and wider legal approaches taken by different countries.

From the ICMEC report it is evident that despite the several international initiatives described earlier, it is still the case that globally many countries simply do not have the basic laws in place which would allow them to act against child abuse images domestically or would allow them to participate in international police actions against child abuse images.

According to the 2008 ICMEC study of the 184 member countries of Interpol, only 29 have what they consider to be 'legislation sufficient to combat child pornography offences'. Ninety-three countries have no legislation that specifically addresses child pornography. Of those that do have legislation that refers to child pornography, 36 do not criminalise possession, regardless of the intent to distribute, and 24 do not have legislative provision to allow for computer-facilitated offences. In the previous edition of the same report, published in 2006, the numbers respectively were 27, 95, 41 and 27 so it is evident that some progress is being made but it is painfully slow: too slow.

As with other types of cybercrime, the possession, manufacture and distribution of child abuse images is often conducted without regard to international borders and therefore requires laws in each country that are comparable or legally equivalent – this is referred to as 'harmonisation'. Criminals, who sexually exploit children, whether it is through the use of computers and the Internet or by travel to other countries, will prefer to victimise children in countries lacking legislation or strict enforcement and in countries that exist outside the framework of international cooperation. The parallels with money laundering spring readily to mind.

Many countries broadly address child exploitation as it relates to labour or other offences. They may have a blanket ban on all kinds of pornography in general; however, these laws are not enough as they do not specifically address the criminal aspects of various forms of child sexual exploitation and child abuse images. The absence of specific laws on child abuse images seems to indicate a lack of understanding of the seriousness of the issues or a lack of political priority for them. Thus whilst laws alone are by no means sufficient, they are a necessary first step. If nothing else they will normally represent some kind of breakthrough in consciousness of the issues among the political leadership of a country.

There may be issues with ICMEC's definition of what constitutes a framework of acceptable legal ingredients. For example, ICMEC's definition does not stipulate that 'pseudo images' are covered. If that were added to the definition the number of countries in the top frame in the 2008 report would be smaller than 29. Moreover it was beyond the scope of ICMEC's extremely valuable review to attempt to make any kind of assessment of the operational effectiveness of the law enforcement agencies within the 29 top countries. Simply because a country has the right laws in place, it does not necessarily follow that within that country the work is properly resourced or given an appropriate priority in policing terms. One suspects that if tests of this kind were applied the overall number gaining top marks would fall again.

In order to be truly effective, countries should be encouraged to adopt specific legislation to criminalise child abuse images and include offences specific to the use of technology and the Internet as it relates to child abuse images; otherwise criminals will take advantage of loopholes in the law. There should also be provisions in the law for a greater commitment to enforce these specific laws and for training for judicial, prosecutorial and law enforcement officials who will invariably be challenged to keep up with the use of technology by offenders. Fundamental areas of concern and guidance for the adoption of legislation include:

- Defining a 'child' in a precise and clear manner in accordance with the UN Convention of the Rights of the Child.
- Defining 'child abuse images' to include specific computer and Internet terminology.
- Creating criminal offences specific to: possession, manufacture and distribution of child abuse images, including pseudo images, and deliberately downloading or intentionally viewing such images on the Internet.
- Creating criminal penalties for parents or guardians who agree to or who facilitate their child's participation in child abuse images.
- Creating penalties for those who make known to others where to find child abuse images.
- Making attempts at crimes related to child abuse images a criminal offence.
- Addressing criminal liability of children involved in child abuse images. Criminal liability must focus on the adult offender, not the child victim.

- Enhancing penalties for repeat offenders, organised crime members and other aggravated factors to be considered upon sentencing.
- Ensure that children are protected through the criminal justice process, that their needs and welfare remain a core concern and that they have access to rehabilitation and welfare.

Practicalities of law enforcement investigations

Aside from requiring a legal framework which would allow for proper law enforcement engagement against child abuse images, law enforcement agencies also need to keep abreast with and be able to deal with how criminals operate in this space.

We have already noted at several points that perpetrators of online sexual offences against children, including persons engaging in the production or exchange of child abuse images, can act from nearly any location in the world and take several different kinds of measures to mask their identity. The equipment and instruments needed to investigate these kinds of online crimes can be quite different from those used to investigate more traditional crimes committed offline.

The Internet, computers, cell phones, Personal digital assistants (PDAs), digital still and video cameras and digital devices of all types have become indispensable tools for certain types of predators seeking to exploit children sexually. The technology on which these devices operate is increasingly complex and changes at a rapid rate. Simply trying to stay up to date can present challenges to even the best resourced and most modern police departments, as discussed by Taylor in Chapter 6.

In order to capture and preserve important evidence left by offenders it is essential for law enforcement authorities to have the training and technical expertise to retrieve such evidence in a way which is consistent with their domestic legal requirements or that complies with the standards required by foreign police or judicial services whose cooperation may be required at some point or other within an investigation. Therefore training must be made available to law enforcement, judicial and prosecutorial officials to help them understand how to conduct forensic analysis of computer hard drives and other digital devices. This training must give them hands-on experience and be constantly updated to keep up with ever-changing technology.

There are many software suites which provide the tools to carry out appropriate examinations of seized media, and training is often included in the purchase price of the suite. Unfortunately these solutions and the associated training can be quite expensive and beyond the reach of the police services in a number of countries. Many companies in the private sector have the expertise to assist with this type of work, consequently partnerships between the public and private sectors for training and technical support may be able to provide critical assistance.

Microsoft has made an important contribution in this area in two ways: it has helped ICMEC to establish an international training programme specifically aimed at overseas police forces, and it has also helped develop Child Exploitation Tracking Services (CETS) which it describes as being:

> ... a database tool that enables agencies to avoid duplicate effort. Sharing information over a secure network, officers can match up investigations that reference the same people or online identities. Using CETS, police agencies can manage and analyze huge volumes of information in powerful new ways, such as cross-referencing obscure data relationships and using social-network analysis to identify communities of offenders.[29]

International law enforcement activity

There is no doubt that the momentum behind international police cooperation in the field of child protection is building up. There certainly have been spectacular examples of successful cooperation across borders by national and local law enforcement agencies which have led to the break up of large networks and to large numbers of arrests of persons involved in downloading child abuse images. Yet, for example, the numbers of children being identified and rescued and the number of arrests of the people behind the large scale commercial production and distribution of child abuse images remains disappointingly low in all parts of the world.

The principal focus for much international law enforcement activity against child abuse images is Interpol, although associated regional initiatives such as Europol are playing an increasingly important role.

Through its network of 187 countries Interpol[30] specialises in facilitating the exchange of information between police forces. With its i24/7 system the Interpol network allows the instant exchange of information between countries, typically directly to specialist law enforcement units.

Mutual cooperation on international criminal investigations is normally accomplished within the framework of bilateral mutual legal assistance treaties or multilateral conventions. Yet in spite of treaty agreements and conventions which might have been entered into by Governments, if they have not been followed through and enacted into a corresponding domestic law in the country from which cooperation is being sought, assistance may not be provided at all, or it may be accorded a low priority, resulting in unhelpful delays or assistance provided only on a very restricted basis. The party providing the information may place conditions upon its use; for example it may require confidentiality.

One of the key offshoots of the G8's engagement with online child protection was the emergence and development of the Virtual Global Taskforce.[31] It was championed by the UK's Child Exploitation and Online Protection centre, CEOP, and currently, in addition to Interpol, it also has member agencies in the USA, Canada, Australia and Italy. The Virtual Global Taskforce (VGT) claims that law enforcement agencies, including members of the VGT, have made 'substantial headway' in facilitating cross-jurisdictional investigations and information sharing. It adds that 'This has been achieved at practitioner level, rather than as a result of multilateral agreements or cooperation between governments at national level.'[32] Such developments are very much to be welcomed but there must always be a risk that this kind of bottom-up approach could easily be displaced or its efficiency reduced by simple things such as changes in key personnel in one or more of the central players. Some kind of formal institutional or other kind of entrenchment would not guarantee ongoing or even necessarily long-term success but it can help shore up and reinforce the strengths of established successful patterns of working.

We may be witnessing the development of an elite 'club' of a comparatively small number of national police forces from the industrialised economies. These are well equipped, well trained and have broadly similar domestic laws. They have the travel budgets to allow them to meet together frequently. They work together easily bilaterally and multilaterally on issues related to child abuse images. Then there is the rest of the world where police forces can act only intermittently, if at all, handicapped by a lack of trained personnel, a lack of other sorts of resources, a lack of clear laws, or some permutation of all three.

To the extent that, hitherto, the elite 'club' consisted of the countries with higher levels of Internet penetration and usage, and were the same countries where most of the perpetrators lived, perhaps its emergence was understandable, even desirable. However as usage levels in the rest of the world start to mirror those in the already industrialised economies, it is of the utmost importance that the current divide is rapidly narrowed. If it is not narrowed, it is likely to expand.

Effective international law enforcement cooperation is essential if we are to address fully and in a timely way several key aspects of child protection concerns on the Internet in relation to child abuse material. The parallels with money-laundering are once again very obvious. Many of the criminals involved in the acquisition and distribution of child abuse material will be fully aware of the legal loopholes and jurisdictional issues which can make their lives easier and that of the police harder. In terms of the manufacture and storage of child abuse material we will see a drift towards countries with few or no laws or few if any trained police officers with the means or inclination to pursue this type of crime.

To develop the necessary collaboration we need to build a consensus, both in relation to basic laws but also, crucially, in relation to police or judicial investigative procedures. The initial focus needs to be on those elements which are likely to be part of any, or at any rate most, of the proceedings concerned with child abuse images exchanged or published over the Internet.

An enduring issue is that, at the moment, all of the key investigative police units are based within national jurisdictions, and to that extent they will always, potentially, be subject to the vicissitudes of political, resource and other pressures within their national territory. A national police agency can suddenly drop out of or slow down an international police action for reasons which are entirely unrelated to the investigation itself. To some extent the risk of this kind of small 'p' politics is inevitable in every kind of human institution and collaborative project, particularly where sovereign governments are involved. However it ought to be possible for Governments to come together with Interpol to consider establishing an internationally based investigative unit, perhaps with a specific remit to focus on the criminal networks behind a very high proportion of the trade in commercially available child abuse images. Such a unit could conceivably reduce the operational costs of several national policing operations and it would certainly aid the development of all the different parts of the collaborative chain. The key challenge for such a unit would be in maintaining the sense of engagement and support of the national police units it was serving. In the end, all policing is local. Perhaps the embryo of such a unit already exists in the shape of the VGT.

New technology to support police work and help protect children

The EU's Safer Internet Programme (EC SIP) has become a major source of funding for the development of new technologies that will assist law enforcement both to process the huge amounts of materials that are seized in police operations involving child abuse images, and to ensure that the intelligence gleaned from it is routed to the appropriate police agencies as swiftly as possible. The EC SIP also funds research into offender online behaviour and victim experience.

The I-Dash project is developing a set of automatic tools to support police professionals in their investigations involving large quantities of child sexual abuse material contained in videos. Thousands of hours of video can be seized in a single arrest. Viewing every frame can present huge challenges, yet vital evidence may be contained within a single frame. The MAPAP (Measurement and Analysis of P2P Activity Against Paedophile Content) project is designed to help analyse illegal content on peer2peer networks. The FIVES (Forensic Image and Video Examination Support) project (a project co-funded by the European Union) helps by identifying and distinguishing new material from already known material. The European Commission also co-funds the establishment and maintenance of an International Child Sexual Exploitation Image Database (ICAID), managed by Interpol. This will be an upgrade of and shall greatly enhance the existing database. It will be able to receive input from police forces worldwide.

The Commission is also funding a project called CIRCAMP (Cospol Internet Related Child Abusive Material Project) that, under the auspices of Europol and Interpol, was established to encourage organised, extensive cross-border exchange of best practice in the fight against the production and online distribution of child sexual abuse material within Europe and internationally. Currently CIRCAMP brings together police forces from 11 countries. Already they have the capability to interrogate in real time a shared database of known images, and at the time of writing six countries had already developed the capability to use it.[33]

ISIS is a software development project jointly funded by the EPSRC (Engineering and Physical Sciences Research Council) and the ESRC (Economic and Social Research Council). It is another example of how cutting edge researchers are seeking to deploy technological solutions both to combat online sexual predators and those engaged in the distribution of child abuse images.[34]

Disruption methods

There is widespread agreement that as soon as a child abuse image or website is discovered it is important to move as quickly as possible to remove the image or have the website taken down or rendered inaccessible. This reduces the chance of that image or website being discovered and downloaded by someone coming to this type of material for the first time, perhaps setting them off on a path which ultimately leads to the real world abuse of a child. Getting the image removed as quickly as possible also acknowledges the harm being done to the child depicted.

In order to facilitate this process of take down, a system of national hotlines has been developed. Currently they are operational in over 30 different countries coordinated by the International Association of Internet Hotlines (INHOPE). They are growing in number[35] although quite slowly. Growth in the number of hotlines is highly desirable as part of a global campaign to end the traffic in child abuse images online. Within the UK the national hotline is the Internet Watch Foundation (IWF), which was established by the Internet industry in 1996. At that time over 18 per cent of all child abuse images being found in the UK were also being published from within the UK. Today it stands at less than one per cent.[36] There are several reasons why the IWF was able to achieve this reduction but, clearly, if other hotlines in other countries could do something similar that would make a very welcome contribution to the overall effort. That is not to say that there is no room for improvement on the part of the IWF.

Slow takedown times

Typically the IWF or another national hotline will receive information from the public about an image that has been found on the Internet and is believed to be illegal. Some hotlines will also actively seek out child abuse images themselves. Normally the hotline's first job is to confirm that the image is illegal[37] and determine where it is being housed, that is, the jurisdiction. The hotline will then pass on information about the address of the image to their local law enforcement agency and, if it is abroad, also to the appropriate overseas law enforcement agency. If the image is found to be in a jurisdiction where there is an existing hotline the image will normally be sent to the sister hotline and it is left to the hotline to inform local law enforcement.

If the child abuse image is found within their own national jurisdiction the hotline will issue a notice to the company hosting it to take it down from the Internet. Within the EU, and in many countries outside the EU, providing that the hosting organisation acts promptly on the notice they will escape any kind of liability for it.

Thus, within the UK for example, where an image is found on a UK-based server the image will be gone within hours. However, where the IWF has to notify an overseas agency, as it does in over 99 per cent of all cases it handles, the speed at which an image is removed can be very different. Despite work undertaken by the INHOPE network to address this, progress in speeding up the take down of identified illegal images has been very patchy.

In June 2008, academics from Cambridge University published the results of their research[38] into the amount of time it took for different forms of illegal content on the Internet to be taken down once notified to the relevant authorities within the UK.

The best performance was achieved by the banks acting on reports of phishing (identity theft) websites, where the mean lifetime of over 300 identified websites was between 3.5 and 4.3 hours. Seemingly one of the ways that these impressive takedown times were achieved was through the simple expedient of using the telephone to ring up the online service providers identified as unwittingly hosting the phishing site. Almost the worst performing section was child sex abuse images, where the mean lifetime of over 2,500 identified websites was 719 hours. In some instances, child sex abuse websites that had been notified to the authorities by the IWF were still up on the web 12 months later.

Reinforcing the Cambridge University study, in March 2009 a German non-governmental organisation (NGO) called Care Child published the results of a collaboration with the Danish police. The police handed them a small random sample of 20 overseas sites, taken from their main list of 3,500 known sites. Rather like the banks grappling with phishing sites, the German NGO simply contacted the website hosts directly, bypassing the traditional routes.

Seventeen website hosts were in the USA and one each was in Holland, the UK and South Korea/Portugal (HTML [Hyper Text Markup Language] coding in South Korea images in Portugal). Sixteen of the 20 sites were closed down within 12 hours; eight within three hours. Three sites said that they had documentary evidence that the 'models' employed on the site were over 18 years of age, as required by US law. Fourteen days after the test it was learned that some of the sites had moved location and were back in business, but almost half had not.

We have commented earlier about the reasons why fast takedown times are imperative.[39] Getting the images removed or blocking access to the sites containing them – whichever can be achieved sooner – has to be a major priority.

Pictures of children being sexually abused should not knowingly be left on view for extended periods, yet that is precisely what can happen. In several overseas jurisdictions the current delays in getting material taken down are overwhelmingly linked to local police workloads. It is understood that nothing should be done that might jeopardise a potential prosecution of an offender, but that is rarely the real reason for delay.

While the Cambridge report clearly suggests that there is room for improvement in the way that the UK's IWF works, the UK otherwise has an exemplary record in getting child sex abuse websites or other content speedily taken down once discovered on any UK-based hosting service. The IWF can do this in part because it is the sole recognised body for first deciding whether or not a given image is illegal and then for following through on all the related processes. By contrast, in many other countries in the world where hotlines[40] exist, the law seems to require that all reports of illegal content go first from the hotline to the police. The police then have the responsibility for deciding whether or not the image is illegal and, assuming it is, for notifying the relevant ISP or hosting company. This appears to be where the bottleneck and the delays occur. This is clearly not a criticism of any individual hotline within the EU or elsewhere, but it does raise concerns about how effectively different national law enforcement agencies relate to their national hotlines.

Blocking technology – reducing the availability of child abuse images

The proliferation of child abuse images on the Internet has created a public outcry for action. Given the scale and nature of the illegal activity relating to child abuse images it is clear that pro-active policing is not on its own a solution to the problem. The jurisdictional and policing issues discussed earlier have given added impetus to the search for better technical ways of disrupting and reducing the availability of, and traffic in, child abuse images.

Blocking is another means of disrupting the viewing and distribution of child abuse images. It involves ISPs and other Electronic Service Providers (ESPs) using software to 'block' access to websites, or Usenet Newsgroups, or both, where they are known to contain or advertise the availability of child abuse images. This means that anyone attempting to reach them to view or download material will be unable to do so through that particular ISP. The geographical location of the web server or the Usenet server becomes irrelevant because all of the decisive activity – the blocking – takes place on the ISP's or the ESP's server.

Part of the theory behind blocking is that if the purveyors of child abuse images cannot reach their customers, because their sites are blocked, the business will become less and less profitable, more and more difficult to manage and so, in the end, those criminals who are in it only to make money will give up and move on to something else.

Where they exist, blocking mechanisms function on a national basis and therefore can differ from country to country. In the UK, ISPs and other ESPs use a list of known addresses which has been generated and is maintained by the IWF. In the case of websites, the IWF provides a list of the uniform resource locators (URLs).[41] With Usenet Newsgroups the IWF simply lists the names of the Newsgroups to be blocked.

In most other countries it tends to be law enforcement, rather than the hotline, that deals directly with ISPs and ESPs in relation to blocking. For example in Italy police from the 'Centre against Child Pornography on the Internet' maintain the list of sites to be blocked. This list is sent to Italian ISPs. They then have 6 hours to block a site newly added to the list. In the UK, although the matter has never been tested, the assumption has always been that up to 24 hours is a reasonable period.

There are a number of key arguments in favour of blocking[42]:

- Blocking is a way of interfering with and disrupting the commercial trade of child abuse material.
- Blocking helps to prevent accidental access to this illegal and harmful content by helping the public.
- It helps to prevent deliberate access to child abuse material on the Internet.
- It helps to reduce the customer base of illegal websites.
- It helps to prevent the re-victimisation of those children who are or have been the victims of abuse.

Blocking technology will not, however, be a substantial obstacle for someone who is both determined to access or share child abuse material and has the right kind of technical knowledge. A determined, technically literate perpetrator could, for example, log onto an overseas server. Many hardened users will also be sharing images via Peer2Peer networks or other forms of closed groups. However, blocking does have a role in helping to prevent the casual, domestic consumer from stumbling across child abuse images by accident and in preventing those who might have a misplaced sense of curiosity from gaining access. Perhaps such persons are at an early stage of developing or feeding a sexual interest in children.

Overall there is a growing consensus that the implementation of blocking helps to undermine and disrupt the commercial trade of child abuse images.

The more countries that use blocking systems the less successful and active the trade will become.

There have been various attempts made to estimate what wider benefits there might be from the introduction of blocking technology. In Norway the police estimated that the Norwegian ISPs that were using blocking technology were preventing between 15,000 and 18,000 attempts per day to access illegal web pages containing child abuse images. In Denmark approximately 2,500 unique users were being blocked per day.[43] In the UK, when BT first introduced their blocking solution, known as 'Cleanfeed', they estimated that on their very large system they were blocking up to 35,000 attempts per day to access illegal sites.[44]

Each of these blocked attempts in Scandinavia and at BT could represent the successful prevention of a crime from being committed. The only problem is knowing who exactly attempted to commit the crime. It seems unlikely, for example, that in the UK on BT's system there are 35,000 subscribers who, every day, try to access child abuse images. What is possible, however, is that there could be a large number of computers that have botnets or other forms of malware working on them which are being controlled by other computers without the owners' knowledge. These botnets or the malware are likely to be attempting to harvest the illegal images to forward on to collectors who, in turn, could be part of an organised criminal gang trading, whether trading for financial gain or not.

Blocking technology has now been widely available for a number of years. While there has been a commitment from the global GSM Association (GSMA) to blocking access to child abuse images from the mobile phone networks[45] and several well known search engines also deploy the lists, there has been no similar kind of commitment from the European Internet Service Providers Association (Euro ISPA) or any global networks of ISPs. There is no reasonable technical argument against implementing such a policy and neither can cost be acknowledged as an important consideration. Blocking access to child abuse images has to be accepted as part of the basic cost of doing business.

Creating a unified list of websites of child abuse material

As already noted, in the UK the IWF maintains a list of all known child abuse websites, irrespective of where in the world the material is hosted. The IWF offers a copy of this list to ISPs or web-filtering companies that wish to deploy it as part of a planned policy of blocking access to such sites According to estimates provided by ISPA UK, over 95 per cent of all UK domestic Internet users are with an ISP that deploys the IWF list. It is anticipated that this percentage will rise to nearer 100 per cent as the industry struggles to fight off legislation to make its use compulsory.

There is a need to establish a single list of all known child abuse websites and Newsgroups, or a list that is as large as possible, drawing on any and all national lists that are not encumbered by local legal constraints. An increasing number of overseas ISPs and web-filtering companies are using the British IWF list because it is recognised as being one of the largest, and because there is a high level of confidence in its quality and accuracy. However, industry representatives in all parts of the world have repeatedly called for a single list that consolidates the lists of as many national hotlines or police agencies as possible.

With appropriate security surrounding its deployment, this resource should be made available to all relevant online service providers, filtering companies and others with an appropriate interest in blocking access to or investigating websites containing child abuse images. Most elements within the industry seriously and genuinely want to keep child abuse images off their networks and are frustrated by the lack of cooperation in this respect by some of the national hotlines.

While one such list could not be taken to constitute the only valid source of information on online child abuse images, work towards establishing a single list will help to avoid the probably considerable duplication of effort that is currently taking place among hotlines and national police forces, and help with the overall project of increasing closer international working in this field.

For example, in relation to child abuse images, even if it was not possible to construct a single database of all images which will be illegal in every country in the world, there is very likely to be a body of images which are illegal almost everywhere, for example, images showing the rape of pre-pubescent children. It is also likely that there is a second identifiable group of images which are illegal in many other countries and there may well be a third category of those images which are illegal only in a smaller number of countries with very strict laws on these matters, for example, the UK.

The Financial Coalition Against Child Pornography

Initially all or most of the commercial trade in child abuse images over the Internet was made possible by the use of credit cards. Again, while it is hard to be precise about it, there is no doubt that the picture has now changed very substantially. The credit card companies have made major investments in developing systems to detect and block the use of their cards by sites dealing in child abuse images, and tracking down the organised groups behind the sites. In part this is thanks to the important work undertaken by the financial services industry, through the Financial Coalition Against Child Pornography and the work of ICMEC.[46] They have recently launched a European counterpart which is administered by CEOP, with financial support from the EU.

Nonetheless, the recent emergence of prepaid credit cards, or stored value cards, which can be obtained anonymously for cash, potentially threaten to undermine some of that work.

The lack of international political mechanisms: ICANN's role

The credit card industry was not the only unwitting ally in the initial development of the criminal exchange of child abuse images. In its annual report for 2008, the IWF noted that child abuse images were being made available commercially on websites from within a comparatively small number of domains:

> 75% ... (some 850 unique domains) are registered with just 10 domain name registries.[47]

This speaks of a regulatory failure by the Internet Corporation for Assigned Names and Numbers (ICANN), the global body responsible for the operation of the naming system on which the Internet depends. The EU, national governments and others should make representations to ICANN to deal more effectively with this issue. It is important that Governments and others make representations to ICANN with a view to securing a substantial improvement in the regulatory performance of those individual domain name registries that currently appear to be ineffective in preventing child abuse images from being published under their auspices. One very obvious policy which ICANN should adopt and enforce on a global basis is a resolution which forbids the use of any form of words which advertise the availability of child abuse images on any website.

Victim identification and care

In the law enforcement sphere the importance of victim identification from child abuse images posted on the Internet has gained ground. Processes and systems are being put in place nationally which means images seized during investigations or otherwise coming into the hands of investigators are being examined with a view to identifying the victim of the abuse and also the perpetrator. Materials which have not been seen before and cannot be marked as locally generated are floated into an international network of investigators and national specialists. This network has evolved around ICAID, which is now also supported by the EU[48] and is coordinated at the Trafficking in Human Beings section of Interpol along with the Interpol Specialist Group on Crimes against Children.

ICAID was formed in 2001 and has since developed into the G8-sponsored International Child Sexual Exploitation (ICSE) Database. As indicated above,[49] the aim of this database is to capture in one place all of the child abuse images that exist on the Internet that come into the hands of law enforcement. This material is examined by the network of specialised officers worldwide and, where possible, is referred to the presumed country of origin for an investigation into the identity of the child being victimised or the perpetrator. Where this is not possible, for example, where it is not possible to determine a potential country of origin, the material is filed in the database with details as to where it was found, by whom and when.

Powerful retrieval tools indicate whether these images have been seen before and, as is often the case, images found in one country can often hold clues which can help identify an abuse case in another. Sometimes the face of the abuser can be seen in the images, leading to their apprehension. As a matter of best practice we need to encourage the formation in every country of a centralised, national resource which can manage all the material being seized inside its borders, creating a national database of hash sets[50] and contributing to the international efforts being made in this area. All this reduces effort for investigators worldwide, avoids duplication of efforts, and ultimately will lead to the identification of more victims and the apprehension of more offenders.

The ability to use hash sets is a critical breakthrough. The use of hash sets allows for rapid comparisons to be made between newly acquired collections of images and the existing stock of known images. Not only does this save valuable police time by helping them to avoid reinvestigating images that might have already been investigated in another part of the world, or indeed have been investigated by another police force within their own country, it also helps to identity new images that have not previously been investigated. Any new image carries with it the possibility that it has been produced recently and that therefore there are children currently being abused who, if they can be identified and located, might be swiftly rescued from the abusive situation they are clearly in. However, what these databases of digital images could also do is allow for the possibility of proactively searching the Internet for replicas. This type of activity should be fully supported and encouraged by both Government and law enforcement.

Slow progress on victim identification despite joint working

Despite these technical breakthroughs it is still fair to say that children's rights and child protection NGOs have considerable concerns about the progress that needs to be made to identify, locate and help to recover the victims of online child abuse images. Only a small number of children have been successfully identified from images held in the Interpol database, and the same is true for many of the databases held at national level.[51]

Building on the technical research currently being funded by the EU's Safer Internet Programme and others, it is essential that Governments and international institutions provide more resources and impetus to help develop ways for law enforcement to achieve a higher rate of detection and location in the real life of children who have appeared in child abuse images on the Internet.

Ongoing care for children

It is also important to recognise issues relating to the long-term consequences for, and therapeutic needs of, children who have been sexually abused where images of that abuse have appeared on the Internet. Children who have been abused to produce child abuse images have particular needs: as well as the traumatic effects of the sexual abuse itself there are specific and probably long-term therapeutic needs that are especially difficult to resolve. These include the impotence felt by the child because of their lack of control over the disclosure process (their images have already been seen by the authorities working with them) and the non-resolution of the abuse – the fact that they must live with the knowledge that their images can probably never be destroyed and may be viewed again and again by many thousands of people (Quayle *et al.*, 2008).

An enduring challenge then for all public authorities is how we move beyond the policing aspect – identifying children and removing them from immediate harm – to the work that needs to be done to deliver a more holistic package of care. We need to ensure that children subject to these forms of abuse do not suffer further through the criminal justice processes. Staff working with them need to have the skills to understand this form of abuse and know how best to enable such children to recover and rebuild their lives.

There is a need to fund more research into the long-term consequences for, and therapeutic needs of, children who have been sexually abused where images of that abuse have appeared on the Internet. Governments should also ensure that appropriate resources are developed to address these needs and that the children's workforce is trained to understand the potential psychological consequences of online forms of sexual abuse and knows how best to manage them. They should ensure that those working with children know how and where to refer children who have been exploited in an online environment in order to ensure they receive support. The response should include a child-centred approach from the police and other criminal justice agencies when gaining evidence and it should be ensured that children feel safe when giving evidence.

Conclusion

This chapter first described the emergence and growth of a new and greatly enlarged market for child abuse images which has been facilitated by the development of the Internet as a mass consumer product. We have also looked at progress to date on trying to deal with this growth and examined some of the key, relatively straightforward technical and legislative measures which can have an impact on the prevalence of the images or the profits associated with them.

While the susceptibility of children to sexual exploitation the world over often seems to be inextricably linked to the larger and sometimes apparently intractable problems of poverty, social disintegration and a lack of support mechanisms or welfare services in relation to the distribution of images via the Internet, there are, by contrast, concrete ways of dealing with the problem that are technically feasible and have been shown to work with a high level of efficiency.

The point has been made many times that the children who are abused in the production of child abuse images are invisible from mainstream society and risk becoming 'forgotten children'.[52] In the UK the role of the Children's Charities' Coalition on Internet Safety (CHIS), a collaboration between Britain's major national children's charities,[53] has been essential in highlighting the issues related to children abused in images online and in pressing for the laws and policies which address their predicament. CHIS has also played a central role in leveraging resources from the Government for enhanced police resources, and more generally in lobbying industry to improve their policies and practices.

The value of this kind of advocacy work by civil society has been recognised by the EU who have agreed the funding for a European network of NGOs to work together to promote child protection and children's rights on the Internet in international arenas.[54] No comparable body exists on a global basis and yet, in the evident absence hitherto of effective or intergovernmental action, mechanisms for establishing some sort of global accountability in relation to child protection in the online environment are clearly essential.

The environmental movement is one of the few which has managed to reproduce a high level of engagement on the international stage which has also translated into laws and policies which are adopted or implemented at the national or regional level.

Notes

1 In this chapter we use the term 'child abuse images' although the terms 'indecent images of children' and, much more commonly, 'child pornography', are all still in everyday use in many countries and used in international or legal agreements. They will therefore also be referred to in different contexts here. We prefer the term 'child abuse images' as it provides a more accurate description of the nature of the content. Video material is also included within the scope of each of these definitions.

2 As explained below, there is still a significant non-monetary online trade in child abuse images, but according to reports from the Internet Watch Foundation the majority of the images available online are still provided through sites which sell the images.

3 We would support the Council of Europe Convention on the Protection of children against sexual exploitation and sexual abuse which defines 'child

pornography' as 'any material that visually depicts a child engaged in real or simulated sexually explicit conduct or any depiction of a child's sexual organs for primarily sexual purposes'. Although it should be noted the Convention allows parties not to apply the relevant parts in relation to 'images consisting exclusively of simulated representations or realistic images of a non-existent child', Article 20 (3). It is also worth noting that this definition excludes textual as opposed to visual material whereas the UN Optional Protocol to the CRC on the sale of children, child prostitution and pornography has been praised for using the term 'any representation, by whatever means'; see Akdeniz, Y. (2008) *Internet Child Pornography and the Law: National and International Responses.* Aldershot: Ashgate Publishing Ltd.

4 It is also legitimate to ask, are collectors of such material at all concerned only to download pseudo images, as opposed to genuine ones? Would they eschew or shun real child abuse images and insist on only collecting pseudo images in preference? It seems highly unlikely that they would be so discriminating, which further calls into question the value of making this kind of distinction in the first place.

5 www.statistics.gov.uk/pdfdir/intacc0702.pdf

6 www.statistics.gov.uk/cci/nugget.asp?id=8.

7 Offending and Criminal Justice Group (RDS), Home Office, Ref: IOS 503–03.

8 www.iwf.org.uk

9 http://www.iwf.org.uk/media/page.70.554.htm

10 See, for example, *Self-Reported Contact Sexual Offenses by Participants in the Federal Bureau of Prisons' Sex Offender Treatment Program: Implications for Internet Sex Offenders, Hernandez, November 2000,* presented at the Association for the Treatment of Sexual Abusers (ATSA) in San Diego, California; Kim, C. (2004) *From Fantasy to Reality: The Link Between Viewing Child Pornography and Molesting Children*, based on data from the US Postal Inspection Service, and Wilson and Andrews (2004) *Internet traders of child pornography and other censorship offenders in New Zealand: Updated Statistics.*

11 Middleton, D., Elliott, I. A., Mandeville-Norden, R. and Beech, A.R. (2006) 'An Investigation into the Applicability of the Ward and Siegert Pathways Model of Child Sexual Abuse with Internet Offenders Psychology', *Crime & Law* Dec, p598.

12 Endrass et al., 2009, 'The consumption of Internet child pornography and violent and sex offending'. http://www.pubmedcentral.nih.gov/articlerender.fcgi?artid=2716325

13 Two of the most prominent researchers in the field have reached rather different conclusions in their analysis of offender risk. Compare for example, Seto M.C. (2009) 'Assessing the Risk of Child Pornography Offenders', Paper Prepared for G8 Global Symposium, University of North Carolina, Chapel Hill, April 6–7, with the emphasis of Andres Hernandez in Hernandez, A. (2009) 'Psychological and Behavioural Characteristics of Child Pornography Offenders in Treatment', Paper Presented for G8 Global Symposium, April 5–7. Although both agree that more research is needed and that there is a great deal that is simply not yet known about the relationship between viewing child abuse images and online and contact sexual offending against children.

14 HMSO, 1997.

15 According to correspondence with the authors in the same year, Interpol's database of images contained only 4,000 pictures.

16 Although it is by no means illegal in all countries. We explore below a report by ICMEC – The International Centre for Missing & Exploited Children on 'Child Pornography' which it published in April 2006. The purpose of the report, which

is now in its 5th edition, was to gain an understanding of existing Child Abuse Material legislation in different jurisdictions.

17 In its annual report for 2007, the IWF maintained that fewer than 3,000 English-language websites accounted for the bulk of child abuse images available online. Three years earlier, the Computer Crime Research Center said the number was greater than 100,000.

18 See details of the 'Reg Pay' case: www.usdoj.gov/criminal/ceos/Press%20Releases/ICE%20Regpay%20PR_080906.pdf

19 In correspondence with Interpol it was disclosed that their database contained over 500,000 unique child abuse images. Telefono Arcobaleno, in their report, speak of 36,000 children of whom '42% are under 7 years of age and 77% are under the age of 12' (see www.telefonoarcobaleno.org/pdf/tredicmoreport_ta.pdf). Clearly the real numbers of both images and children involved are likely to be higher. These figures relate solely to what is currently known by the authorities from images already seized and processed.

20 Quayle, E., Loof, L. and Palmer, T. (2008) 'Child Pornography and Sexual Exploitation of Children Online', A contribution of ECPAT International to the World Congress III against Sexual Exploitation of Children and Adolescents.

21 Ibid, p91.

22 The EU's Safer Internet Programme has also made a significant contribution including through funding the network of hotlines, and the next generation of the programme (2009–13) will prioritise child protection.

23 Proposal for a Council Framework Decision 'on combating the sexual abuse, sexual exploitation of children and child pornography, repealing Framework Decision 2004/68/JHA', COM(2009)135final of 25th March 2009.

24 https://wcd.coe.int/ViewDoc.jsp?id=1470045& Site=CM

25 http://ecpat.net/Ei/Updates/WCIII_Outcome_Document_Final.pdf

26 http://www.itu.int/osg/csd/cybersecurity/gca/cop/index.html.The objectives of COP are to:

- identify risks and vulnerabilities to children in cyberspace
- create awareness
- develop practical tools to help minimise risk
- share knowledge and experience.

27 There then remains the equally, some would say even more important, challenge of making a reality the provision of the necessary care and protection for children.

28 http://www.icmec.org/en_X1/English – 5th_Edition_.pdf

29 http://www.csreurope.org/solutions.php?action=show_solution&solution_id=291

30 Interpol also coordinates a working party on crimes against children which meets once a year in a group session. There are five sub-groups within the working party and members of this group meet virtually throughout the year in an effort to work on projects. Four of the five sub-groups are: Internet facilitated crimes against children; Sex Offenders; Child Trafficking; and Serious and violent crimes against children. The fifth sub-group is a victim identification sub-group which facilitates the international cooperation which is a daily fact around the International Child Sexual Exploitation database.

31 www.virtualglobaltaskforce.com/what_we_do.asp

32 CEOP evidence to 3rd World Congress against the Sexual Exploitation of Children and Adolescents, November, 2008, page 1, see http://ec.europa.eu/information_society/apps/projects/logos//1/SIP-2007-HL-111701/080/publishing/readmore/Annual Report-2008.pdf.

33 For the full text of the EU's Safer Internet work programme, see http://ec.europa.eu/information_society/activities/sip/docs/call_2009/wp_09.pdf

34 Led by the University of Lancaster, and involving Middlesex and Swansea Universities. See http://tiny.cc/LeUjO

35 See www.inhope.org

36 See http://www.iwf.org.uk/media/news.268.htm

37 Strictly speaking what they are doing is confirming that, in their opinion, were the matter to go before a court it would be likely to be found to be illegal. When acting in this way the hotline is acting in a quasi judicial capacity.

38 *The Impact of Incentives on Notice and Take-down*, Moore and Clayton, www.cl.cam.ac.uk/~rnc1/takedown.pdfspeeds

39 See above http://ec.europa.eu/information_society/activities/sip/index_en.htm

40 The IWF is the UK's 'hotline'. According to the international association of hotlines, INHOPE, there are currently hotlines in 30 countries around the world.

41 URL stands for Uniform Resource Locator. It is an Internet address (for example, http://www.iwf.org.uk/reporting), usually consisting of the access protocol (for example, http), the domain name (for example, www.iwf.org.uk), and optionally, the path to a file or resource residing on that server (for example, reporting). The URLs contained in the IWF list may be addresses for an individual web page or a whole website.

42 Europol's (COSPOL) working group on 'Internet related child abusive material', named CIRCAMP is focusing on the commercial sexual exploitation of children, in removing or limiting the customer base of commercial sites distributing child sexual abusive material. This is being done via the deployment of 'The Child Sexual Abuse Anti-Distribution Filter' (CSAADF). The national law enforcement agency deals directly with national ISPs to ensure that blocking technology is implemented and they use the list of URLs which has been scrutinised against the national legislation on child sexual abuse material.

43 Correspondence with authors with Interpol.

44 http://www.theregister.co.uk/2006/02/07/bt_cleanfeed_iwf/ (accessed on 14th August, 2009).

45 http://www.gsmworld.com/our-work/public-policy/protecting-consumers/mobile_alliance.htm

46 http://www.missingkids.com/missingkids/servlet/PageServlet?LanguageCountry=en_US&PageId=3703

47 www.iwf.org.uk/media/news.258.htm

48 See above p. 75.

49 See https://www.interpol.int/Public/ICPO/speeches/20011219.asp

50 Every image generates its own unique digital signature, known as a 'hash set'.

51 The US-based National Center for Missing and Exploited Children said, in September 2008, that they knew of 1,660 children who had been identified from child abuse images, not all of which had been distributed on the Internet (see 'Child Pornography and Sexual Exploitation of Children Online', paper for 3rd World Congress, www.ecpat.net).
From correspondence with the authors, Interpol estimate that they have identified around 900 children from the images that have been sent to them by police forces around the world.

52 Save the Children (2006) 'Visible Evidence – Forgotten Children' the need for a child protection and children's rights focus in identifying children who have been sexually abused for the production of child abuse images. Brussels: Save the Children Europe Group.

53 www.chis.org.uk
54 www.enacso.eu

References

Child Exploitation Tracking Services, http://www.csreurope.org/solutions.php?action=show_solution&solution_id=291. Clayton, www.cl.cam.ac.uk/~rnc1/takedown.pdf-speeds.

Endrass, G. and Urbaniok, K. (2005) 'The Consumption of Internet Child Pornography and Violent and Sex Offending', http://www.pubmedcentral.nih.gov/articlerender.fcgi?artid=2716325.

Hernandez, A. (2000) Self-Reported Contact Sexual Offenses by Participants in the Federal Bureau of Prisons' Sex Offender Treatment Program: Implications for Internet Sex Offenders, November 2000, presented at the Association for the Treatment of Sexual Abusers (ATSA) in San Diego, California.

Hernandez, A. (2009) 'Psychological and Behavioural characteristics of Child Pornography Offenders in Treatment', Paper Prepared for G8 Global Symposium, April 5–7.

The International Centre for Missing & Exploited Children report on Child Pornography (2006), 5th edn, http://www.icmec.org/missingkids/servlet/PublicHomeServlet.

Internet Watch Foundation Annual Report (2008) www.iwf.org.uk Internet Watch Foundation http://www.iwf.org.uk/media/page.70.554.htm

Kim, C. (2004) *From Fantasy to Reality: The Link Between Viewing Child Pornography and Molesting Children.* Child Sexual Exploitation Update, Vol 1, 3, 2004.

Middleton, D. (2006) 'An Investigation into the Applicability of the Ward and Siegert Pathways Model of Child Sexual Abuse with Internet Offenders Psychology', *Crime & Law*, Dec, 598.

Offending and Criminal Justice Group (RDS) Home Office, Ref: IOS 503–03 www.statistics.gov.uk/pdfdir/intacc0702.pdf www.statistics.gov.uk/cci/nugget.asp?id=8.

Quale, E., Loof, L. and Palmer, T. (2008) Child Pornography and Sexual Exploitation of Children. Online – thematic paper written on behalf of ECPAT International as a contribution to the World Congress III against sexual exploitation of Children and Adolescents.

Seto, M.C. (2009) 'Assessing the Risk of Child Pornography Offenders', Paper Prepared for G8 Global Symposium, University of North Carolina, Chapel Hill, April 6–7.

Chapter 4

Stage model for online grooming offenders

Petter Gottschalk

Introduction

'I am Stian 15' said the Norwegian man on the Internet and made young girls take off their clothes in front of their web cameras at home. He had sex with two girls and made 60 girls aged 10–16 strip in front of their cameras. In 2008, the man (33) was sentenced to four years in prison in Norway. The same year, pictures of child abuse in Asia by a Canadian were found on a PC in Norway. Norwegian police informed Interpol in Lyon in France. While raping boys younger than 10, the Canadian had taken and later distributed pictures of himself and the boys (NRK, 2008).

Online victimisation has been a serious problem for many years. Children and young people are active users of online technologies, and have in many instances more expertise and experience in the use of information technology than their parents, teachers or other adults. However, as a consequence of the possibilities that lie within the services offered online, such as social network services, their own behaviour and the behaviour of people with a sexual interest in children in terms of harmful conduct, children and young people are vulnerable and may become victims of sexual abuse. The numbers of children are targeted or become victims in the online environment and the dynamics of children's own behaviour and that of the perpetrators is only known to a certain extent (European Commission, 2008).

Risks for and negative impacts on children online can result from being exposed to illegal content, harmful conduct and harmful content (European Commission, 2008):

- *Illegal content* is defined by national law. Illegal content is primarily dealt with by law enforcement agencies, prosecuting offenders and bringing them to trial. The main type of illegal content which falls under our scope is child abuse material.
- *Harmful conduct* includes conduct preparatory to committing a sexual offence against a child by contacting them online (grooming) and harassment happening in the online environment (cyber-bullying). The preparatory

acts for committing sexual offences are not, as such, yet considered as an offence in most European countries, but grooming is a criminal offence in the UK and in an increasing number of other countries.

- *Harmful content* is content which parents, caretakers, teachers and other adults responsible for children consider to be harmful for them. The conception of what is harmful varies across countries and cultures. A variety of means exist to deal with harmful content, such as enforcement of legal provisions where they exist.

This chapter represents a knowledge enhancement effort in law enforcement. According to the European Commission (2008), knowledge enhancement projects are important projects within the general field of safer Internet and online technologies in electronic government. The aim of such projects is to strengthen the knowledge base relevant to the policing work, law enforcement work and government work in general. Specifically, our project aims to enhance the knowledge of online-related sexual abuse and victimisation, in particular online grooming. Grooming is the process by which a person befriends a child with the intention of committing sexual abuse.

Stages of growth models

Stages of growth models have been used widely in both organisational research and management research. According to King and Teo (1997), these models describe a wide variety of phenomena – the organisational life cycle, product life cycle, biological growth, and so forth. These models assume that predictable patterns (conceptualised in terms of stages) exist in the growth of organisations, the sales levels of products, and the growth of living organisms. These stages are (i) sequential in nature, (ii) occur as a hierarchical progression that is not easily reversed, and (iii) evolve a broad range of organisational activities and structures.

Benchmark variables are often used to indicate characteristics in each stage of growth. A one-dimensional continuum is established for each benchmark variable. The measurement of benchmark variables can be carried out using Guttman scales (Frankfort-Nachmias and Nachmias, 2002). Guttman scaling is a cumulative scaling technique based on ordering theory that suggests a linear relationship between the elements of a domain and the items on a test.

Various multistage models have been proposed for organisational evolution over time. For example, Nolan (1979) introduced a model with six stages for information technology maturity in organisations, which later was expanded to nine. Earl (2000) suggested a stage of growth model for evolving the e-business, consisting of the following six stages: external communication, internal communication, e-commerce, e-business, e-enterprise, and transformation, while Rao and Metts (2003) describe a stage model for electronic commerce development in small- and medium-sized enterprises. In the area of knowledge management, Housel and Bell (2001) developed a five-level model. In the area of knowledge management systems, Dean and Gottschalk (2007) present a four-stage model applied to knowledge management in law enforcement. Gottschalk and Tolloczko (2007) developed a maturity model for mapping crime in law enforcement, while Gottschalk and Solli-Sæther (2006) developed a maturity model for IT outsourcing relationships, and Gottschalk (2009) presented maturity levels for interoperability in digital government. Each of these models identifies certain characteristics that typify firms in different stages of growth. Among these multistage models, models with four stages seem to have been proposed and tested most frequently.

A recent example is a stage of growth model for corrupt organisations, where the four-stage model proposed by Pfarrer et al. (2008) is concerned with organisational actions that potentially increase the speed and likelihood that an organisation will restore its legitimacy with stakeholders following a transgression. The four stages are labelled discovery, explanation, penance, and rehabilitation respectively.

The concept of stages of growth has been widely employed for many years. Already two decades ago, Kazanjian and Drazin (1989) found that a number of multistage models had been proposed, which assume that predictable patterns exist in the growth of organisations, and that these patterns unfold as discrete time periods best thought of as stages. These models have different distinguishing characteristics. Stages can be driven by the search for new growth opportunities or as a response to internal crises. Some models suggest that organisations progress through stages while others argue that there may be multiple paths through the stages.

Kazanjian (1988) applied dominant problems to stages of growth. Dominant problems imply that there is a pattern of primary concerns that firms face for each theorised stage. In criminal organisations, for example, dominant problems can shift from lack of skills to lack of resources to lack of strategy associated with different stages of growth, as suggested by Gottschalk (2008) in his stage model for organised crime.

Kazanjian and Drazin (1989) argue that either implicitly or explicitly, stages of growth models share a common underlying logic. Organisations undergo transformations in their design characteristics, which enable them to face the new tasks or problems that growth elicits. The problems, tasks or environments may differ from model to model, but almost all suggest that stages emerge in a well-defined sequence, so that the solution of one set of problems or tasks leads to the emergence of a new set of problems and tasks that the organisation must address.

Online grooming offence

In the UK, the Sexual Offences Act clarifies the position with regard to sexual abuse of children, as discussed by Davidson in Chapter 1. Meeting a child following sexual grooming applies to the Internet, other technologies such as mobile phones and also to the real world. Grooming involves a process of socialisation during which an offender seeks to interact with a child (and sometimes the child's family), possibly sharing their hobbies, interests and computer slang in an attempt to gain trust in order to prepare them for sexual abuse. The process may also involve an attempt to persuade a child that sexual relations between adults and children are acceptable.

Sex offenders use the Internet to target and groom children for the purposes of sexual abuse, to produce and/or download indecent illegal images of children for distribution, and to communicate with other sex offenders. Internet sex offender behaviour includes (Davidson, 2007):

- construction of sites to be used for the exchange of offender and victim information
- experiences and indecent images of children
- organisation of criminal activities that seek to use children for prostitution purposes
- production of indecent images of children at a professional level
- organisation of criminal activities that promote sexual tourism

The demand for indecent images through, for example, the use of file-sharing technologies, has expanded so much that law enforcement agencies are finding it difficult to identify and track down all child victims and the perpetrators involved. Possible motivations of online child sex abusers are many. It is suggested that sex offenders perceive the Internet as a means of generating an immediate solution to their fantasies. Factors including presumed anonymity, interactivity and ready accessibility might encourage offenders to go online. The unique structure of the Internet may play a major role in facilitating online child abuse. Offenders' Internet use is not limited to abuse; the Internet often plays a significant role in other areas of their lives.

Typologies of Internet child sex offenders have been developed to guide the work of police officers. One typology does include those offenders targeting and grooming children online, a group largely excluded from other typologies. For example, nine categories of offenders might be identified (Davidson, 2008): (i) the browser is an offender who accidentally comes across indecent images and saves them; (ii) the dreamer applies fantasy to digital image; (iii) the networker is an offender engaging in exchange with others; (iv) the collector looks for indecent images in open search to update his collection; (v) the member belongs to an online, hidden sex offender network; (vi) the connector targets children via peer-2-peer technology and chat rooms; (vii) the abuser enjoy images of their own abuse; (viii) the producer records sexual abuse of children, while (ix) the distributor is an offender who distributes indecent images for financial gain or as part of their collecting behaviour.

Child pornography represents indecent images. However, what is 'indecent' differs among legislations, and it is often left to the courts to decide. In some countries, a jury has to decide. The jury is shown the images and asked to consider whether they believe that they are indecent images of children. Traditionally, definitions of child pornography emphasise the sexual nature of the representation and, as such, seek to distinguish child pornography from innocent images of children (Gillespie, 2005).

The definition of grooming in the UK legislation is such that (Davidson, 2008):

- The offence only applies to adults over 18.
- There must be a meeting with the victim.
- The communication can take place anywhere in the world.
- The offender must either meet the child or travel to the prearranged meeting.
- The meeting or at least part of the travel must take place within the jurisdiction.
- The person must have an intention to commit any offence under the sexual offences act or any act which would be an offence in the jurisdiction. This may be evident from the previous communications or other circumstances, for example, an offender travels in possession of ropes, condoms or lubricants.
- The child is under 16 and the adult does not reasonably believe that the child is over 16. However, if this is not the case, for example, the child's place has been taken by an undercover police officer, an attempt could be charged.

In sentencing under the sexual grooming category, judges are advised to consider the following aggravating case circumstances (Davidson, 2008):

- The seriousness of the intended offence (which will affect both the offender's culpability and the degree of risk to which the victim has been exposed).
- The degree to which the offence was planned.
- The sophistication of the grooming.
- The determination of the offender.
- How close the offender came to success.
- The reason why the offender did not succeed, that is, was it a change of mind or did someone or something prevent the offender from continuing.
- Any physical or psychological injury suffered by the victim.

Stages of online offending

While most stages of growth models are concerned with the organisational level, this research is concerned with the individual level. In the following, we propose a stage of growth model for online grooming offenders. Our model represents a stage hypothesis for offenders. The idea of stages of growth is that it might be assumed that the offender starts at stage 1 and over time develops into higher and more serious stages. This assumes that an offender found to be at stage 4 was at a lower stage some years ago.

The model suggests escalation to more serious contact offending over time. This model suggests a possible link between the possession and collection of indecent child images and the propensity for contact abuse. Given the lack of empirical evidence in this area, the development of any stage of growth model must be tentative; the work of Hernandez (2009) and Taylor (Chapter 6) suggests a link, whilst Seto's (2009) research is less conclusive. There is, however, some evidence of escalation from relatively minor offences including indecent exposure to serious contact offences in the general sex offender literature (Finkelhor, 1984), which is pertinent here. The stage of growth model presents a possible behavioural movement or escalation from the use of indecent images of children towards contact abuse. It is not suggested that all Internet sex offenders will follow this route, and categories are not mutually exclusive, but the model offers one possible offending route or 'pathway' (Ward and Siegert, 2006).

In this tentative model the offender begins at stage 1 as a user or consumer of online indecent images. These images are used to fuel fantasy. The role of deviant sexual fantasy in fuelling offending is well documented in the sex offender literature and has formed a cornerstone of sex offender treatment programmes in the US and the UK. Over time the offending behaviour escalates into higher and more serious stages facilitated by the Internet and possibly in conjunction with other online abusers.

The stages in the stage model for online grooming offenders are as follows (Figure 4.1):

- *Stage 1: Online Consumer.* This person may start as a browser who accidentally comes across indecent images and saves them. This is also a person who seeks indecent images and saves them. After a while, such images are purchased via credit card. Indecent images are used to satisfy private fantasies. Digital images are consumed for personal use. As a consumer, the sex offender is mainly concerned with combining image impression and personal fantasy to achieve personal satisfaction. Indecent images are used to satisfy personal fantasies, and such offenders will have an existing sexual attraction to children. Consumption of indecent images of children on the Internet is the main activity of the abuser. In some cases, the person has experienced prior contact abuse. Some offenders may stop at level 1, while others may progress to level 2.

According to Davidson (2007), sex offenders use the Internet to access indecent images of children, to select victims for abuse and to communicate

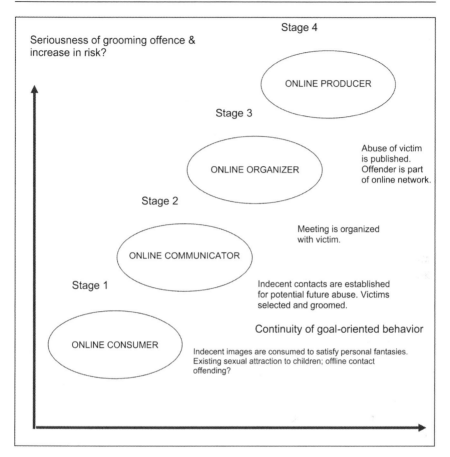

Figure 4.1 Stages of online grooming

with other sex offenders. This activity has expanded so much that law enforcement agencies have difficulties tracking down the child victims and perpetrators involved.

According to Kierkegaard (2008), every second about 30,000 Internet users are viewing pornography. Internet is aiding sexual sex offenders, stalkers, child pornographers, child traffickers, and others with the intent of exploiting children. Child pornography is defined in Norwegian criminal law as sexual presentation of real children (Skybak, 2004).

The online consumer at stage 1 is similar to Krone's (2004) 'browser', who uses indecent images to satisfy private fantasies (Wortley and Smallbone, 2006).

- *Stage 2: Online Communicator.* This person searches indecent images through open browsers and may engage in some networking. Also, this person looks for indecent images in open areas of the Internet such as chat rooms and peer-2-peer networks and may engage in some networking. As a communicator, the person might communicate with other sex offenders and/or potential victims. For example, the person may both exchange and trade in indecent images with men having the same interest. Here we find collection of certain images (same victim time and same level of seriousness).

According to Kierkegaard (2008), Internet bulletin boards, chat rooms, private websites, and peer-2-peer networks are being used daily by sex offenders to meet unsuspecting children. Teenagers are especially vulnerable because they are often trusting, naive, curious, adventuresome, and eager for attention and affection.

Online sex offences and online contacts leading to offline sex offences against children in Sweden were studied by Brå (2007). In a school survey of a representative Swedish sample aged 15, 31 per cent reported online sexual contact from someone they 'know or believe is an adult' over the past 12 months (46 per cent of girls, 16 per cent of boys).

The online communicator at stage 2 is similar to Krone's (2004) 'trawler', who searches for indecent images through open browsers and may engage in some networking. It is also similar to Krone's (2004) 'non-secure collector', who looks for indecent images in open areas of the Internet such as chat rooms. It is entirely possible that the online communicator has already committed offline contact offences.

- *Stage 3: Online Organiser.* This person uses peer-2-peer technology, interactive Internet games and chat rooms to organise meetings. The person is grooming online for the purposes of abuse or could remain an indecent image organiser. If a meeting is organised, personal sexual abuse of a child or children is the goal. Here we find online abuse or possibly that abuse is ongoing with family children or other children known to the offender.

According to Wolak et al. (2008), most Internet-initiated sex crimes involve adult men who use the Internet to meet and seduce underage adolescents into sexual encounters. The offenders use Internet communications such as instant messages, email, and chat rooms to organise meetings and to develop intimate relationships with victims.

'Stian 15' is one of the few offenders caught in Norway in recent years. Twenty-two per cent of all Norwegian children between 9 and 16 years of age (about 70,000 children) have met someone on the Internet. Most of these meetings were with persons of their own age and occurred without any problems. However, in some cases the children met adults who claimed to be children on the Internet. Only 10 per cent of those children who have gone to such meetings report that they experienced anything unpleasant in terms of words or physical abuse. It is mostly girls of 15–16 years who have unpleasant experiences. Most of those children who have unpleasant experiences in terms of physical or psychological abuse at such meetings with adults report that they are dissatisfied with friends, school and/or own family. Most of them have parents born in a country other than Norway. A total of 6,000 children aged 9–16 had unpleasant experiences at meetings following Internet contact in 2006 in Norway (Justis, 2007).

The online organiser at stage 3 is similar to Krone's (2004) 'groomer', who targets and grooms children via peer-2-peer technology, interactive Internet games and chat rooms. These offenders may send indecent images to children as part of the grooming process and become what Krone (2004) labels 'physical abusers', who have an interest in indecent images as part of their fantasy cycle. These offenders may photograph their abusive behaviour for their own use (Wortley and Smallbone, 2006).

- *Stage 4: Online Producer.* This person records the sexual abuse of children for the purposes of distribution to networks and to satisfy their own fantasy. Also, the person may distribute indecent images and contact details either for financial gain or as part of an exchange relationship. The person may expand into a more business-focused role by use of children for prostitution and by promoting sexual tourism as part of a larger personal fantasy scheme.

Members of an Internet criminal organisation called 'Fun Club', 25 men were arrested, mainly fathers photographed or filmed with web cameras, as they abused their daughters, aged between 2 and 14. One father had contacted Sergio Marzola, an Italian producer of child pornography, who offered 250 Euros for the daughters to be filmed dressed in sex offender lingerie, 500 Euros to film them naked and 750 Euros for him to rape one of them (Croy, 2006). Sergio Marzola is an example of an offender at stage 4, being an online producer. He had his own photo studios where he abused children who he first contacted on the Internet. In his photo studio in Ukraine, for example, many poor children were abused. Before he was arrested, he managed 30 Internet sites intended for the exchange of child pornography.

A 51-year-old man was sentenced to 60 years in prison in the US. He had videotaped himself sexually abusing three children aged under six. A laptop computer was seized and was found to contain over 16,000 images and over 1,000 video files depicting children – many of whom were between the ages of two and ten years old – being sexually assaulted. The suspect admitted to sexually assaulting the children. He pleaded guilty to manufacturing child sexual abuse images in Federal court and was sentenced to 60 years in US Federal prison, without parole, the highest possible sentence under Federal law (IWF, 2007).

The online producer at stage 4 is similar to Krone's (2004) secure collector who belongs to an online hidden sex offender network. These offenders are highly organized and likely to be collectors and employ sophisticated security to conceal their offending.

(Wortley and Smallbone, 2006)

A typical offender at stage 2 (online communicator) potentially developing into higher stages (online organiser and online producer) is described by O'Connell (2003) as follows, where 'the child' is an adult:

'The child' is befriended by another chat room user who claims to be slightly older in age than the child, and to have similar likes and dislikes. These similarities are discerned throughout the course of a conversation (s) about music, sports, computers etc. These topics can be discussed during one on-line conversation or the process may span a number of on-line encounters, which can occur over a number of days, weeks or even months. The duration of the 'friendship-forming' stage can vary quite a bit but the effect is the creation of a shared virtual friendship. Typically, the 'virtual friend' presents him or herself as slightly older in age than 'the child' and therefore often assumes the role of advisor, confidant or teacher who guides a child toward increasing his or her self-knowledge and self-confidence. Naturally 'the child' feels comfortable confiding with this 'virtual friend', because the 'virtual friend' understands and often proclaims a 'deep love' for 'the child'. When the virtual friend begins to ask 'the child' about issues relating to e.g. sexuality, sexual development or sexual experiences, the child may not interpret these questions as a deviation from mutuality. It is important to recognize the psychological dynamics underpinning the shift in the tone of a conversation into these realms, which serves a number of functions for an alleged sex offender. It seems reasonable to suggest that this kind of conversation is sexually titillating for an adult with a sexual interest in children. Furthermore, the conversation serves to prime the child for the sexual suggestions, which typically follow these introductory remarks. In addition, the disclosures 'the child' makes in response to such requests for intimate insights into 'the child's' developing sexuality serves to lure the child into an emotionally abusive arena, which they may feel complicit in creating. It seems reasonable to suggest that similar to off-line sex offender grooming practices, the typical net result is that a child feels unable to inform a responsible person about the on-line activities because of a mixture of shame and guilt. The adult with a sexual interest in children may engage in these activities for any number of reasons and may choose to disengage at any number of points. The adult may simply engage in these activities out of curiosity, to hone his grooming skills, or for masturbatory purposes. Alternatively, the adult with a sexual interest in children may wish to meet the young child in the real world and the encounters may escalate to an off-line meeting. The incidence and outcomes of these meetings have been well documented by the press over the course of the last year. Therefore, it seems reasonable to suggest that there is a need to educate children to be able to detect these shifts in conversation. These activities are very similar to off-line grooming practices except the child often has far fewer cues with which to discern the identity of the person with whom they are conversing.

However, O'Connell's (2003) sample was small, and police officers dealing with hundreds of 'hits' every week tend to have a somewhat different story to tell. For example, Police Officers working as undercover children in High Tech Crime Units in the UK have suggested that Internet grooming can be and often is different from 'real world' grooming in that offenders spend little time chatting and will come straight to the point, sometimes instantly, for example, 'would you like to meet for sex?' This would suggest that the Internet might act to remove inhibitions associated with face-to-face contact (Davidson, 2007).

Potentially dangerous contacts with strangers through the Internet are intriguing to many children. Even the appearance of a meeting suggestion is often not treated as something that can cause anxiety. Sometimes it even inspires imagination. It is more alarming to children when the Internet interlocutor wants to learn specific personal details such as name, surname, and address. Most children know that they are not supposed to provide such information. The exception is if the person they are talking to has a web cam. This is often the proof they need that the person is who they say they are (MMI, 2007).

This finding from Norway by the polling institute MMI (2007) was included in a pan-European qualitative study Eurobarometer (2007) covering 29 European countries, where children of 9–10 and 12–14 years of age were interviewed in-depth about their use of online technologies. In the interviews, the children were told a story of a young person of their age who, after putting his/her profile online on the Internet and gradually giving personal details, had established a relationship with someone unknown.

The participants were asked to react to this story. One Danish boy responded (Eurobarometer, 2007: 47).

> I met him at a station and then it was an old, nasty, 44 years old man. Then I walked away! I have never told my parents about it! They would get angry. It might have consequences. I might have my mobile phone taken from me.

In almost all groups in a large majority of countries, the study collected a number of personal anecdotes like this one. These anecdotes attested to real, potentially dangerous, contacts. It therefore seems that some children adopt riskier behaviour than they say and think they do. In particular, young people aged 12 to 14 can show themselves to be very confident, both in their own insight in unmasking false identities and in being wary of interlocutors who are especially 'friendly' towards them. They are reluctant to warn their parents.

Offender-related perspectives on online victimisation of children include: (1) understanding the ways in which sexual abuse is caused with the help of online technologies; (2) understanding how offenders use online technologies to find and target children; (3) the changing nature of grooming behaviour; (4) the link between consumption of child abuse material and contact sexual abuse; and (5) the changing profiles of online child abusers (European Commission, 2008).

Whilst it is very difficult to identify key stages in the grooming process, the case files we have seen on these men demonstrate very different approaches and styles. However, it could be that we have simply not yet seen enough of these men (no women yet) to be sure about their behaviour, and that is why we think our proposed stage hypothesis is so important.

According to Seto and Eke (2005), the likelihood that child pornography offenders will later commit a contact sexual offence is unknown. In their study, a sample of 201 adult male child pornography offenders was identified. Fifty-six per cent of the sample had a prior criminal record, 24 per cent had prior contact sexual offences, and 15 per cent had prior child pornography offences.

Whether a child pornography offender will progress into higher stages of victimisation could depend on the kind of pornography consumption. A distinction can be made between two groups of offenders depending on whether or not the sex offenders masturbate while looking at child pornography on the Internet. The masturbating group seems more sexually motivated and thus more likely to move to higher stages, as compared to the non-masturbating group that seems less sexually motivated. The masturbating group is assumed to be closer to hands-on sexual offending (Elliott and Beech, 2009).

It is indeed relevant to assume that child pornography exposure may influence the development of contact sexual offending in some sex offenders, in particular when images are used to stimulate sexual satisfaction in terms of masturbation. The hands-on theory suggests that a progression is more likely among masturbating consumers. However, it can be argued that the move from viewing abusive images of children on the Internet to contact offending is a massive one. Therefore, not every offender who masturbates to indecent images of children will inevitably progress to contact sexual offences. However, we argue that the risk of them doing so will increase as the conditional pairing of online fantasy with masturbation and physical satisfaction will lower their inhibitions for doing so.

This is in line with research by Elliott and Beech (2009), who base their study on sexual offence theory consisting of multi-factor models, single factor models, as well as models of offence processes. According to this theory, two developmental resources combine and interact to shape an individual's unique psychological functioning: (1) biological factors – essentially genetic and evolutionary factors, and (2) social learning factors – that is, the social, cultural and physical environment along with an individual's personal circumstances.

It is important to stress here that stages of growth models are very different from life cycle models. While stage models define and describe accumulated progression and escalation by online groomers, life cycle models represent a cycle of birth, growth, decline, and eventually death of sex offenders.

In future research there is a need to validate the stage model both theoretically and empirically. Furthermore, there is a need for benchmark variables that will have different content for different stages. In the current research, the stages are lacking both theoretical background and practical situations. While stage 4 may seem understandable and viable, the remaining stages are in need of further conceptual work. Core questions in future research will be whether consumer, communicator, organiser, and producer are valid, practicable, and accountable.

In future research, strengths and weaknesses to the suggested model have to be taken into account. We need to provide a more critical analysis of a stage model such as the one suggested. It is not at all intuitively obvious to all readers that the progression over time is from consumer, via communicator and organiser, to producer. Why not communicator, consumer, organiser, and producer; or producer via organiser and communicator to consumer? Thus, the conceptual research presented here is lacking empirical evidence. Only a questionnaire based on Guttman scaling rather than Likert scaling can verify the suggested sequence or alternatively identify another sequence.

The important contribution of this chapter, however, is the introduction of the stage hypothesis to our understanding of online grooming behaviour. Rather than thinking of online grooming behaviours in terms of alternative strategies, we suggest an evolutionary approach where the future is building on the past, rather than the future being a divergent path from the past. Rather than thinking that what was done in the past is wrong, past actions are conceived of as the only available foundation for future actions. If past actions are not on the path to success, direction is changed without history being reversed when online groomers are developing their strategy.

Police investigations

While the expansion of the Internet and the proliferation of information technology has created new opportunities for those who engage in illegal activities (Taylor and Quayle, 2003), the area of digital forensics has grown rapidly as well (Ferraro and Casey, 2005). This has helped in the discovery of new ways of criminal activities. According to Davidson (2007), sex offenders use the Internet to access indecent images of children, to select victims for abuse and to communicate with other sex offenders. This activity has expanded so much that law enforcement agencies have difficulty tracking down child victims and perpetrators involved unless they have the capability of professional digital forensics and intelligence (Smith, 2008).

Rapid growth of the Internet and advances in technology mean enormous benefits to society, and children should be able to enjoy the benefits that the Internet offers safely. However, it is necessary to recognise that with the spread of the Internet comes the growth in the possibility of the system being abused by sex offenders; making contact with children with intent to groom the youngsters through chat rooms and social Internet sites (RMA, 2007).

Dealing with illegal content, on the one hand, and harmful content, on the other, may require using different methods, strategies and tools. However, some tools can be used for all categories. For instance, awareness raising can be used in respect to illegal content and harmful conduct (crime prevention) as well as for harmful content (European Commission, 2008).

Successful cybercrime investigations require computer skills and modern systems in policing. Furthermore, modern information systems in policing with access to all relevant electronic information sources require a modern electronic government. Digital government infrastructure must be in place to support the breadth and depth of all government activities, including computer forensics in cybercrime investigations by law enforcement agencies.

Online victimisation of children is a global issue in need of international law enforcement solutions. This is particularly true for illegal content. Material depicting child sexual abuse may be produced in one country, hosted in a second, and accessed and downloaded all over the world. Commercial payment systems operating worldwide may be used to fund sale and purchase of the images (European Commission, 2008).

Digital forensics is the art and science of applying computer science to aid the legal process. It is more than the technological, systematic inspection of electronic systems and their contents for evidence or supportive evidence of a criminal act. Digital forensics requires specialised expertise and tools. As a term, digital forensics refers to the study of technology, the way criminals use it, and the way to extract and examine digital evidence (Ferraro and Casey, 2005).

Digital forensics is an approach to identifying evidence from computers that can be used in trials. A typical forensics investigation consists of two main phases, exploration and evidence respectively. During the exploration phase, investigators attempt to identify the nature of the problem and what exactly happened or is expected to happen at the crime scene. The evidence phase takes place after the exploration has been concluded. It consists of accumulating all documentation, which will work in court.

From a data viewpoint, this two-phase procedure can be broken down into six stages: preparation, incident response, data collection, data analysis, presentation of findings, and incident closure. Some of these stages may be so complex in certain circumstances that they are divided into sub-stages. The most time-consuming tasks in digital forensics investigation are searching, extracting, and analysing. Therefore, there is a need for a forensics model that allows formalisation of the digital forensics process, innovative data-mining techniques for the forensics process, and a dedicated infrastructure for digital forensics.

Mitchell *et al.* (2005) explored the extent and effectiveness of proactive investigations in which investigators pose as minors on the Internet to catch potential sex offenders. Results suggest that proactive investigations represented a significant proportion (25 per cent) of all arrests for Internet sex crimes against minors. The online personas assumed by investigators paralleled the ages and genders of real youth victimised in sex crimes that started as online encounters.

Internet red buttons

Today, nearly all service providers use information technology in order to make parts of their service production virtual rather than physical. There is a widespread excitement about the prospects of the Internet to make more service activities virtual.

In the early days of the information technology era, there was a widespread euphoria about the prospects of information technology, in general, and the Internet, in particular, for virtualisation of various service activities. Apocalyptic predictions declared that in many service sectors, a large part of the service production would move from the traditional, face-to-face channel to the Internet and that this shift would be linear and irreversible – some researchers assumed that the Internet would downplay a large share of traditional market actors, a phenomenon which was referred to as 'disintermediation' (Benjamin and Wigand, 1995) or an 'electronic brokerage effect' (Lewis and Talalayevsky, 1997).

However, researchers are increasingly debating such euphoria, excitement and prediction for the future. Maybe virtual service production on the Internet is like a two-edged sword. In a service marketing context, a more sober and, we argue, realistic approach to information technology and the Internet has begun to emerge; one which acknowledges that the move from face-to-face service production to technology-mediated service production is far from linear. In fact, there seems to be little evidence supporting the disintermediation hypothesis. Balasubramanian *et al.* (2005, p. 13) argue that 'predictions that nimble, virtual sellers will replace inefficient brick-and-mortar retailers are fading as analysts realise that markets of the future will contain a mix of channels'. Research on consumers' channel choice indicates that consumers often choose the Internet for purchasing a service when the complexity of the service is perceived to be low. When purchasing services that are perceived to be more complex in nature, consumers' adoption of the Internet has remained low, and the proximal, face-to-face service encounter is still preferred (Coelho and Easingwood, 2004; Osterlund et al., 2005; Frambach et al., 2007). Furthermore, research in channel strategy has found that companies using a combination of physical channels and the Internet are more successful than actors with a virtual presence only, and that such a strategy may generate synergies and higher profitability (Berman and Thelen, 2004; Harridge-March, 2004; Rangaswamy and Van Bruggen, 2005). Today, the Internet is therefore increasingly considered as a complement to, rather than as a substitute for, traditional service production channels (Kumar and Venkatesan, 2005; Rangaswamy and Van Bruggen, 2005).

Taken together, the infusion of the Internet has led to a new distribution of tasks between service production channels. Whereas the Internet is taking over an increasing amount of the simple, standardised, transaction-based services, more complex ones require the proximal, face-to-face interaction between consumer and service provider. Some researchers have argued that this new division of tasks will place an increased importance on face-to-face service production and the physical branches, thereby creating a need to redefine their roles (Bekier et al., 2000; Laing et al., 2002). Yakhlef (2005) argues that virtualisation should not be interpreted as synonymous to a de-materialisation of the concrete world. Instead, he suggests that it should be viewed as liberating places and humans from certain tasks, but simultaneously introducing others. However, few studies have been devoted to exploring this new distribution of tasks (Rangaswamy and Van Bruggen, 2005), and Grove et al. (2003, p. 115) called for more research investigating 'the impact of high tech service dimensions on the demand for high touch features'. In her doctoral dissertation, Värlander (2007) shows how attempts at virtualisation trigger off changes in the physical realms of service production.

In this section, we build on these initial findings and extend our study to the empirical context of Norwegian police services and 'the red button', which has the purpose of reporting online grooming and groomers to prevent victimisation of children by sex offenders. In order to gain insights into the physical–virtual service production interplay in this context we will apply the concepts of 'framing' and 'overflowing' (Callon, 1998), which are introduced below, followed by a description of the empirical context. Finally, the section discusses the empirical context in light of the theoretical concepts and draws conclusions and implications for researchers and practitioners.

Rhetorically, 'virtual' is one of the most important marketing terms for the development of an assumed high-tech, knowledge-oriented 'virtual society' (Shields, 2003). The Internet has commonly been referred to as a 'virtual' channel, which is contrasted to 'physical channels', where services are provided in the presence of the parties involved. The virtual is often seen as a possible way of suppressing, compressing and reducing the cost of place and time, giving rise to a new type of profit: customers save time and travel costs, while providers save the cost of owning and running physical branches and provide possibilities for economies of scale and lower wage-rate locations (Alexander, 1997). But how can the virtual be defined? A useful definition, which forces us to critically reflect upon the definitions of the virtual as a move away from place, is the definition by Shields (2003). Shields (2003) defines 'virtual space' as a recasting of communication as a space or environment. For example, the telephone has intervened in our sense of the world by providing virtual auditory spaces where a person in one place is brought into the earshot of a person in a distant place (Ronell, 1989). Calling a telephone conversation a type of virtual space challenges the idea of 'virtual space' as something enduring and independent of geographical space. Instead, this definition of the virtual leads us to think of the virtual as attached to, and dependent upon, physical places and human bodies. Thus, the transcending possibilities attributed to virtual communication technology should not be viewed as a one-directional movement from physical place to virtual space. Graham (1998, p. 167) claims that 'little conscious thought is put to thinking about how new information technologies actually relate to the spaces and places bound up with human territorial life'. Fearing the consequences of a too narrowly defined view of the physical–virtual interplay, he argues that 'without a thorough and critical consideration of space and place, and how information technology relates to, and is embedded in them, reflections on cyberspace and the economic, social and cultural dynamics of the shift to growing telemediation seem likely to be reductionist, deterministic, over simplistic and stale' (Graham, 1998, p. 167). Hence, it is suggested that the interaction between physical and virtual is a back-and-forth move rather than a linear movement from physical to virtual. A useful conceptualisation of this back-and-forth move is provided by Lévy who argues that virtuality involves movements of deterritorialisation and detemporalisation; but without the existence of alternative places, virtuality cannot be conceived. The virtual demands the physical, because even if it may liberate places and humans of certain tasks, it redistributes tasks to others. This is the reason why virtualisation does not only imply deterritorialisation but also reterritorialisation. The physical exchange of objects and values is virtualised, deterritorialised and reterritorialised into the physical realms. Thus, territorial and spatial re-definitions seem to be implicated in the interplay of the physical and the virtual. This implies that the virtualisation of activities may also have effects on the ways in which the physical realm is conceived.

Callon's (1998) concepts of 'framing' and 'overflowing' are also illustrative for the phenomenon of how virtualisation of service production may affect the physical service production. Drawing on Goffman (1971), Callon (1998) shows how encounters take place in frames, which establish a boundary within which interactions take place. However, framing necessarily involves overflowing. 'It is essential that something should cross or break through the boundary drawn up round the commercial interaction within the frame' (Callon, 1998, p. 256). In the context of information technology, the concept of overflow suggests that technologies constantly create uncertainties in relation to identities, institutions, and practices. This is not due to any intrinsic property of a particular technology. Rather, it stems from the way that technologies are enmeshed with society. Overflows emerge from the 'turbulence' of human encounters, which make them difficult to standardise, manage and predict (Fuchs, 2001, p. 203). There are certain features of encounters that cannot be framed in a technological code – 'Encounters have many more results, outcomes, and effects than contained in the minutes' (Fuchs, 2001, p. 236). Therefore, when attempting to standardise or frame service production through information technology, overflows on the proximal, face-to-face service production process are generated. Those features of the service encounters that are not possible to frame, or virtualise, will generate physical overflows that are often unexpected.

In this section we explore the overflows that are generated through the virtualisation of Norwegian police services by introducing 'the red button', which was launched in September 2008. The red button is located on web pages for children where online grooming may occur. The red button can be pressed by children and others who experience abusive behaviour on that website. When the button is pressed, an automatic message is sent to the national criminal police (Kripos) in Norway (Døvik, 2008). Kripos is open all year day and night.

Before providing a more detailed description of this, we present a short note on the background to the introduction of the 'red button' and provide a deeper insight into the problem of online grooming.

It is Microsoft in Norway who has taken the lead to install this system, which is to be found on all websites used by children. By pressing the red button marked police, abuse can easily be reported directly to the police (Døvik, 2008).

When the red button is pressed, the police tip page tips.kripos.no automatically opens on the screen. Three alternatives emerge on the screen: Sexual exploitation of children (*Seksuell utnytting av barn*), human trafficking (*Menneskehandel*), and Racial expressions on the Internet (*Rasistiske ytringer på Internett*).

If sexual exploitation of children is ticked, then instructions on the screen say that the tip registration will occur in three steps:

Step 1: What is the tip about?
Step 2: Where did the act occur?
Step 3: Who is the sender of the tip?

Next, there is a choice between ticking: (i) web pages that have pictures or films sexualising children, (ii) sexual exploitation of children on the Internet (grooming), and (iii) sexual offence against children.

The purpose of this section is to develop a conceptual link between the literature and the case in terms of criteria for evaluating the red button approach. In the following we list criteria for red button evaluation that emerge from our literature review:

1. *Complementary approach.* Internet is a complement, rather than a substitute, for traditional service production. Research in channel strategy has found that organisations using a combination of physical channels and the Internet are more successful than actors with a virtual presence only, and that such a strategy may generate synergies and higher profitability (Berman and Thelen, 2004; Harridge-March, 2004; Rangaswamy and Van Bruggen, 2005). Today, the Internet is therefore increasingly considered as a complement to, rather than a substitute for, traditional service production channels (Kumar and Venkatesan, 2005; Rangaswamy and Van Bruggen, 2005). Therefore, we would expect to find face-to-face contact information for Kripos on red button pages.

2. *Simple requests.* Whereas the Internet is taking over an increasing amount of the simple, standardised, transaction-based services, more complex ones require the proximal, face-to-face interaction between respondent and service provider. Therefore, we would expect to find a stepwise approach distinguishing between simple and complex responses on red button pages for Kripos.

3. *Virtual role.* Some researchers have argued that this new division of tasks in simple versus complex tasks will place an increased importance on face-to-face service production and the physical branches, thereby creating a need to redefine their roles (Laing *et al.*, 2002). Therefore, we would expect to find a virtual role perception by respondents using the red button. A virtual role perception includes a perception of the red button being a liberating place as compared to face-to-face places. This is in line with Yakhlef (2005), who argues that virtualisation should not be interpreted as synonymous to a de-materialisation of the concrete world. Instead, he suggests that it should be viewed as liberating places and humans from certain tasks, but simultaneously introducing others. While communication on the Internet might be personal in content, it is not perceived as interpersonal in meaning. A typical example is email, where the sender might feel completely disconnected from the time and place that the receiver reads the message. Even when chatting in real time, sender and receiver may perceive both involvement and disconnectedness at the same time. Some people unconsciously change their personality when

moving from face-to-face communication to email communication (Weber, 2004). Internet grooming can be and often is different from 'real world' grooming in that offenders spend little time chatting and will come straight to the point, sometimes instantly, for example, 'would you like to meet for sex?' This would suggest that the Internet might act to remove inhibitions associated with face-to-face contact, which can be explained by the disconnected nature of personal communication on the Internet, thereby avoiding unpleasant emotional states (Quayle *et al.*, 2006). This is what we define here as the virtual role for individuals sending messages to Kripos.

4. *Physical role.* In her doctoral dissertation, Värlander (2007) shows how attempts at virtualisation trigger off changes in the physical realms of service production. Therefore, we would expect to find changes in Kripos after the red button introduction. While we define the virtual role for the sender, we define the physical role for the receiver of messages communicated on the Internet.

5. *Frame overflow.* An Internet service establishes a boundary within which interactions take place. However, framing necessarily involves overflowing. 'It is essential that something should cross or break through the boundary drawn up round the commercial interaction within the frame' (Callon, 1998, p. 256). In the context of information technology, the concept of overflow suggests that technologies constantly create uncertainties in relation to identities, institutions, and practices. This is not due to any intrinsic property of a particular technology. Rather, it stems from the way that technologies are enmeshed with society. Overflows emerge from the 'turbulence' of human encounters, which make them difficult to standardise, manage and predict (Fuchs, 2001, p. 203). There are certain features of encounters that cannot be framed in a technological code – 'Encounters have many more results, outcomes, and effects than contained in the minutes' (Fuchs, 2001, p. 236). Therefore, when attempting to standardise or frame service production through information technology, overflows on the proximal, face-to-face service production process are generated and have to be identified by Kripos.

We can formulate our criteria in terms of the following five research hypotheses:

Hypothesis 1. *More face-to-face contact information found on a red button page will increase the number of messages about suspected online grooming activities received by the police.*

Hypothesis 2. *More stepwise approach distinguishing between simple and complex responses on red button pages will increase the number of messages about suspected online grooming activities received by the police.*

Hypothesis 3. *More virtual role perception for individuals sending red button messages will increase the number of messages about suspected online grooming activities received by the police.*

Hypothesis 4. *More physical role perception for police officers receiving red button messages will increase the number of messages about suspected online grooming activities received by the police.*

Hypothesis 5. *More overflows on the proximal, face-to-face service production process (generated from attempting to standardise or frame service production through information technology) handled by the physical red button role of police officers will increase the number of messages about suspected online grooming activities received by the police.*

In this conceptual research, links were established between the use of the Internet in cyber policing and the use of red buttons by the public. The case of online groomers illustrates the seriousness and importance of efficient and effective communication with both cyber police and face-to-face police. In the early days of the information technology era, there was a widespread euphoria about the prospects of information technology, in general, and the Internet, in particular, for virtualisation of various service activities. However, researchers are increasingly debating such euphoria, excitement and prediction for the future. Recent advances in computer technology have been aiding sexual sex offenders, stalkers, child pornographers, child traffickers, and others with the intent of exploiting children. In this section, cyber policing online groomers was discussed. Specifically, the red button case was presented to illustrate the need for both virtual and face-to-face policing. Future empirical research needs to test hypotheses developed in this section.

Sex offender progression

Contrary to the populist view, Wolak *et al.* (2008) argue that most Internet sex offenders are not adults who target young children by posing as another youth, luring the children to a meeting, and then abducting or forcibly raping them. Rather, most online offenders are adults who target teens and seduce victims into sexual relationships. This is supported in the Norwegian findings, where mainly 15 and 16-year-old girls have unpleasant experiences in terms of physical or psychological abuse at such meetings with adults (Justis, 2007).

While this chapter presents a stage model where it is assumed that many sex offenders move from one stage to the next over time, several researchers have developed typologies which implicitly seem to indicate an underlying stage hypothesis. An example is O'Connell (2004), who developed a typology of child cyber exploitation and online grooming practices. Her typology really represents stages: the friendship-forming stage, the relationship forming stage, the risk assessment stage, the exclusivity stage, and the sexual stage.

Only future research can validate the stage hypothesis presented in this chapter. Empirical studies are needed to evaluate developmental behaviour by offenders over time.

A stage model for offender behaviour in victimisation of children was presented in this section. By identifying development and escalation in individual abuse, social and law enforcement authorities may gain new insights into contingent approaches. Future empirical research is needed to validate and potentially revise the suggested model; Chapters 5 (Martellozzo) and 6 (Taylor) offer a different perspective on online offending behaviour.

References

Alexander, M. (1997). 'Getting to Grips with the Virtual Organization', *Long Range Planning*, 30 (1), 122–24.

Balasubramanian, S., Raghunathan, R. and Mahajan, V. (2005). 'Consumers in a Multichannel Environment: Product Utility, Process Utility, and Channel Choice', *Journal of Interactive Marketing*, 19 (2), 12–30.

Benjamin, R. and Wigand, R. (1995). 'Electronic Markets and Virtual Value Chains on the Information Superhighway', *Sloan Management Review*, 36 (2), 62–72.

Berman, B. and Thelen, S. (2004). 'A Guide to Developing and Managing a Well-integrated Multi-channel Retail Strategy', *International Journal of Retail and Distribution Management*, 32 (3), 147–56.

Callon, M. (1998). *The Laws of the Markets*, Blackwell Publishers, Oxford.

Coelho, F. J. and Easingwood, C. (2004). 'Multiple Channel Systems in Services: Pros, Cons and Issues', *The Services Industries Journal*, 24 (5), 1–29.

Brå (2007). Vuxnas Sexualla Kontakter med Barn via Internet (Adults' Sexual Contacts with Children via Internet), Brottsförebyggande rådet (Crime prevention council), Stockholm, Sweden, www.bra.se.

Croy, J. (2006). From Operation Hamlet to Operation Video Child, Droit Fundamental, http://droitfondamental.eu.

Davidson, J. (2007). Current Practice and Research into Internet Sex Offending, Risk Management Authority Research, Department of Social & Political Studies, University of Westminster, UK.

Davidson, J. (2008). *Child Sexual Abuse – Media representations and government reactions*, Routledge, Abingdon, UK.

Dean, G. and Gottschalk, P. (2007). *Knowledge Management in Policing and Law Enforcement – Foundations, Structures, Applications*, Oxford University Press, Oxford, UK.

Døvik, O. (2008). Rød Knapp skal Stanse Overgripere (Red button shall stop offenders), NRK (Norwegian Broadcasting Corporation), www.nrk.no, published 11.08.2008.

Earl, M.J. (2000). 'Evolving the E-business', *Business Strategy Review*, 11 (2), 33–38.

Elliott, I.A. and Beech, A.R. (2009). 'Understanding Online Child Pornography use: Applying Sexual Offense Theory to Internet Offenders', *Aggression and Violent Behaviour*, 14 (3), 180–93.

Eurobarometer (2007). Eurobarometer on Safer Internet for Children: qualitative study 2007, ec.europa.eu/information_society/activities/sip/eurobarometer/.

European Commission (2008). *Safer Internet plus: A Multi-annual Community Programme on Promoting Safer use of the Internet and New Online Technologies*, Information Society and Media Directorate-General, European Commission, http://ec.europa.eu/saferInternet.

Ferraro, M.M. and Casey, E. (2005). *Investigating Child Exploitation and Pornography: The Internet, the Law and Forensic Science*, Elsevier Academic Press, New York.

Finkelhor, D. (1984). *Child Sexual Abuse: New Theories and Research*, New York: The Free Press.

Frambach, R.T., Roest, H.C.A. and Krishnan, T.V. (2007). 'The Impact of Consumer Internet Experience on Channel Preference and Usage Intentions acros The Different Stages Of The Buying Process', *Journal of Interactive Marketing*, 21 (2), 26–41.

Frankfort-Nachmias, C. and Nachmias, D. (2002). *Research Methods in the Social Sciences*, 5th edn, Arnold, UK.

Fuchs, S. (2001). *Against Essentialism: A Theory of Culture and Society*, Harvard University Press, Cambridge, MA.

Gillespie, A.A. (2005). 'Indecent Images of Children: The Ever-Changing Law', *Child Abuse Review*, 14, 430–43.

Goffman, E. (1971). *Frame Analysis: An Essay on the Organization of Experience*, Northeastern University Press, Chicago.

Gottschalk, P. (2008). 'Maturity Levels for Criminal Organizations'. *International Journal of Law*, Crime and Justice, 36, 106–14.

Gottschalk, P. (2009). 'Maturity Levels for Interoperability in Digital Government', *Government Information Quarterly*, 26, 75–81.

Gottschalk, P. and Solli-Sæther, H. (2006). 'Maturity Model for IT Outsourcing Relationships, *Industrial Management & Data Systems*', 105 (6), 685–702.

Gottschalk, P. and Tolloczko, P. (2007). 'Maturity Model for Mapping Crime in Law Enforcement'. *Electronic Government, an International Journal*, 4 (1), 59–67.

Graham, S. (1998). 'The End of Geography or the Explosion of Place? Conceptualizing Space, Place and Information Technology', *Progress in Human Geography*, 22 (2), 165–85.

Grove, S.J., Fisk, R.P. and John, J. (2003). 'The Future of Services Marketing: Forecasts from Ten Services Experts', *Journal of Services Marketing*, 17 (2), 107–21.

Harridge-March, S., (2004). 'Electronic marketing, the new kid on the block', *Marketing Intelligence and Planning*, 22 (3), 297–309.

Hernandez (2009). Psychological and Behavioral Characteristics of Child Pornography Offenders in Treatment, Global Symposium for Examining the Relationship between Online and Offline Offenses and Preventing the Sexual Exploitation of Children, University of North Carolina, April 6–7.

Housel, T. and Bell, A.H. (2001). *Measuring and Managing Knowledge*, McGraw-Hill Irwin, New York.

IWF (2007). 2007 Annual and Charity Report, Internet Watch Foundation, Cambridge, UK, www.iwf.org.uk.

Justis (2007). På vei Imot et Tryggere Norge – noen Tall og Fakta (On the road to a safer Norway – some numbers and facts), Justis-og politidepartementet (Ministry of Justice and Police), Oslo, www.regjeringen.no.

Kazanjian, R.K. (1988). 'Relation of Dominant Problems to Stages of Growth in Technology-based New Ventures', *Academy of Management Journal*, 31 (2), 257–79.

Kazanjian, R.K. and Drazin, R. (1989). 'An Empirical Test of a Stage of Growth Progression Model', *Management Science*, 35 (12), 1489–503.

Kierkegaard, S. (2008). 'Cybering, Online Grooming and Ageplay', *Computer Law & Security Report*, 24, 41–55.

King, W.R. and Teo, T.S.H. (1997). 'Integration Between Business Planning and Information Systems Planning: Validating a Stage Hypothesis', *Decision Sciences*, 28 (2), 279–307.

Krone, T. (2004). A Typology of Online Child Pornography Offending, Trends and Issues in Crime and Criminal Justice, No. 279, Australian Institute of Criminology, Canberra, Australia.

Kumar, V. and Venkatesan, R. (2005). 'Who are the Multichannel Shoppers and how do they Perform? Correlates Of Multichannel Shopping Behavior', *Journal of Interactive Marketing*, 19 (2), 44–62.

Laing, A., Lewis, B. Foxall, G. and Hogg, G. (2002). 'Predicting a Diverse Future: Directions and Issues in the Marketing of Services', *European Journal of Marketing*, 36 (4), 479–94.

Lewis, I. and Talalayevsky, A. (1997). 'Travel Agents: Threatened Intermediaries?' *Transportation Journal*, 36 (3), 26–30.

Mitchell, K.J., Wolak, J. and Finkelhor, D. (2008). 'Are Blogs Putting Youth at Risk for Online Sexual Solicitation or Harassment?' *Child Abuse & Neglect*, 32, 277–94.

MMI (2007). Safer Internet for Children, Qualitative Study in 29 European Countries, National Analysis: Norway, Eurobarometer Qualitative Study, MMI Univero, Oslo, Norway.

Nolan, R.L. (1979). 'Managing the Crises in Data Processing', *Harvard Business Review*, March–April, 115–26.

NRK (2008). Etterlyser Pedofil Mann (Searching paedophile man), Norsk rikskringkasting (Norwegian Broadcasting Corporation),www.nrk.no.

O'Connell, R. (2003). Be Somebody Else but be Yourself at all Times: Degrees of Identity Deception in Chatrooms, Cyberspace Research Unit, University of Central Lancashire, http://www.once.uclan.ac.uk/print/deception_print.htm.

O'Connell, R. (2004). A Typology of Child Cybersexploitation and Online Grooming Practices, Cyberspace Research Unit, University of Central Lancashire, UK, www.fkbko.net.

Osterlund, D., Wikstrom, S. and Yakhlef, A. (2005). 'Channel Integration: An Organisational Perspective', *International Journal of Financial Services Management*, 1 (1), 26–40.

Pfarrer, M.D., DeCelles, K.A., Smith, K.G. and Taylor, M.S. (2008). 'After the Fall: Reintegrating the Corrupt Organization', *The Academy of Management Review*, 33 (3), 730–49.

Quayle, E., Vaughan, M. and Taylor, M. (2006). 'Sex offenders, Internet Child Abuse Images and Emotional Avoidance: The Importance of Values', *Aggression and Violent Behaviour*, 11, 1–11.

Rangaswamy, A. and Van Bruggen, G.H. (2005). 'Opportunities and Challenges in Multichannel Marketing: An Introduction to the Special Issue', *Journal of Interactive Marketing*, 19 (2), 5–11.

Rao, S.S. and Metts, G. (2003). 'Electronic Commerce Development in Small and Medium Sized Enterprises: A Stage Model and its Implications', *Business Process Management*, 9 (1), 11–32.

RMA (2007). Current Practice and Research into Internet Sex offending, Risk Management Authority Briefing, St. James House, St. James Street, Paisley, Scotland, UK, www.rmascotland.gov.uk.

Ronell, A. (1989). *The Telephone Book: Technology, Schizophrenia, Electric Speech*, University of Nebraska Press, Lincoln.

Seto, M. (2009). Assessing the Risk Posed by Child Pornography Offenders, Global Symposium for Examining the Relationship between Online and Offline Offenses and Preventing the Sexual Exploitation of Children, University of North Carolina, April 6–7.

Seto, M.C. and Eke, A.W. (2005). 'The Criminal Histories and Later Offending of Child Pornography Offenders', *Sexual Abuse: A Journal of Research and Treatment*, 17 (2), 201–10.

Shields, R. (2003). *The Virtual*, Routledge, New York.

Skybak, T. (2004). Ofre for Seksuelle Overgrep på Internet: Hva GjøRes for å Identifisere Barn? (Victims of Sexual Assaults on the Internet: What is Done to Identify Children?) Redd Barna (Save the Children Norway), www.reddbarna.no.

Smith, A.D. (2008). Business and E-government Intelligence for Strategically Leveraging Information Retrieval, *Electronic Government, an International Journal*, 5 (1), 31–44.

Taylor, M. and Quayle, E. (2003). *Child Pornography: An Internet Crime*, Brunner-Routledge, Taylor & Francis Group, New York.

Värlander, S. (2007). Framing and Overflowing: How the Infusion of Information Technology Alters Proximal Service Production, Dissertation, Stockholm University School of Business.

Ward, T. and Siegert, R.J. (2006). Ward and Siegert's Pathways Model, in: T. Ward, D., Polaschek, B. and Beech, A. (editors), *Theories of Sexual Offending*, Chichester, UK.

Weber, R. (2004). The Grim Reaper: The Curse of E-mail, Editor's Comments, *MIS Quarterly*, iii–xiii.

Wolak, J., Finkelhor, D., Mitchell, K.J. and Ybarra, M.L. (2008). 'Online "Sex offenders" and Their Victims – Myths, Realities, and Implications for Prevention and Treatment', *American Psychologist*, 63 (2), 111–28.

Wortley, R. and Smallbone, S. (2006). *Child Pornography on the Internet*, US Department of Justice, Office of community Orientated Policing Services, Washington D.C.

Yakhlef, A. (2005). Virtual Organisation as Spatial and Temporal Innovations, Forthcoming in *Space and Culture*.

Chapter 5

Understanding the perpetrators' online behaviour

Elena Martellozzo

Introduction

Understanding sex offending against children is a difficult task, mainly because of 'the secrecy which typically surrounds the commission of these offences' (Smallbone and Wortley, 2001:1). The majority of research data on child sexual offending derives from studies of convicted offenders undergoing treatment. However, this chapter explores perpetrators' modus operandi by focusing on data collected during covert police investigations, where suspects' behaviour and offences are recorded and observed live. It portrays a virtual world in which sex offenders can anonymously and simultaneously target large numbers of victims within a very short period of time. Whilst there is no such thing as a typical online child groomer, it is nevertheless both possible and instructive to identify a range of distinctive child grooming behaviours. The chapter explores a spectrum of grooming behaviours from online fantasists who groom for immediate sexual gratification in the virtual world, to persistent predators who groom online to lay the foundations for child sexual abuse (CSA) in the physical world.

Background and context

Online child sexual abuse comprises not only the production and the distribution of indecent images of children, but also that of 'online grooming'. As argued by Davidson in Chapter 1, online grooming involves the process of socialisation during which an offender interacts with a child in order to prepare him/her for sexual abuse (Sexual Offences Act 2003). This emergent online offence, facilitated by the anonymous nature of cyberspace and its vague boundaries, has grown exponentially during the past four years, and the government, the police and other agencies such as the Internet Watch Foundation (IWF) and the Child Exploitation and Online Protection Centre (CEOP) have been training and developing new tactics and awareness programmes to protect children from sexual abuse, as discussed by Carr and Hilton in Chapter 3.

Like the production of child abuse images, the process of grooming is not a new phenomenon. It dates back to when child sexual abuse was first identified and defined (Conte, Wolf, *et al.* 1989), and it may take place offline as much as it does online (Gillespie 2004). However, there has been little systematic research on the process whereby adults identify, recruit and maintain the compliance of child victims (Conte, Wolf, *et al.* 1989).

Studies have generally focused on the victims' or offenders' characteristics and the type and frequency of deviant sexual acts (Groth, Longo, *et al.* 1982; Abel, Becker, *et al.* 1987; Stermac, Hall, *et al.* 1989), despite the significance of offenders engaging in repetitive patterns of behaviour (Groth 1978), carefully planning their offences (Herman 1981; Laws 1989; Salter 1995), and repeating these patterns with multiple victims (Abel, Becker, *et al.* 1987). Interestingly, children who are victimised in the realm of the cyber show characteristics similar to those abused in the real world. The IWF found that 80 per cent of the child victims in all the Uniform Resource Locators (URL) since 2003 are female. Ninety-one per cent of all these children appear to be 12 years of age or under (Internet Watch Foundation, 2006:9) and are lonely, trusting, and vulnerable (Wolak, Mitchell, *et al.* 2003).

It is imperative to highlight that the main difference between the real world and cyberspace is anonymity. Although it can be exciting and fun for children to go online and form new friendships, what should not be underestimated is that the Internet allows people to be whoever they want to be, at any time and in any place (Davidson and Martellozzo, 2007). In a small number of cases young people thought that they had met someone special who they could implicitly trust, but in reality they had been talking to an adult who had a sexual interest (O'Connell, Price, *et al.* 2004).

These adults target children and young people with the intention of making the child feel loved and comfortable enough to eventually meet so they can take advantage of them. The Home Office Task Force (2007), together with practitioners and consultants, put together a list of techniques that they believed sex offenders could use to make contact and establish relationships with children or young people. These are:

- gathering personal details, such as name, address, mobile number, name of school and photographs
- offering opportunities for modelling, particularly to young girls
- promising meetings with pop idols or celebrities, or offers of merchandise
- offering cheap tickets to sporting or music events
- offering material gifts including electronic games, music or software
- offering virtual gifts, such as rewords, passwords and gaming cheats
- suggesting quick and easy ways to make money
- paying young people to appear naked and perform sexual acts via web cams.

- gaining a child's confidence by offering positive attention and encouraging him or her to share any difficulties or problems they may have at home, and providing a sympathetic and supportive response
- bullying or intimidating behaviour, such as threatening to expose the child by contacting their parent to inform them of their child's communications or postings on a social networking site, and/or saying they know where the child lives or goes to school
- using webcams to spy and take photographs and movies of victims
- asking sexually themed questions, such as 'Do you have a boyfriend?' or 'Are you a virgin?'
- asking children or young people to meet offline
- sending sexually themed images to a child, depicting adult content or the abuse of other children
- masquerading as a minor or assuming a false identity to deceive a child
- using schools or hobby sites to gather information about a child's interests, likes and dislikes.
   (Home Office Task Force on Child Protection on the Internet, 2007:15)

In her doctoral research, the author (Martellozzo, forthcoming) came across hundreds of cases where individuals engaging with children adopted a number of different approaches to those highlighted by the Home Office Task Force on Child Protection on the Internet. A more comprehensive overview of these particular online behaviours is provided in the following sections of this chapter.

Methodology

This chapter is a product of doctorate research conducted with the Metropolitan. Police Officers working at the High Technological Crime Unit and the Paedophile Unit – the foremost online Internet abuse policing units in Europe. The analysis of the data obtained throughout this ethnography focuses primarily on 22 interviews with key police officers across the whole rank and on the analysis of 23 cases from a Metropolitan Police operation.

Offenders creating a profile

Social Networking Groups such as Hi5, MySpace and Bebo have become the favourite playground for Internet sex offenders. When sex offenders set up their profiles, they do so through the requirements of standardised electronic membership forms (name, sex and age) of social networking and similar websites and the verification processes of service providers. The data they insert is checked electronically through a website and not physically by someone. Therefore, offenders can make any desired claim about their identity, including the use of any profile picture. These profiles are designed to attract either children or like-minded people. Therefore, the visual (in terms of pictures, list of friends, links to favourite sports, pop singers, and so forth) is essential, as it draws children's interest and may help them decide whether to add the new 'virtual friend' to their contact. However, it is very dangerous to accept a new friend on the basis of an online profile. Often very little information is posted publicly. Offenders who are very reserved and cautious about their personal details may be more dangerous than perpetrators who openly post their photographs or other types of images, listings of hobbies, interests in children, their location, their age, or their sex.

Indeed, whilst there is no such a thing as a typical online groomer using a typical profile, it is possible to identify a distinctive grooming behaviour. Here, the grooming behaviour is understood – as feminists have sought to understand male violence (Kelly, 1988) – as existing across a spectrum of confidence. The author has purposively avoided using a positivistic approach underpinned by the often pseudo-scientific classification of people or objects into discrete typologies with rigid boundaries. Positivistic typologies would not have worked in this context; they would have placed online sex offenders' profiles into boxes, categorised them and reinforced a stereotypical notion overlooking the nuance and fluidity of human characteristics and behaviours.

Sex offenders who target young children form a diverse group that cannot be 'accurately characterised with one-dimensional labels' (Wolak, Finkelhor, et al. 2009:1). It can be noted that, at one end of the spectrum of openness, some groomers are 'hyper-confident' and will declare their sexual intentions to children from the outset. The hyper-confident individual is usually open about his identity; in his profile he posts a picture and details of himself.[1] It was found, however, that most of the online groomers lied about their age.

Hyper-confident groomers

Hyper-confident groomers may create a decent or indecent profile. They would create a decent profile by, for example, posting a photo of themselves, to make the child feel comfortable but at the same time curious about the person depicted in the profile. Friendships normally develop after the profile is added to the child's list of friends.

Hyper-confident indecent groomers would choose their profile to be indecent, by, for example posting a picture of themselves naked, probably hoping that the child would be curious and inquisitive about the profile and accept a virtual friendship. Furthermore, the profile may explicitly state the sexual interest of the person. For example, a groomer in one of the profiles examined in previous research explicitly wrote: 'I am a nice, decent, very loving caring guy with a pervy side – daddy/daughter, incest etc.' Some had listed their interests under categories such as 'incest', 'cherry popping Daddies' and 'dreamer of teens'. One suspect's profile contained a picture of a young female performing oral sex on him and a link to a 'paedo paradise' website. In these cases the subjects are ignoring any element of risk, drawing attention to themselves by making their interest in children extremely explicit. As this police officer highlights:

> These types of offenders are also the most familiar with the Internet. From their behaviour it is clear they have experience in chatting with a lot of people. Newer ones to the 'game' are more cautious and may explore the risk further.
>
> (Police Officer: ID 3)

At the other end of the spectrum, hyper-cautious groomers will not post any abusive images or declare any sexual interest in children until interaction takes place. Hyper-cautious groomers post cartoons or toys as their pictures and spend time establishing that individuals are genuine. They do so because they are concerned that someone in society may report their inappropriate behaviour or that they are wasting time with perverts that fantasise about being young girls. In this way they play a passive role in the sense that they require the child to make the majority of approaches. For example, if they were speaking to an adult they would ask for indecent images of children believing that law enforcement agencies would not post them based 'on legal and moral ground' (Gallagher, 2007:112). It resulted, however, that when they communicate with someone they believe to be a young girl, they would not ask for indecent images of children.

The hyper-cautious groomer

The hyper-cautious groomer is the one 'who could possibly be the most dangerous; they are not easy to identify and lie from start to finish' (Police Officer: ID 2). Hyper-cautious groomers are so concerned about being caught that they are not willing to furnish details about themselves until completely sure. This type of offender may insist on viewing the potential victim on web cam, hearing her voice over the phone and receiving more photographs. Eventually, when they feel they are chatting to someone real, they start grooming the child. However, this is not always the case. If they do not feel comfortable in establishing a closer relationship, because of a lack of credentials, they may decide to move on to the next victim. This contention was supported by the majority of the police officers working in the field:

> Hyper-cautious online groomers are the ones that we don't know how dangerous they are, we don't know if they're sex offenders, we don't know anything about them because we don't have the tactics or technology to go up against them. We're not able to prove at a very early stage that we are an authentic child and they switch off and go elsewhere and quite possibly go elsewhere to real children.
>
> (Police Officer: ID 20)

This spectrum should be interpreted as fluid, as a wide range of grooming behaviours exists at every stage in between. That said, despite the fluidity of grooming behaviours, it is possible to discern certain characteristics that are common to all groomers, regardless of levels of confidence. The key common characteristic across the spectrum is suspiciousness.

Understanding online offenders

By using the Internet individuals have the opportunity to explore the dark side of their sexuality by pretending to be whoever they feel like being, and by disclosing as much or as little about themselves as they wish to others (Cooper, McLaughlin, *et al.* 2000). A man can be younger or older, a woman, a child, or a cartoon character. Moreover, by hiding behind their fictitious profile, they explore any opportunity cyberspace may offer, including that of sexually abused children.

During one of the first Metropolitan Police undercover operations, more than 1,300 individuals visited the fictitious girl's profile. Of these, more than 450 individuals with adult male profiles initiated contact with the child, and 80 became virtual friends and prolonged their relationship. Experience with covert Internet investigators suggests that the vast majority of male adults contacting the girl's profiles would do so for sexual purposes. Some are simply interested in having sexual conversations. Young (2001: 300) defines these individuals as 'fantasy users', and distinguishes those who utilise online chat room and instant messaging for the express purpose of role-playing in online fantasy sex chat. However, many suspects go beyond the fantasy stage; they distribute indecent images, expose themselves and travel to meet a child to sexually abuse.

Research and experience have repeatedly shown that sex offenders cannot be easily 'picked out' of a crowd (Stanko, 1990; Grubin, 1998). There is no consistent model or typology into which they can be accurately placed for the purpose of identification and isolation – and public denunciation. In other words, 'it is not possible to describe the "typical" child molester' (Grubin, 1998:14). This contention can also be applied to online forms of child sexual abuse. As this police officer claims:

> I couldn't describe to you necessarily a person who I would say he is, or she is a typical groomer but I can describe to you, in my experience, what typical grooming is. The gain and the trust being the big friend and doing things for that child beyond the cause of duty. So, there's certainly a typical grooming mythology but I certainly couldn't sit here and if there's 100 people there point to one and say he's a groomer, unless I've interacted with that person on line.
>
> (Police Officer: ID 17)

Online police investigations have shown that online groomers come from diverse backgrounds and are a heterogeneous group.

Case study: an offender operationalising a profile

This case study involves a hyper-cautious suspect and shows how an offender operationalises a profile. The profile provided by this suspect lacks information regarding the individual's interests, work, and location. It simply shows the suspect's ID name, his age (which rarely reflects reality [see Martellozzo 2007]), his marital status, and his hobbies: 'smd looking to chat with attractive female of any race etc'. However, the person behind this plain 'cyber-profile' was a specialist crime detective. The individual introduced himself to undercover police officers pretending to be a girl. During their interaction, the suspected offender sent a number of sexual movie files in the form of emoticons.[2] The CII maintained a periodic, passive online relationship with the suspect over a period of a few months. This was with a view to identifying the suspect and obtaining evidence of his online activities. During the course of the online relationship, the suspect managed to obtain the girl's mobile number and sent a number of text messages declaring his love for her:

> He became obsessed with the girl calling her 'babe' and telling her she was beautiful and repeatedly insisting he loved her.
>
> (Police Officer: ID 21)

When he was arrested, his home address was searched and his computers forensically examined. A total of 510 indecent images of children were recovered. The images ranged across all five COPINE (Combating Online Paedophile Information Networks in Europ) levels. He was charged with 10 counts of attempting to cause a child to look at an image of a person engaging in sexual activities and one count of attempting to cause or incite a child to engaging in a sexual activity (both offences are contrary to Section 1 Criminal Attempts Act 1981).

He pleaded guilty to one count of attempting to persuade an underage child to engage in sexual activity and to ten counts of trying to incite a child to view indecent material. He also admitted five charges of making indecent images of children and one of possessing 168 similar pictures. Judge Christopher Hardy told the defendant:

> In passing a custodial sentence upon you. I do so not only to punish you – although you have already been visited by the shame of this incident and the loss of your career – but perhaps more importantly as a deterrent to others from accessing and using this sort of material.
>
> (Taylor, 09/03/07)

He received an 18 month custodial sentence.

This case is one of the many cases to highlight that the danger for children and young people is present in cyberspace and that it is not feasible to solely rely on the police or new jurisdictions for protection. Education and media literacy form a critical part of keeping children safe online. As Carr *et al.* and Davidson suggest in this book, technology should be combined with education and awareness amongst children, parents and teachers, and effective inter-agency partnership, all working together. This strategy would help maximise the few available resources and move one step closer to making cyberspace a safer place for young and vulnerable Internet users.

Offender research: justifying the offence

Sex offenders tend to share similar distorted assumptions about their victims, the nature of the offences committed, and their responsibility for their offending behaviour. Furthermore, they are often not cognisant of their wrongdoing (Middelton, 2004), as they neutralise the consequences of their actions (Matza and Sykes, 1961). However, to enhance understanding of online offending, another key characteristic could be added to the list, that of Internet addiction (Young, 2008).

Based on the analysis of forensic interviews ($N = 22$) with virtual sex offenders, Young's (2008) research on Internet addiction found that all her clients met the basic criteria of Internet addiction. She claims that, 'similar to an alcoholic who consumes greater level of alcohol in order to achieve satisfaction, clients routinely spent significant amounts of time online' (Young 2008:301). She used a model which follows five stages of developing Internet addiction: discovery, exploration, escalation, compulsion, and hopelessness or regret (Young 2008:301). Unlike classic sex offenders who go through cycles of abusive behaviour by their distorted thinking (denial, blaming, omitting and believing the child enjoys and wants to be sexually active) (Salter, 1995; see also Chapter 3 this volume), Young's offenders were first time offenders, with no previous history of sexual activity towards children (however the research was based on a small sample and the results may not be typical). This characteristic was found in the great majority of offenders explored in this research. Furthermore, the offences committed by Young's sample were not entirely confined to the realm of cyberspace. That is to say, offenders went beyond the fantasy and discovery stages and committed some serious offences in the real world. They detached themselves from the Internet and travelled with the intention to sexually abuse a child.

It was found that the models proposed by Young and other scholars (Salter, 1995; Salter, McMillan, *et al.* 2003; Sullivan and Beech, 2004; 2008) contain key emergent themes also present in the case studies examined in this research. Some of these have been selected and used as guidelines to inform the analysis of the 12 in-depth interviews conducted by police officers from the Metropolitan Police paedophile unit. Thus, the key themes identified for this analysis are:

1) Discovery
2) Denial
3) Distorted attitudes towards children online
4) Conflict in adult relationships
5) Conflict with cyberspace and reality

Each theme was explored separately with reference to grooming children online for the purpose of sexually abusing them, and to producing and distributing indecent images of children. Sex offenders' accounts sought to directly address these key themes and focused upon online offending behaviour.

Exploring discovery

As in Young's study, police interview transcripts indicate that sex offenders satisfied their fantasy by engaging in erotic dialogues. This took place first on social networking sites, and then moved to MSN online chat, where conversations were believed to be more private, anonymous, and safe. As Young (2008:303) claimed: 'the fantasy theme began and progressed as a novelty created through cyberspace chat rooms and their anonymous availability'. As discussed previously, the undercover profile initially attracted more than 450 adult males. Of these, 80 had a prolonged and persistent contact on MSN. After the first few interactions, 23 suspects went beyond the discovery and exploration stages. Their fantasy escalated to the point of continuing through the whole cycle of abuse (Sullivan and Beech, 2004) and eventually to committing offences contrary to the Sexual Offences Act 2003. The great majority of sex offenders recognised their dependence on the Internet and on their online relationships. As this convicted offender explains:

> [...] you just get sucked into it, its fantasy, role play, inquisitiveness called it whatever its just, I don't know, I honestly don't know how it ever got to this, I really don't.
>
> (Sex Offender: ID 1)

Some sex offenders discussed the process of how their behaviour escalated from discovery or boredom to the point of becoming entangled in the web of the Internet. They felt that the Internet could continuously feed their curiosity and alleviate their boredom without risks:

> Yeah, it was curiosity in the same way that probably a 14, 15 years old boy want to look at a copy of playboy. Curiosity growing up. It progressed from that curiosity later in life to being this new thing called the

Internet and there seems to be unregulated. There is that newsgroup there, lets have a look and see what all the fuss is all about.

(Sex Offender: ID 2)

I was bored, browsing the Internet, I went into Yahoo there's various groups that I joined on there and when you see people on there I just started chatting using instant messaging system.

(Sex Offender: ID 3)

Other sex offenders saw the discovery process as an experiment:

It was experiments, it was just that I saw them and just clicked and read and joined the group [...] they were called 'younger girls for older men'.

(Sex Offender: ID 4)

Even when a more direct and provocative approach was taken by the officers and supported by recorded evidence of offenders' behaviour, the respondents would continue to maintain justificatory strategies built around notions of boredom and fantasy. One sex offender (ID 3) suggested to the undercover officer posing online as a young girl that she should open a bank account so he could transfer money to her. During his online interaction he told the undercover officer that he had bought her a number of presents worth £170: an ipod nano, a web cam, a Motorola mobile phone. This behaviour was probed by the officers after his arrest:

Q 'A man with no intentions would not have sent presents down to her like a web cam.'
SO: ID 3 'I was never gonna go down there.'
Q 'Would never say "Cannot wait to have sex with you 15, 20 times" '.
SO: ID 3 'There was never going to be any sexual act it was just stupidity.'

From this stage, 'their habitual behaviour becomes more ingrained and develops into a compulsive obsession' (Young, 2008:304). It emerged that sex offenders' lives seem to be dependent on their interaction with their virtual targets or virtual like-minded friends. In other words, as also found in Young's research, the Internet does not represent a tool any longer, but a form of psychological escape. As this sex offender explains:

The reason why I started was because my wife had a major drinking problem ... it's a big mistake, she got violent when she got drunk; it's because of the non-sexual nature of our relationship is why I went onto the Internet. I used to talk with anybody and everybody.

(Sex Offender: ID 4)

The concrete manifestations of such forms of psychological escape varied considerably among respondents. Some offenders blamed other people or the Internet, one blamed his alcohol addiction, and others justified their behaviour as fantasy. This shows that sex offenders do not form a homogeneous group of individuals and tend to be affected differently by situational/external factors (McGuire, 2000; Quayle, Erooga, *et al.* 2006). Whilst there is a large number of a situational/external factors that may trigger their online abuse, their common denominator is sexual attraction to children.

Exploring denial

Gudjonsson (1988) claims that offenders tend to blame society, the circumstances of the offence, and the victim for their offending behaviour. This contention was reinforced by Davidson (2002) during her study on the context and practice of community treatment programmes for convicted sex offenders in England and Wales.

Confronted by the recorded evidence, the respondents of the present study admitted their offence, but appeared to be inclined to blame external circumstances. One of the fundamental questions that the author focused upon in analysing the interview transcripts was: How far did offenders deny responsibility for their offending at the moment of arrest despite offenders being faced by recorded evidence? Denial here is linked to the intention to meet a child for sexual purposes after having groomed him or her online. Levenson and Macgowan (2004) claim that, whilst denial of offending behaviour, to the offender himself and to others, is a prominent theme in all types of offending, it is a particular pertinent feature in sex offending. Furthermore, denial is common to virtually every convicted child abuser. As rehearsed previously in the literature, denial is often used as a means to avoid punishment or as a coping strategy (Abel, Becker, *et al.* 1987).

The majority of offenders, primarily those who did not travel to meet potential victims, denied their grooming offence and their involvement with the online offences, claiming that their online behaviour was pure fantasy. The majority of the offenders used the excuse that they did not believe they were interacting with a child. Some believed that the child was an adult male or female fantasising. As these sex offenders claim:

> I believed it was another bloke role playing sexual fantasy of some sort, and in moments of boredom I would go along with it, however as regards to inciting a child, one to look at pornographic images, and two to indulge in some sort of sexual act contrary to sexual offences act, I never genuinely believed that person was a child and certainly had no intent of any sort as regards to committing any of these offences.
>
> (Sex Offender: ID 6)

I didn't actually believe she was 12. It was just a wind up, it was just a laugh, there was not actual intention there. It was just a case of its something to kill the boredom.

(Sex Offender: ID 3)

Interestingly one sex offender claimed he thought he was interacting with a police officer:

so I believe her to be probably about 21 and probably someone in the police force connected to.
Q Can I just ask have you always thought she was 21 year old police officer?
so At first you have a bit of doubt but as soon as they talk back you understand, you think there is something funny, she was talking to adult I think being a father of a 13 year old boy and how he talks. I hope this is helping you (laughs) she didn't seem to be talking the way that he would talk and a 10 year old I know the way they talk. It is father instincts, so I just played with her.

(Sex Offender: ID 7)

There are various aspects of denial, some of which can be applied to the realm of the cyber. As argued by Mezey (1981, cited in Prins 1995) the first ones are denial of the child as a victim and as a person. In relation to the grooming process, the majority of sex offenders claimed they did not believe they were talking to a child, even when some travelled to meet the child. Indeed, the great majority arrested at the meeting point claimed that they would never commit contact abuse of a child even when they were found to be in possession of lubricants, toys, condoms, Viagra, and so forth. As this sex offender claims:

[...] its all fantasy and role play really. You have heard all this before obviously but I mean I've never asked, I had no intention of meeting anybody so its all over the computer, that's what started off titillation has gone too far.

(Sex Offender: ID 7).

There is little concrete evidence to suggest that any of the subjects were contact abusers, although the intention was certainly there for those who came to meet the undercover officer posing as a young girl as they were equipped with toys, condoms and pornography. One of the subjects was believed to possibly have been committing or planning to commit contact abuse. He was involved in grooming a friend's 13-year-old sister, persuading her to view pornography. The police were particularly concerned as this male had 165 friends listed in his account, 95 per cent of them being young girls. The subject had also been cohabiting with his 16-year-old girlfriend, showing a sexual preference for young girls.

Of the 23 suspects, nine turned up to meet the undercover officer posing as a young girl, a further five had arranged to meet 'her' but had not turned up or had cancelled at the last minute. It would be interesting to establish what made some of the subjects turn up to meet the 'girl' and others cancel, but unfortunately it was not possible for the author to interview offenders and probe these issues. If any factors or warning signs could be explored and identified through further research, they could help assess the risk a certain subject poses and help prioritise the running order of covert operations. Fear of apprehension alone may have prevented some subjects from turning up to a pre-arranged meeting. Some of the subjects were guarded and suspicious and well aware of the penalties. During a conversation with the undercover officer one stated:

> Do you realise if the police even knew I'm talking to you about sex I'd get 3 years in jail.
>
> (Sex Offender: ID 6)

This same suspect had been looking up grooming legislation on his home computer, assessing what he could be prosecuted for. He failed to appear at the arranged police meeting. As has been argued in the previous chapters, online behaviour and the risk that a suspect may pose to a child can only be understood and analysed through individual online interaction and on a case by case basis. It is dangerous to assume, for example, that 'high risk' indecent image collectors are not contact abusers.

Denial and indecent images

In relation to indecent images of children, all offenders arrested during this research were found to be in possession of child abuse images. At the time of the interview, the great majority of the offenders recognised the illegality of the images but failed to understand the damage caused to the child by downloading, viewing and distributing them. For example, one Sex Offender (ID 8) explained:

> I never saw them (indecent images) in the way you are describing them to me. To me it was just a file [...] it was an individual having sex on camera to me. I separated myself away from that.
>
> (Sex Offender: ID 8)

> I didn't go hunting for anything in particular. I wasn't like that's the real turn to me. I will go for the title, that you know it has to be that type of girl or that age or anything, I never saw it like that I never saw the twist thing. To me it was something to add to the collection.
>
> (Sex Offender: ID 8)

The analysis of this suspect's computer revealed a large amount of indecent images and a developed and select network with other individuals with similar inclinations. For this sex offender, collecting and distributing images was simply a passion, similar to collecting and trading old stamps for new ones. To his eyes, the children depicted in the images found in his computer were not vulnerable victims but tradable objects. This finding supports Finkelhor's (1986) suggestion that abusers are able to justify their actions by objectifying children.

Moreover, from this particular offender's account, it is possible to claim that there is no necessary link between the viewer and the child. As also argued by Quayle *et al.* (2006:45), if the viewer is not the producer, the offender tends to distance himself, in place and time, from the person photographed. Unlike the person making the images, the viewer does not actively become involved in the act of the actual abuse.

Furthermore, Quayle argues, 'viewing abuse images can be associated with sexual behaviour of the viewer, notably masturbation' (Quayle, Erooga, *et al.*, 2006:45). Interestingly, what emerged from observing the interactions between police officers and sex offenders was that indecent images of children were not only used to become closer to and to sexually desensitise children (Durkin and Bryant, 1977), but also to feed fantasies and for masturbatory purposes. This was noticeable when offenders used a web cam to expose themselves to show their masturbatory acts to the child or when there were long pauses during online interaction to masturbate. It can be argued that, viewing indecent images is not a passive act, as it involves sexual behaviour (for example masturbation or exposure or both). However, this was not perceived as damaging by the sex offenders who were arrested and interviewed.

SO: ID 7   '[...]Yes I do receive some porn and I receive some porn and I know it is bad things its really bad. But I would never meet, honestly I never would.'

Q   'But you would send it to someone who you believe to be a young girl thinking they might want to know.'

SO: ID 7   'Possibly yes, possibly.'

Q   'Concentrating on the moment at the sending of the image to and correct me if I am wrong who you've now said you believe would be a young girl and that's the sort of thing she would like to learn from, had I said it right?'

SO: ID 7   'Possibly.'

(Sex Offender: ID 7)

Moreover, what they do not appear to consider is the harm they cause by downloading and distributing the images of these children over and over again.

I'd love to be able to convince you that I am not a danger, its just something (downloading and distributing) really, really stupid that I've being doing for a couple of years, I've got no intention of harming children.

(Sex Offender: ID 9)

During the interviews, many of the offenders arrested for production and distribution of indecent images, when asked whether they have ever physically abused a child or if they are attracted to children, expressed a high level of indignation:

None whatsoever no. I would die for the child [his granddaughter who lived with him at the time] I would never do anything that is even remotely sexual or even think it.

(Sex Offender: ID 8)

I am sure everybody says this, I don't consider myself being a paedophile. I do not look for instance at my girlfriend's daughter and think anything of a sexual nature.

(Sex Offender: ID 2)

Viewers rarely consider the suffering or torment of the children depicted in their images and the repercussion that the abuse and its permanent record on photographs, film, or videotape may have in their lives (Martellozzo and Taylor, 2009). Many seem to think that their own actions in 'merely' viewing the images are much less serious than those who are abusing the children in the videos and still images.

Exploring distorted attitudes towards children

As argued by Hudson and Ward (1997), cognitive distortions play an important role in the explanation of CSA. These distortions overcome internal inhibitions to offend. This leads to offending behaviour usually being persistent, premeditated and accompanied by firmly entrenched cognitive distortions concerning the legitimacy and beneficial nature of child–adult sexual contact. Abel *et al.* (1984) identified different distortions common to the offenders, some of which can be used to explain online behaviour. The first one is about physical resistance; a child who does not physically resist really wants sex. Due to the nature of the operation, it was not possible to establish physical resistance, as there was no physical contact between the victim and the offender. However, what can be analysed in this context is the online interaction between an undercover officer posing as a young girl and a potential sex offender. In this operation, the undercover police officer never refused indecent images, never reacted negatively to online exposure, and never refused meeting after the online interaction. This behaviour may be interpreted by the sex offender as a positive sign of acceptance, as there was no resistance. What would have been interesting to observe is the reaction of the potential offender if the child refused to continue the online relationship.

The second distortion (Abel, Becker, *et al.* 1984) is about having sex with a child with the aim to teach the child about sex. This, in a way, can be applied to cyberspace, in the sense that sex offenders would use pornography or indecent images of children to teach them about sexual intercourse and to normalise sexual intercourse either between adults or between a child and an adult:

> Maybe I did think she is younger and she wants to learn these things [sexual acts from child abuse images].
>
> (Sex Offender: ID 9)

Another cognitive distortion that had been identified during the analysis of the online interaction is that, when an adult is asked about sex, it is interpreted as the child wanting to see the adult's sex organs or have sex with the adult. Because of entrapment issues, the undercover officer posing as a young girl could not ask for sex. However, when 'she' was asked whether 'she' wanted to know more about sex, her answer was usually positive. During a conversation with the undercover officer one of the sex offenders (ID 10) sent 'her' an image showing a male naked from the waist down and asked her:

SO   'Do you want it? U can say no, I won't b offended.'
OFFICER   'Suppose, yeah.'
SO   'Ok, getting naughty (slap my wrist), if u were here now, what would you do to it?'
OFFICER   'Dunno. U tell me.'
SO   'Like u 2 touch it, stroke it, ok with that?'

Interestingly, after a few minutes of this conversation, the suspect undressed and masturbated in front of the web cam. Another interesting element that emerged in almost all interviews was the sudden memory loss. According to Wyatt and Powell (1988), memory loss may be real and reflective of a traumatic recent event. In this case, being caught and arrested can be perceived as traumatic for some. This was present during the initial stage of the interview.

Q   'Do you remember on one occasion whilst web camming with her you actually got up, undressed yourself and then masturbated towards the webcam?'
SO ID: 10   'I don't remember doing that, I have done that before yes to people with adults but I honestly don't remember doing that.'

However, as the police officers intensified their probing and presented the suspects with recorded evidence, they seem to remember their acts more clearly. It can therefore be noticed that rather than memory loss or trauma, sex offenders are in denial from the moment of the arrest.

Exploring sex offenders' adult relationships

The literature suggests that sex offenders tend to be socially isolated individuals (Marshall 1996; Pithers 1999; Davidson 2002) incapable of maintaining successful adult relationships. This concept is based upon Finkelhor's (1986) assertion that abusers are more emotionally and sexually congruent with children than with adults. The literature suggests that sex offenders may be characterised as socially incompetent as a group, having difficulty in forming the most basic adult relationships (Groth, Longo, *et al.* 1982). Although, as explained previously, this issue was not addressed directly by the officers, some offenders volunteered information regarding the problems they had with their wives or partners. There was some evidence to support the concept of 'low self-esteem' which was explored during the in-depth interviews with practitioners. As argued by this police officer:

> I just think that our sort of the demographics of our clientele are normally 21 years old to 75 year old white men. Some are single, typically sad individuals who live at home have poor social circles, have the inability to form relationships with people, find it very difficult to have interpersonal relationships with members of the opposite sex. They use the Internet as their sort of way of connecting with people because they have a sexual interest in children they can meet like minded people and go onto forums and that's how they get their enjoyment out of life. Otherwise there's the person who is a professional. You will find vicars, teachers, policemen, magistrates who all have a respectable veneer but they all share a common secret which is this dirty little secret that they have and they will do anything to try and keep it hidden.
>
> (Police Officer: ID 5)

In the literature, low self-esteem has been identified as a characteristic of sex offenders. For example, Pithers (1999) states that 61 per cent of child sexual abusers in his research had low self-esteem. It is also suggested that offenders are weak, inadequate, unassertive, socially isolated individuals with intimacy deficits (Bell and Hall, 1976; Peters, 1976; Ames and Houston, 1990; Bumby and Hansen, 1997).

These characteristics have also been identified by the majority of police officers who regularly interview and debrief them after the arrest:

There is a reasonable cross section of people that gets nicked but it tends to be the saddo living with mummy and daddy because they're like 30 years of age, they've got a job going nowhere fast, or no job. They're a social misfit, they've got no social skills, they can't integrate, they can't form relationships. If I go back to the times I was in the paedophile unit, I say the majority of the people were either those types of people, who had nothing better to do all day long, or you had the professional people the teachers and Magistrates who were married but were probably unhappy.

(Police Officer: ID 7)

This is consistent with other research which has suggested that, for offenders, establishing online relationships provides important social support that often replaces unsatisfactory relationships in the offline world (Quayle, Erooga, *et al.* 2006).

Conclusion

On the basis of the evidence presented in this chapter, a number of proposals can be advanced about sex offenders' modus operandi: First, it is clear that the Internet is more than just a medium of communication. There is overwhelming evidence presented here to suggest that the Internet constitutes a complex virtual reality with its own roles and language. For example, to be able to interact successfully with their victims, sex offenders learn the appropriate computer language (Davidson and Martellozzo, 2004), and learn about children's educational development at school, music groups, and so forth. Furthermore, the Internet provides the supportive context within which the child abuser is no longer a lonely figure, but forms part of a larger community that shares the same interests (Davidson and Martellozzo, 2008).

Moreover, as it has been argued, the Internet provides offenders with the opportunity to hide their real identity, as in the case of the hyper-cautious offender. The majority of practitioners interviewed in this study acknowledged that it is not possible to identify a typical online groomer using a typical profile. Online behaviour and the risk that a suspect may pose to a child can only be understood and analysed through online interaction and not simply on the basis of the information provided in online profiles. However, all practitioners supported the notion that regardless of levels of confidence and despite the fluidity of grooming behaviours, it is possible to distinguish certain characteristics that are common to all groomers explored in this study.

In broad terms, it can be concluded that there is considerable behavioural diversity and psychological complexity among adult online sex offenders. Both in the real world and in cyberspace, offenders are willing to exploit children's trust and integrity 'for the abuser's own gratification, profit or selfish purpose' (Wurtele and Miller-Perrin, 1993:20).

Notes

1 It is important to note that all offenders in the sample were male.
2 Emoticons are text-based faces and objects that are often seen in emails and online chat. They help give the reader a sense of the writer's feelings behind the text. For example, the classic smiley or sad faces show that the writer is happy or unhappy about something. However, emoticons can also be moving images, either cartoon or real life. The emoticons sent by the suspect were real life images of adults kissing, a male ejaculating, and female masturbation.

References

Abel, G. G., Becker, J. et al. (1984). 'Complications, Consent and Cognitions in Sex Between Adults and Children.' International Journal of Law and Psychiatry 7: 89–103.

Abel, G., Becker, G. et al. (1987). 'Self-reported Sex Crimes of Non-incarcerated Paraphiliacs.' Journal of Interpersonal Violence 2: 3–25.

Ames, M. and Houston, D. A. (1990). 'Legal, Social, and Biological Definitions of Paedophilia.' Archives of Sexual Behaviour 19: 333–42.

Bell, A. P. and C. S. Hall (1976). The Personality of a Child Molester. Sex research: Studies from the Kinsey Institute. M. S. Weinberg. Oxford, Oxford University Press.

Bumby, M. K. and J. D. Hansen (1997). 'Intimacy Deficits, Fear of Intimacy, and Loneliness among Sexual Offenders.' Criminal Justice and Behaviour 24(3): 315–31.

CEOP (2006). 'Thinkyouknow', www.thinkyouknow.co.uk.

Conte, M., Wolf, S. et al. (1989). 'What Sexual Offenders Tell Us About Prevention Strategies.' Child Abuse and Neglect 13: 293–301.

Cooper, A., McLaughlin, I. P. et al. (2000). 'Sexuality in Cyberspace: Update for the 21st Century.' Cyber Psychology and Behaviour 3(4): 521–36.

Davidson, J. and Martellozzo, E. (2004). Educating Children about Sexual Abuse and Evaluating the Metropolitan Police Safer Surfing Programme. London, University of Westminster and Metropolitan Police.

Davidson, J. and Martellozzo, E. (2007). Child Security Online: A Shared Responsibility IPES. Urbanization & Security Dubai. 8–12 April. Unpublished Conference Paper.

Davidson, J. and Martellozzo, E. (2008). 'Protecting Vulnerable Young People in Cyberspace from Sexual Abuse: Raising Awareness and Responding Globally.' Police Investigations Police Practice & Research: An International Journal 9(4): 277–89.

Davidson, J. C. (2002). The Context and Practice of Community Treatment Programmes for Child Sexual Abusers in England and Wales. Department of Social Policy. London, London School of Economics and Political Science: 435.

Donmoyer, R. (2000). 'Generalizability and the Single-Case Study.' Case Study Method: Key Issues, Key Texts. R. Gomm, M. Hammersley and P. Foster. London, Sage.

Durkin, K. F. and Bryant, C. D. (1995) 'Log on to sex: some notes on the carnal computer and erotic cyberspace as an emerging research frontier' Deviant Behaviour: An Interdisciplinary Journal, 16: 179–200.

Finkelhor, D. (1986). Child Sexual Abuse; New Theory and Research. New York, Free Press.

Finkelhor, D. (1984). Four Conditions: A Model. Child Sexual Abuse: New Theories and Research. New York, The Free Press.

Finkelhor, D. (1986). *A Sourcebook on Child Sexual Abuse*. Beverly Hills, Sage Publications.

Finkelhor, D., Araji, S. *et al.* (1986). *A Sourcebook on Child Sexual Abuse*. California, Sage.

Freeman-Longo, R., Bays, L. *et al.* (1996). *Empathy and Compassionate Action Issues and Exercise: A guided Workbook for Clients in Treatment*. Bandon, VT: Safer Society Press.

Freeman-Longo, R. and Wall, R. V. (1986). 'Changing a Lifetime of Sexual Crime.' *Psychology Today* 3: 58–64.

Gallagher, B. (2007). 'Internet-Initiated Incitement and Conspiracy to Commit Child Sexual Abuse (CSA): The Typology, Extent and Nature of Known Cases.' *Journal of Sexual Aggression. An International, Interdisciplinary Forum for Research, Theory and Practice* 13(2): 101–19.

Gallagher, B., Fraser, C. *et al.* (2006). International and Internet Child Sexual Abuse and Exploitation. Research report. Huddersfield, Centre for Applied Childhood Studies. University of Huddersfield.

Gillespie, A. A. (2004). 'Tackling Grooming.' *The Police Journal* 77(3): 239.

Gomm, R., Hammersley, M. *et al.* (2000). 'Case Study and Generalization.' *Case Study Method: Key Issues, Key Texts*. R. Gomm, M. Hammersley and P. Foster. London, Sage.

Groth, A. N. (1978). 'Patterns of Sexual Assault Against Children and Adolescents.' *Sexual Assault of Children and Adolescents*. A. W. Burgess, A. N. Groth, L. L. Holmstrom and S. M. Sgroi. Lexington, MA, Lexington Books: 3–24.

Groth, A. N., Longo, R. E. *et al.* (1982). 'Undetected Recidivism Among Rapists and Child Molesters.' *Annals of Sex Research* 1: 485–99.

Grubin, D. (1998). 'Sex Offending against Children: Understanding the Risk.' *Police Research Series* 99.

Gudjonsson, G. (1988). 'Attribution of Blame for Criminal Acts and in Relationship with Type of Offence.' *Medical Science Law* 28(4): 301–3.

Herman, J. L. (1981). *Father–Daughter Incest*. Cambridge, MA, Harvard University.

Hernandez, A. E. (2009). Psychological and Behavioural Characteristics of Child Pornography Offenders in Treatment. Global Symposium: Examining the Relationship between Online and Offline Offences and Preventing the Sexual Exploitation of Children. The Injury Prevention Research Centre, The University of North Carolina, Chapel Hill.

Home Office Task Force on Child Protection on the Internet (2007). Good Practice Guidance for the Providers of Social Networking and Other User Interactive Services, www.homeoffice.gov.

Hudson, S. M. and T. Ward (1997). 'Intimacy, Loneliness and Attachment Style in Sex Offenders.' *Journal of Interpersonal Violence* 12(3): 199–213.

Internet Watch Foundation (2006). Annual and Charity Report.

Kelly, L. (1988). *Surviving Sexual Violence*. Oxford, Polity Press.

Laws, D. R. (1989). *Relapse Prevention with Sex Offenders*. New York, Guilford.

Levenson, J. S. and Macgowan, M. J. (2004). 'Engagement, Denial, and Treatment Progress Among Sex Offenders in Group Therapy.' *Sexual Abuse: A Journal of Research and Treatment* 16(1): 49–63.

Lieberson, S. (1992). 'Small N's and Big Conclusions: an Examination of the Reasoning in Comparative Studies Based on a Small Number of Cases.' *What is a*

Case? Exploring the foundations of social inquiry. C. Ragin and H. S. Becker. Cambridge, Cambridge University Press.

Marshall, W. L. (1996). 'Assessment Treatment and Theorizing About Sex Ofenders: Developments Over the Last Twenty Years and Future Directions.' *Criminal Justice and Behavior* 23(162–99).

Marshall, W. L. (1997). The prevalence of convictions for sexual offending. London, Home Office.

Marshall, W. L., Anderson, D. *et al.* (1999). *The Development of Cognitive Behavioural Treatment of Sex Offenders.* England, John Wiley and Sons, Ltd.

Martellozzo, E. (2007). Policing Child Sexual Abuse On Line: Understanding Grooming in the 21st Century. Crime, crime prevention and communities in Europe. September 26–29, Bologna, Italy.

Martellozzo, E. (forthcoming). Metropolitan Police Practice: Protecting Chidlren Online. Exploring the work of the High Technological Crime Unit, University of Kingston.

Martellozzo, E. and Taylor, H. (2009). 'Cycle of Abuse.' Index on Censorship 38(1): 117–22.

Matza, D. and Sykes, G. (1961). 'Juvenile Delinquency and Subterranean Values.' *American Sociological Review* 26(5): 712–19.

McGuire, J. (2000). Cognitive-Behavioural Approaches: An Introduction to Theory and Research. London, Home Office: 11–121.

Middelton, D. (2004). Current Treatment Approaches. Child Sexual Abuse and the Internet. Tackling New Frontier. M. Calder, Russell House Publishing: 99–112.

O'Connell, R., Price, J. *et al.* (2004). Cyber Stalking, Abusive Cyber Sex and Online Grooming: A programme of Education for Teenagers. Lancashire www.FKBKO. net, University of Central Lancashire.

Peters, J. J. (1976). 'Children who are Victims of Sexual Assault and the Psycology of the Offender.' *American Journal of Psycotherapy* 30: 398–421.

Pithers, W. D. (1988). Relapse Prevention. A Practitioner's Guide to Treating the Incarcerated Male Sex Offender. B. Shchwarz. Washington DC, National Institute of Corrections: 123–40.

Pithers, W. D. (1999). 'Empathy: Definition, Enhancement, and Relevance to the Treatment of Sexual Abusers.' *Journal of Interpersonal Violence* 14(3): 257–84.

Prime, J., White, S. *et al.* (2001). Criminal careers of Those Born Between 1953 and 1978 March 2001. Statistical Bulletin, 4/01. London, Home Office.

Prins, H. (1985) 'Will They do it again? Risk assessment and management in criminal Justice', Routledge.

Quayle, E., Erooga, M. *et al.* (2006). *Only Pictures?* Dorset, Russel House Publishing.

Salter, A. C. (1995). *Transforming Trauma.* Newbury Park, CA, Sage.

Salter, D., McMillan, D. *et al.* (2003). 'Development of Sexually Abusive Behaviour in Sexually Victimised males: a Longitudinal Study.' *The Lancet* 361: 9356–9471.

Smallbone, S. and Wortley, R. (2001). 'Child Sexual Abuse: Offender Characteristics and Modus Operandi.' *Trends and Issues in Crime and Criminal Justice* 193: 1–6.

Soothill, K. and Walby, S. (1991). *Sex Crime in the News.* London, Routledge.

Stanko, E. (1990). *Everyday Violence.* London, Unwin Hyman.

Stermac, L. E., Hall, K. *et al.* (1989). 'Violence Among Child Molesters.' *Journal of Sex Research* 26(4): 450–59.

Sullivan, J. and Beech A. (2004). *Are Collectors of Child Abuse Images a Risk to Children?* London, The John Grieve Centre for Policing and Community Safety.

Taylor, M. (09/03/07). Flying Squad Officer Jailed for Child Sex Offence on Internet. The Guardian Online. Accessed on 3/10/08.

West, D. (1996). *Sexual Molesters. Dangerous People.* London, Blackstone Press Limited.

Wolak, J., Finkelhor, D. *et al.* (2005). 'Internet-initiated Sex Crimes against Minors: Implications for Prevention Based on Findings from a National Study.' *Journal of Adolescent Health* 35(5): 424–37.

Wolak, J., Finkelhor, D. *et al.* (2009). Trends in Arrests of 'Online Predators'. Crime Against Children Research Centre. University of New Hampshire.

Wolak, J., Mitchell, K. J. *et al.* (2003). 'Escaping or Connecting. Characteristics of Youth Who Form Close Online Relationships.' *Journal of Adolescence*: 105–19.

Wolf, S. (1985). 'A Multi Factor Model of Deviant Sexuality.' *Victimology: An Internal Journal* 10: 359–74.

Woods, J. (1997). 'Breaking the Cycle of Abuse and Abusing: Individual Psycotherapy for Juvenile Sex Offenders.' *Clinical Child Psychology and Psychiatry* 2(3): 379–92.

Wurtele, S. K. and Miller-Perrin C. L. (1993). *Preventing Child Sexual Abuse: Sharing the Responsibility,* Lincoln: University Nebraska Press.

Wyatt, G. and Powell G. (1988). *Lasting Effects of Child Sexual Abuse.* London, Sage.

Young, K. (2008). 'Understanding Sexually Deviant Online Behaviour from an Addiction Perspective.' *International Journal of Cyber Crimminology* 2(1): 298–307.

Young, K. S. (2001). *Tangled in the Web: Understanding Cybersex from Fantasy to Addiction.* Bloomington, IN, Authorhouse.

Chapter 6

Policing social networking sites and online grooming

Jon Taylor

Introduction

This chapter describes research undertaken by the author in his capacity as undercover police officer at the Metropolitan Police High Technology Crime Unit during 2009. The aims of the research were: to advance understanding of the use of Internet Social Networking Sites that sex offenders use to source, groom and sexually abuse children; to assess the link between social networking sites and instant messaging systems; to explore the proactive strategies for policing online Child Sexual Abuse (CSA) with particular reference to the work of the Metropolitan Police High Technological Crime Unit (HTCU); and to identify the link between non-contact offenders and contact offenders through the phenomenon of 'virtual offending'.

Historical context of Internet abuse and policing

As discussed in previous chapters (Davidson, Chapter 1; Carr and Hilton, Chapter 3) concern fuelled by extensive media coverage regarding sex offenders (Soothill and Walby, 1991) has been matched with frantic political and legislative activity in recent years. Yet this is not a new phenomenon; previous research has extensively explored the historical and cultural evidence of historical child abuse (Demause, 1976, 2002). Sex offenders' use of computers is also not new; the Meese Commission Report (1986) provided the first evidence that this group of offenders have been using computer networks to circulate child abuse images since 1985 in the United States. In the UK, references to child pornography were made within a computer bulletin board system as early as 1985[1] (Akendiz, 2000).

Research conducted on child sexual abuse (CSA) online is without doubt a developing area. However, CSA online is increasing as a result of technological development, as technological advancements continue the ability for offenders to remain anonymous and disappear within the virtual world has become a policing problem. This has not only affected the way in which Law Enforcement Agencies police the cyberworld but also police and government response to the phenomenon. Early research into online risks to children quickly established that sex offenders and children interact in chat rooms (O'Connell, 2003). However, the Internet has advanced rapidly; the creation of social networking sites (SNS) and instant messaging sites (IMS) has meant interaction can take place in many more areas. Some researchers such as O'Connell have argued that sex offenders spend a long time grooming a child before disclosing their sexual interest. However, more recent research has suggested that this is not always the case (Webster and Davidson *et al.*, 2009; Martellozzo, forthcoming). Social Networking Sites have allowed very easy access to vulnerable victims, some of whom readily supply personal information about themselves, making the rapport stage of grooming all but redundant. This gives cause for concern particularly in the light of recent research which suggests that many young people are willing to divulge personal information to online strangers (Davidson et al., 2009; see Chapter 1).

Commentators have suggested that since the advent of the Internet child abuse 'phenomenon' the police have reacted passively and tentatively (Gillespie, 2009) through lack of knowledge and resources. Operation Cathedral in 1998 and Operation Ore in 1999 were examples of reactive policing by the UK Police as a result of information from Law Enforcement Agencies in the US (Gillespie, 2009). Operation Cathedral was the largest ever international raid and followed months of surveillance of the notorious Wonderland Club whose members swapped indecent images of children. On 2 September 1998 an international police operation involving 12 countries successfully seized nearly a million indecent child images as well as 1,800 'computerised videos' depicting children suffering sexual abuse. Operation Ore was a British police operation that commenced in 1999, following information from US law enforcement, and it intended to prosecute thousands of users of websites reportedly featuring indecent child images.

However, covert policing has identified proactive capabilities in identifying and successfully prosecuting sex offenders online (Sanderson, 2004). *R v Sadowski* 2003 resulted from the dissemination of information from US authorities to the Metropolitan Police Sex Offender Unit and highlighted the need for dedicated covert police officers to operate within dedicated units. This research will analyse and discuss new police methods, particularly proactive online policing. Current guidelines are in place that attempt to protect children whilst online. Furthermore, the Virtual Global Taskforce (VGT) in conjunction with the Child Exploitation Online Protection (CEOP) service, have instigated 'report abuse online'. This reporting process allows victims of CSA to electronically report online sexual inappropriateness, bullying and abuse.

Social networking sites

Social networking sites are web-based sites, which allow users to set up online profiles or personal homepages, and develop an online social network

(Gillespie, 2008). It is important to note that the term 'friend', as used on a social networking site, is different from the traditional meaning in the offline world. Whilst it can be argued that the personal information provided on profiles assists the online groomer to identify a child victim, SNS and Instant Messaging services are far more important in establishing the rapport stage during the grooming process. By definition, SNS let users meet new people online and are designed for this purpose (Gillespie, 2008).

These sites encourage and enable people to exchange personal information, share pictures and videos, and use private messaging to communicate with friends and share interests, either with individual contacts or all site users. This indicates that it is important to maintain a level of awareness concerning the possible pitfalls associated with online social networking sites. The British Office of Communications (Ofcom, 2009) recently determined that half of all British minors between the ages of 8 and 17 who use the Internet have a profile on an online social networking site. Despite the fact that the minimum age for most major social networking sites is usually 13 (14 on MySpace), 27% of 8–11-year-olds who are aware of social networking sites say that they have a profile on a site. While some of these younger users are on sites intended for younger children, the presence of underage users on social networking sites intended for those aged 13 or over was also confirmed by qualitative research conducted by Ofcom. Online social networking grew by 35% in Europe in the last year, with 42 million people using sites regularly, a figure that is expected to more than double by 2012, with 71% of year 7[2] children now admitting that they have created SNS profiles (www.guardian.co.uk, 2009).

In April 2006 the Home Office Task Force on Child Protection on the Internet recommended the implementation of Social Networking guidance and advice for industry, parents and children, showing how to stay safe online (Home Office, 2006). This was developed by a taskforce of representatives from industry, charity and law enforcement agencies including Vodafone, CEOP and the National Society for the Prevention of Cruelty to Children (NSPCC). The Government set guidelines requiring the sharing of the 'email addresses' of registered sex offenders to social networking sites to make it harder for sex offenders to groom children online. Launching the Task Force on Child Protection on the Internet, Social Networking Guidance in April 2008 Home Secretary Jacqui Smith said:

> If the likes of Bebo, Facebook and Myspace had access to this information it would make it easier for them to stop or monitor offenders using their sites ...
>
> (http://police.homeoffice.gov.uk)

However, law enforcement agencies have pointed out that it is easy for people to set up multiple email addresses to bypass these restrictions, and to continue online grooming with essentially new identities. Furthermore this guidance was not implemented, as the Task Force was closed before any advice was offered or legislation passed to place an onus on SNS to proactively monitor their sites. The Task Force has recently been replaced by the UK Council on Child Internet Safety.

Policing child sexual abuse online

Benn (2003:46) has argued that 'child protection is a priority for us all' and thus should be taken seriously.[3] As a result the UK HMIC report[4] provided recommendations including ensuring that child protection be given 'sufficient priority, resources and structures to be effective'. The Victoria Climbié[5] inquiry made a number of recommendations including making child protection a government and policing priority.[6] The Government responded with the 'Keeping Children Safe'[7] report again proposing Child Protection to be a high priority. Indeed this rhetoric is mirrored by senior and influential police officers, both serving and retired; 'Of all the wider policing tasks for the twenty-first century, nothing could be more important than the protection of children' (Grieve, 2003:6). Policing Authorities appear to discharge their responsibility by ensuring that specialist units deal primarily with reactive intra-familial investigations. Thus policing intervention will occur primarily after an offence or sequence of offences has been committed resulting in harm to a child.

Policing the Internet has not only proactively changed over the past five to six years, but has resulted in changes to the UK legislation. The advent of the Internet allowed sex offenders to seek out other offenders to share images and also to justify their thoughts, beliefs and fantasies (Sanderson, 2004). Early policing of the Internet was focused around the viewing, possession and distribution of indecent images. The Sexual Offences Act (SOA) 1956, and the Protection of Children Act (POCA) 1978 were used to identify and prosecute offenders who were downloading such images, this saw such operations as Operation Ore, Operation Cathedral and Operation Orchid (Sanderson, 2004). These operations identified many hundreds of offenders who were willing to purchase and exchange indecent images of children. However, online sex offenders using the Internet to find, groom and sexually abuse children remained largely un-policed. *R v Luke Sadowski* and the SOA 2003 changed all this. *R v Sadowski* saw the first proactive covert operation that brought together covert law enforcement agencies from the US and the UK, and influenced the creation of the SOA 2003. This resulted in the UK pioneering direct legislation to combat online grooming.

UK police forces were able to train officers to become Covert Internet Investigators, who were able to proactively police the Internet by portraying themselves as children. In the UK the Child Exploitation and Online

Protection Centre launched in April 2006. This organisation works across the UK to maximise national and international links. CEOP incorporates dedicated expertise of technological business sectors, government, specialist charities and other interested organisations – all focused on tackling child sex abuse wherever and whenever it happens. This means working with parents, young people and children to safeguard their online experiences. It includes direct support to victims and their families and involves the relentless tracking and prosecution of offenders. This is a new web-based initiative involving law enforcement agencies from across three continents.

Internationally The Virtual Global Task Force (VGT) is an international partnership between law enforcement agencies and industry in the UK, Australia, Canada, the US, and Interpol. This alliance delivers crime prevention and crime reduction initiatives with the aim of making the Internet a safer place for children and a more hostile place for sex offenders. VGT's website acts as a gateway to provide information on how to use the Internet safely, and links to a range of support agencies that can advise and support victims of abuse. It facilitates the ability of Internet users to report online child abuse to appropriate law enforcement agencies in a number of different countries (moves to protect children online have been discussed by Davidson in Chapter 1 and Carr and Hilton in Chapter 3).

However organisations such as CEOP and the VGT rely on victims reporting offenders whilst the grooming process takes place, and research has demonstrated that child victims rarely report or disclose sexual abuse. Furthermore, the political issues concerning how and what to police, due to the unavailability of statistics, coupled with the lack of research into how the SNSs are used by sex offenders, has allowed this area to continue to grow largely un-policed.

> Paedophilia is being dissected, examined, studied, pondered over and pronounced upon. Yet no one can say with any certainty why men of all ages sexually abuse children and few know what can be done to successfully stop, change and cure them [sic].
>
> (www.preda.org)

A second aim of the author's research was to ascertain whether the new technological use of the Social Networking Sites by online sex offenders can shed light upon an exploration into the link between the use of indecent images and the commission of contact sexual offences. The issue of child pornography is an emotional one, and the debate has largely been on moral and political grounds rather than on the development of understanding (Quayle and Taylor, 2003). Although there is a growing bank of knowledge regarding child sexual abusers and there is increasing literature on indecent image users, there is still little known about those who perpetrate contact abuse and who use indecent images of children. It can be argued that there is still little understanding of the motivational factors prompting such behaviour and the risks posed by indecent image collectors. However the author's research sought to explore this link by investigating the use of Social Networking Sites and Instant Messaging services by online sex offenders to groom and sexually abuse children. The research explores what role indecent images play in the offending cycle of such offenders. Examination of this data provides a unique way to learn about the nature of the relationship between child pornography on the Internet and the commission of sexual abuse.

Covert police operations

Covert Internet Investigators (CIIs) were introduced into policing in the UK as a result of the growth of the Internet and the use of the Internet by sex offenders. Initial focus was upon the way in which the Internet was being used to access and distribute indecent images of children. Furthermore, a major concern was that the Internet could be used by sex offenders to share not only indecent images of children but also sexual fantasies (Calder, 2003). This deviant way in which the Internet was used by sex offenders also meant that contact offenders were able to source victims whether by sex tourism, online sexual grooming or through contact with other online sex offenders who already had access to children. The combination of the reluctance of child victims to disclose sexual abuse with that of an un-policed Internet meant that online sex offenders were allowed uninterrupted access to young people and to each other, and were afforded complete anonymity. US law enforcement agencies began covert operations to infiltrate sex tourism by creating 'honey-pot' Internet sites to identify and arrest sex offenders. However, due to the nature of the World Wide Web a number of sex offenders contacting these sites came from outside the US. One such sex offender was Luke Sadowski.

Sadowski was an 18-year-old trainee teacher, who contacted one such site. This saw the first known multi-agency operation between the US and the UK. The Metropolitan Police Sex Offender Unit worked with the US Customs and Enforcement Agency (ICE – now Homeland Security) to interact with and arrest Sadowski. However, the Metropolitan Police Service in 2002 had no undercover officers specifically trained to interact with online sex offenders. In 2003 the National Police Improvement Agency (NPIA) in the UK created a two-week course to train police officers as Covert Internet Investigators. Currently there are 160 CII police officers. Whilst the initial training centred on policing online sex offender activity, the course now includes officers from Intelligence Bureaus and Counter Terrorism.

The case of Luke Sadowski not only created new police training but it also corresponded with the new Sexual Offences Act 2003 which created specific offences related to interaction on the Internet (discussed in Chapter 1). Offences of inciting sexual activity (web cam) to that of online grooming covered by the new act directly influenced how the Internet could be policed.

It can be seen that sections 10–15 of the Sexual Offences Act 2003 may not have been specifically created to link the online world to the offline world but they can be applied to both. Technology now allows the online offender to commit offences that once were considered as contact offences. Software and hardware technology in the form of social networking, instant messaging, chat facilities, Voice over Internet Protocol (VoIP) and web cam allow visual and verbal contact. However, initial online policing concentrated on offenders collecting indecent images, police covert investigation with online sex offenders remains in its infancy. This was due not only to the lack of disclosure by victims, but also, and largely, due to ignorance of online sex offender activity. This in turn lead to differentiating between non-contact offenders and contact offenders. Understanding the differences would assist in identifying how these two offending areas could be correctly risk assessed and as a result correctly policed.

Contact offending and non-contact offending

Some researchers have suggested that a causal link in the aetiology history of individual sexual offenders exists; Wyre claimed that viewing pornography acts as an inciter (Wyre, 1996). Furthermore, Wyre stated: 'If a man buys child pornography he does so for one reason alone … the reason is he wants to have sex with children. The fact that he may not have done so is more likely to be a question on availability or the fear of getting caught than revulsion at the very concept' (www.raywyre.com). Edwards (2000) in her national study of child pornography trials in both Crown Court and Magistrates Court between 1995 and 1997 concluded that there was a 'relationship between child pornography and child sexual abuse'. However, this study predated the Internet boom and dealt with relatively low numbers (Edwards, 2000).

The academic and legal debate regarding potential causal links between child abuse material and child abuse continues today. As discussed by Gottschalk in Chapter 4, a number of researchers working in this area (Bourke & Hernandez, 2009; Hernandez, 2009) recognise that there may be links between those offenders that view child abuse images and those offenders that sexually abuse children. However it has been argued that there is evidence to the contrary (Williams, 2004) suggesting that pseudo-photographs can relax desires, thus rendering the individual less harmful and possibly making the images therapeutic in some way. It was further argued that the use of material as a masturbatory aid is not in itself illegal nor is it dangerous to children (ibid., 2004) and Seto (2009) found little evidence of reconviction for contact offences amongst his sample of child pornography offenders (this study was however based on reconviction data amongst a sample of sex offenders). Furthermore, Wyre altered his view, postulating that the collection of pornography can in itself become addictive, leading those involved to seek more extreme types of material, which include child pornography. Wyre is suggesting that such collectors do not pose a direct threat to children (Wyre, 2003).

Seto *et al.* (2005) have suggested that child pornography offending was a stronger diagnostic indicator of paedophilia than contact sexual offending against children. This research was conducted on data from 685 patients at the Kurt Freund Laboratory of the Centre for Addiction and Mental Health utilising phallometric tests (Seto, 2006). Seto (in an interview with Davidson, 2007) has suggested that greater paedophilic sexual arousal appears to be equated with greater risk of committing a criminal offence, and low non-sexual criminal history lowers the risk of contact abuse. He also stated that people are likely to choose the kind of pornography that corresponds to their sexual interest (Davidson, 2007).

Akdeniz also states that there is ' … no conclusive correlation between individuals who access, view and possess child pornography and offences of sexual abuse'. He cites a statement made by Baroness Scotland of Asthal in the House of Lords: 'People who sexually abuse children are often found to be in possession of indecent images of children. There is evidence to suggest that child pornography can be used in an attempt to legitimise their sexual activities with children and to "groom" or encourage compliance from their victims.' However, no evidence existed to support a direct causal link between the access to child pornography and the commission of sexual offences against children (Akedeniz, 2008).

Some research suggests that fantasy and masturbation to deviant sexual fantasies increases the possibility of moving on to contact sexual offending (Sandberg and Marlatt, 1989). This is interesting as this research was some way before the advent of CFs, SNS and IMS, which have allowed the process of online interaction. The Internet's easy access to child abuse material and the ease of interaction with children may serve to fuel sexual deviancy and contact offending. Sullivan and Beech (2003) conclude that people who download child abuse images from the Internet are in fact more likely to offend with actual abuse by acting out the fantasies. Durkin (1997) suggested that some sex offenders might refine or act upon their deviant proclivities because of their exposure to the Internet.

As discussed, research in this area is difficult as it mainly relies on data and accounts of those offenders within the criminal justice system, and it can be argued that contact offending remains a 'hidden crime'. Hernandez introduced concerning evidence in his testimony to the Sub-committee on the Oversight and Investigation Committee on Energy and Commerce United States House of Representatives, where he stated that between 80 to 85 per cent of the prison population incarcerated for child pornography with no previous convictions of contact offences later admitted to having committed such offences. He concluded that Internet child pornographers are far more dangerous than previously thought (Hernandez, 2009: 162).

Hernandez (2009:3) states 'there was little information about this criminal population and many individuals in the criminal justice system viewed these offenders as mere computer criminals'. Here the criminal population meant those convicted of viewing or downloading indecent images of children. In the Butner Redux study, Michael Bourke and Andres Hernandez (2009) examined the relationship between online and contact sexual offences among a group of incarcerated sex offenders participating in treatment. They observed more similarities than differences between online and offline sex offenders. One dimension in which the two groups appeared similar was their undetected history involving contact sexual offences. Convicted sex offenders who had downloaded child abuse material whilst in treatment routinely disclosed previously undetected contact sexual offences, mimicking patterns frequently observed in research involving contact sexual offenders (Alhmeyer et al., 2000).

However this and other current research relied upon incarcerated child pornography offenders. This type of research is open to criticism due to the incentives offered to participating offenders (Williams, 2004). Incentives, ranging from prison re-location, offender rehabilitation programmes to even early parole are believed to have been offered, influencing offenders' participation. Real time research in the form of complete covert participation, where research is carried out through covert interaction with online sex offenders, allows for research without incentives or consequence. However what the Butner redux study did conclude was that a substantial percentage of offenders who initially claimed to be at low (or no) risk of harm to children because they exclusively collected child abuse images subsequently indicated that they had committed acts of undetected child sexual abuse. This raises the question of whether the advent of the Internet has created a new type of sex offender, or if it merely provides additional outlets for sexually deviant individuals.

Findings: researching offender online behaviour

The methodological approach employed was mixed, combining different techniques. These included ethnography, complete participant observation, and secondary data analysis. Access to a subject can prove most difficult in ethnographic studies, particularly in sensitive research. An important aspect of access concerns the research setting (area), and whether the subject to be researched can be described as 'open' or 'closed' (Bell, 1969). Hammersley and Atkinson (1995) made a similar distinction by referring to 'public' and 'non public' settings, implying how easy and difficult access can be. Research into social networking sites and online sex offending can be regarded as an open public setting, as the Internet is accessible to anybody with a computer and Internet connections. Furthermore, SNS are an open arena; individuals who join SNS and create public profiles forgo any 'expectation of privacy' as other SNS users are capable of viewing and interacting with other users. This access is available without passwords, requests or permission, whether as a law enforcement officer or not. However to be able to interact with online sex offenders then the researcher remains covert whilst becoming a member of SNS.

The researcher is a serving police officer and is currently one of four trained Covert Internet Investigators working within the Metropolitan Police High Tech Crime Sex Offender Unit. The researcher is currently employed full-time to covertly police the Internet, identifying sex offenders utilising CF, SNS and IMS to source, engage and groom child victims. The researcher had the unique position that allowed full participant observation including:

- engagement as an online covert police officer interacting with suspected online child abusers
- real time interaction with suspected online offenders
- direct involvement in discussions as to how, where and which social networking sites and chat forums are being utilised by online sex offenders.

Given the uniqueness of the researcher's access rights the cautious approach has been broken down despite the sensitivity of the subject and the once held belief that sexual abuse is a taboo subject (Greer, 2003). This allows for ease of access and discussion forming qualitative analysis. These types of discussion and the gathering of data is common practice for law enforcement agencies working within specific fields, as it allows for the sharing and dissemination of information.

Despite the researcher working within the field of online covert policing, formal ethical permission was sought and given from the researcher's managers and colleagues within the High Technological Crime Unit and the Sex offender Unit. Once permission was granted, the observational fieldwork began. This comprised:

- creation of child profiles within Social Networking Sites and Chat Facilities
- interacting with suspected online sex offenders via Instant Messaging Services
- involvement in discussions around the effectiveness of existing techniques
- complete participation first hand in the processes and practices of policing CSA online
- comparison of three Covert Operations within Social Networking Sites.

This research data includes chat log interaction with suspected online sex offenders in a covert capacity; obviously given the nature of the covert work of online child sex abusers it was neither feasible nor desirable to seek research permission from the potential offenders. This does raise an ethical issue regarding informed consent, but data has been heavily anonymised to protect the identity of offenders.

The findings discussion has been divided as follows: the first part discusses three major undercover police operations where police officers acted as young girls and interacted with online sex offenders; the second part looks at policing methodologies to combat online child sexual abuse; and the third focuses on the links that may exist between contact and non-contact offending in cyberspace.

Social Networking Sites have quite simply broken down the rapport stage of grooming (Webster and Davidson et al., 2009; Martellozzo, 2009). Introductions are made without the awkwardness of embarrassment, facing a rejection and the high risk of arrest. SNS have become the new park or school playground that allows for easier access to possible victims with relative complete anonymity (www.childnet-int.org).

The researcher in his role as a Covert Internet Investigator was able to create SNS profiles of young girls aged 12, 13 and 14 years of age for three proactive police operations. For these operations, the researcher created virtual identities of 12–14-year-old girls on SNS, chat facilities and instant messaging systems. The researcher was tasked with identifying and interacting with online sex offenders that were using the Internet to sexually groom the girls online and sexually abuse offline. Previous research to date (Gillespie, 2008) has shown how 'chat rooms' are the areas of the Internet used by online sex offenders to find, groom and sexually abuse children (Gillespie, 2008). However, this research has been able to show specifically what rooms, sites or facilities are used by sex offenders to search for possible victims.[7]

It is important to note that for any child or user of SNS, IMS, or CFs email addresses are first required. That is to say that any user has to sign up with an email provider before any interaction on CF or IMS or profile creation on SNS can commence. The two main email providers are Hotmail (Microsoft) and Yahoo; they are also the two leading IMS providers. However, both providers allow users with email addresses from other providers to access and register the IMS facilities. Microsoft and Yahoo up until very recently only allowed those users with Hotmail or Yahoo emails to use their facilities respectively. However now both facilities allow users with any email (for example, AOL [America On-Line], or G-mail etc) to join and use. The researcher created email addresses within Hotmail and Yahoo to allow both facilities to be used.

As stated, Microsoft and Yahoo are the two main providers of IMS; others are available but most Internet IMS users opt for MSN or Yahoo. MSN and Yahoo Messenger are web-based software freely available to members of the public that allows its users to chat online in real time and to also send computer files, including moving and static images. MSN and Yahoo messenger also offer the facility to share and send pictures and movies. This means images do not actually have to be sent, but photos and photo albums can be opened, viewed, shared and saved. Once the free messenger software has been downloaded, and a user has signed up with a unique username, the user can build up a contact list of other users. The messenger facility also allows for images and movie files to be seen and viewed as emoticons.[8] For this research the researcher signed up for both MSN and Yahoo messenger facilities which were utilised in all three covert operations.[9]

As discussed, SNS let users meet new people online (Gillespie, 2008). There are approximately 150 SNS that are regularly used within Europe. The researcher picked six SNS from the top 10 most popular SNS within the UK to join as a 12–14-year-old girl. These SNS were: Hi5, Bebo, Netlog, Face Party, Facebook, and Meet Your Messenger. Whilst SNS can give the user the option for a private profile, meaning that no other user can view the user's profile, the researcher left the profile public to allow other users to view the profile created. The public profile allows other users of the specific SNS to view the girl's email addresses which they can add to their own respective IMS to begin one-to-one interaction. Furthermore, SNS also have their own messaging systems which can be similar to IMS but are used to meet/introduce other users by leaving email type messages.

Once SNS had been created, interaction with online subjects began immediately. The creation of public profiles allowed subjects to send friendship requests or welcome messages via the SNS or IMS. It was found that most of the subjects had provided Internet profiles summarising their personalities and interests. These varied in content and the extent to which a realistic portrayal of the person was presented. Of these some profiles were not particularly informative of the suspect and provided no inclination of the subject's sexual preferences. However, several of the profiles were extremely open about their sexual preferences; for example one male stated: 'I am a nice, decent, very loving caring guy with a pervy side – daddy/daughter, incest etc'; another stated 'age is just a number'. Some had listed their interests under categories such as 'incest', 'cherry popping Daddies' and 'dreamer of teens'. One suspect's profile contained a picture of a young female performing oral sex on him and a link to a 'paedo paradise' website. In these cases the subject is taking a risk in drawing attention to himself by making his interest in children so explicit.

These subjects seemed more likely to meet a young girl less than 14 rather than just engaging in role play or online fantasy. These online predators generally appeared to be less concerned at being identified and arrested; either that or their desire to abuse was stronger and overrides their self-preservation. This supports the notion that online sexual predators are either 'felony stupid' or possess 'desire stupidity' (Tanner, 2009).

This is not to suggest that a suspected offender who does not disclose his personal sexual interests online does not pose any risk to children. Throughout the research, it was noticed that many online offenders made their intentions clear from the outset; however it took some offenders a long time before trusting the potential victim enough to plan a meeting together.

Two of the subjects used exceptionally elaborate ploys to initially groom the researcher into communicating online. One pretended to be an older woman who had an adult male friend who wanted to have sex with a girl aged 13. The other purported to be a teenage girl who was already sexually experienced with older men. Both of these online personalities then introduced the researcher, as a 13-year-old girl, to the subject, and the grooming process began. This appears to be a common technique used by online groomers to make the victim feel more at ease when communicating with the online sex offender. Four other online sex offenders lied about their age and/ or marital status, one claiming to be 43 when he was actually 64 – this did not deter him from turning up to meet with the 13-year-old girl. However not all adults with an inappropriate sexual interest in children pose as teenagers to establish communication. A large proportion of adults will be economical with the truth with respect to their adult status. Some may indeed give accurate information about themselves, their location and their desires and sexual preferences. Thus supporting previous research (O'Connell, 2003; Tanner, 2009) in respect of offender techniques, anonymity offered by the Internet, and the 'desire stupidity' shown by some offenders, overriding their 'self-preservation'.

The duration of time that the subjects communicated with the researcher before their arrest varied from two weeks to five months. The frequency of the chats also varied; some offenders communicated sporadically with the CII, others appeared keener and emailed more frequently. Without exception the suspect had mentioned sex by the second conversation (O'Connell, 2003). Several males suggested meeting up with the young girl early on in the dialogue; it appears that for these offenders meeting the victim was always their desire and therefore they were more likely to turn up.

All of the suspects talked in a sexually explicit way to the victim, although their approaches varied. Some attempted to court the girl, professing to love her: 'I want to kiss you so gently but, so passionately but I know I shouldn't', 'you are my girlfriend and I am dying to see you, love you'. A couple tried to deny their behaviour was inappropriate: 'I am not doing any of that grooming stuff you hear about, just to talk with no intent to do anything else.' The majority were overtly sexual, asking her to perform sexual acts on them or herself and asking her about her sexual experience. Several of the online offenders described how they would like to take her virginity and what they would like to do to her. The progression from initial meeting to that of sexual interaction would always follow the same pattern. Once the offender had identified his victim on a CF or SNS interaction via IMS would occur, a process that could sometimes occur in a matter of minutes. Whilst relationship forming, and risk assessment stages (O'Connell, 2003) would not be bypassed, they would be covered sub consciously. SNS have speeded up the process as the profile created can offer instant credibility. Therefore the offender can move to the exclusivity and sexual stage a lot earlier as a result of SNS.

In addition to online discussion, over half of the subjects also communicated with the victim from their mobile phones using text messages. These texts were a continuation of the grooming process, mainly explicit, but continued the credibility stage. Mobile phones were also used by offenders to arrange the actual face-to-face meeting with the victim once they had arrived at the meeting venue.

The researcher was involved in three operations working alongside two other CIIs; all created profiles of 12, 13, or 14-year-old girls. All used emails, CFs, SNS and IMS to meet and interact with online offenders displaying a sexual interest in these girls. During these operations 150 offenders interacted with the researcher and CIIs; furthermore, 39 offenders groomed a supposed child and travelled to meet the child for sexual abuse of the child (Sec 15 SOA 2003). The remaining 111 either caused or incited a child under 13 to engage in sexual activity (Sec 10 SOA 2003), or engaged in sexual activity in the presence of a child (Sec 11, SOA, 2003), or caused a child to watch a sexual act (Sec 12 SOA 2003). These offences being committed through CFs, SNS, and IMS, used digital cameras, mobile phones and web cams to assist in the commission of the offences. On arrest, all the offenders had their computers seized and analysed to establish further evidence, further offences or to identify further offenders or further victims. Of the 150 subjects, 147 were found to have child abuse images or movies on their computers or on their person when arrested. The collection of such indecent images points to a long-standing interest in children rather than, as often claimed on arrest, a temporary lapse in judgement. This enhances and supports previous research conducted and beliefs held concerning the link between offenders who download child abuse material and the risk of being hands-on offenders (Carr, 2004; Wolak, Finkelhor, and Mitchell, 2005; Bourke and Hernandez, 2009).

Policing contact offences and non-contact offences in the virtual world

Proactive CII interaction and subsequent prosecution of online sex offenders has identified the use of Social Networking Sites, Chat Facilities and Instant Messenger Systems by online sex offenders. Research has shown that sexually compulsive behaviour on the Internet is a recognised problem, with the 'Triple A Engine accessibility, affordability and anonymity being the factors unique to the Internet environment' (Cooper, 2002:6). CII interaction has been able to show the methods employed by sex offenders, to explore their behaviour and types of online interactions.

Figure 6.1 outlines a possible relationship between contact offending (CO), non-contact offending (NCO), and virtual offending (VO). The link between NCO and VO is well researched and accepted, as it deals with those

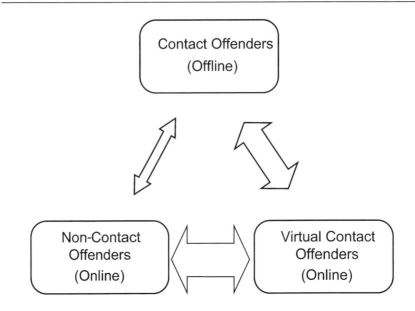

Figure 6.1 Triangle of Association

offenders who download, view and distribute indecent images of children using the Internet; the strong relationship here illustrated by a broad arrow. Furthermore, what has always been believed is it that there has to be a causal link between NCO and CO, this link here represented by a thin arrow of association. However this research suggests that there is a strong link between VO and CO as the Internet is used to commit online and offline sexual offences; this is represented by another broad arrow. This creates the 'Triangle of Association' and shows the link between NCO and CO via the VO.

It is also important to recognise that the links between *consumption* of child abuse images (non-contact offending) and contact sexual abuse crimes against children is an under-researched area. It has previously been argued in this dissertation that many of the individuals arrested for child sexual abuse crimes have been in possession of child abuse images (Healey, 1996). An investigation by the US Postal service in 2000[10] found that around 35% of people who look at child abuse images are also abusers in the real world (Carr, 2004) and Hernandez's (2009) recent research, along with the online grooming model proposed by Gottschalk in Chapter 4 supports this contention, although more research is needed in this area.

There are, however, very different views and research findings on the links between non-contact offending and contact abuse vary. Wolak *et al.* suggest that the rate is 17 per cent.[11] But in reality it is very difficult to accurately estimate the incidence of contact abuse amongst those convicted for indecent image related offences and any estimate will be based upon offender self-report and reconviction data, and the validity of these as indicators is highly questionable. It is thought that a very high proportion of those arrested under operation Ore had no previous contact with law enforcement agencies or social services.

Previous research exploring a causal link has always concentrated on finding a direct link between non-contact offending and contact. This research has become increasingly vital in assessing whether offenders viewing indecent images of children pose as great a risk to children as contact offenders. The concept of 'virtual' offending assists greatly in not only identifying the level of risk posed by offenders who download images, but also in identifying the link between contact and non-contact offending. Previous research has shown that those arrested for possessing child abuse images can be dual offenders who had also sexually victimised children, and the risk that viewers of such material pose to children may be far greater than first thought (Wolak, Finkelhor and Mitchell, 2005; Seto, Cantor and Blanchard, 2006; Bourke and Hernandez, 2009; Hernandez, 2000). However this has not been empirically tested and questions about research validity remain.

Whilst offenders who download and view indecent images for their own sexual gratification can be described as non-contact offenders, the same cannot be said of offenders who use the Internet to interact with children younger than 16. The Sexual offences Act 2003 not only introduced the new offence of grooming but it also introduced the offences of inciting a child under 13 to engage in sexual activity (Sec 10), engaging in sexual activity in the presence of a child (Sec 11), causing a child to watch a sexual act (Sec 12), arranging or facilitating a child offence (Sec 14), and meeting a child following sexual grooming (Sec 15). The SOA 2003 may not have specifically been created to combat online offending, however with virtual offending mirroring contact offending via the advances in technology in the form of Web Cams, Voice over Internet Protocol (VoIP; for example, Skype), the act fits perfectly.

Online sex offenders are able to interact with victims as if they were in the same room (Cooper, 2002). The definition of contact offending in changing, for example, if a sex offender in the same room as a victim incites the victim to masturbate and/or masturbates himself, this would be construed as a contact offence. Furthermore an offender who manipulates the victim to take an indecent image of them whilst in the same room would also be committing a contact type offence. This type of offending would be regarded as an offence conducted in the presence of a child, a 'contact offence'. The Internet, and more importantly technology in the form of web cams (a camera that transmits real time still or moving images over the Internet), and VoIP (a digital telephone service) now allow contact offences to occur through visual, verbal and physical offending whilst being many miles apart. This introduces the concept of 'virtual contact' offending (see Figure 6.1).

It is a well known fact that there have been very few studies that have analysed the link between the consumption of child pornography and the subsequent perpetration of hands-on offences. Furthermore, any research that has been conducted has always involved interviewing convicted consumers of indecent images who either agreed to discuss previous offending or were questioned years ahead concerning recidivist offending (Bourke and Hernandez, 2009). This recent research focused on convicted sex offenders, reducing the validity and reliability of the data. However, this research involved real time analysis of, and with, online sex offenders interacting with children whom the offenders believed to be under the age of 16. This allowed the findings to be conducted in 'real time' to endorse the concept of virtual offending, positively linking contact offenders with non-contact offenders.

In the author's research the study population consisted of 150 online offenders, all of whom had interacted online with the researcher, and were subsequently charged with offences relating to the visual, verbal or physical contact with a girl aged 13 or 14 (albeit an undercover officer). Out of these 150 offenders, 97 per cent had indecent images of children found on their computers (the other 3 per cent had used Internet cafes). There was a 100 per cent conviction rate of all offenders, with 97 per cent pleading guilty on their first court appearance; the 3 per cent of those electing trial were all found guilty by unanimous juries (Taylor, 2009).

As illustrated in Figure 6.1, the 'Triangle of Association' is an important device in risk-assessing online child sex offenders. Whilst previous research has shown a link between Non-Contact Offenders and Contact Offenders, it has not been able to show exactly how the two areas of offending are linked. It has relied on incarcerated offenders opening up about previous offending. The Triangle of Association shows the importance of the 'virtual offender'. An offender who consumes child abuse material combined with the use of SNS, CF and IMS, can be seen to raise the risk of offline hands-on offending. Therefore the offender can be risk assessed accurately. Furthermore, this correct risk assessing allows for the correct policing methods to be employed. The Internet has created and allowed the association between Non-Contact Offenders and Contact Offenders to grow from one of just causal interest to one of deliberate actions.

Consuming child abuse material alone is not a risk factor for committing hands-on sex offences (Quayle and Taylor, 2003), however this research has shown that Virtual Contact Offending provides the link, creating the association and increasing the known risk that Non-Contact Offenders present. This supports the belief that there is a requirement for all agencies involved in child protection to dispense with the distinction between 'online' and 'offline', 'real' and 'virtual' (Crowe and Bradford, 2006).

The section that follows focuses on different strategies to combat online child sexual abuse used by the London Metropolitan Police.

Policing online child sexual abuse

This section explores the different types of police methods available for policing child sexual abuse online and their effectiveness. More specifically, it evaluates reactive and proactive policing methods and how these can be combined with policing online child sexual abuse more effectively. These findings are based on case studies that the researcher has selected, analysed and, because of his unprecedented access, directly policed. During the final 10 months of this research, the researcher was part of a team that identified 273 online sex offenders, all of whom committed offences contrary to sections 10, 11, 12, or 15 of the Sexual Offences Act 2003, via the Internet.

Since early 2006 the Metropolitan Police High Tech Crime Unit[12] has committed considerable time, effort and resources in their effort to counter Internet-based sexual offending against children. These operations have, in the majority, been centred upon the deployment of Covert Internet Investigators in the guise of underage children within a number of Social Networking Sites. Since the inception of these covert initiatives, the Metropolitan Police has expanded its scope of CII operations to include a number of innovative and long-term strategies to target those offenders who adopt alternative methods and tactics in order to achieve sexual gratification; these objectives may range from engaging in the distribution of indecent images of children through to engaging in the facilitation of children for hands-on sexual abuse (Internet Grooming). It is within the field of Internet Grooming that CIIs have been innovative and have identified the importance of Actual Proactive Covert Internet Policing (Jewkes and Andrews, 2005). CIIs have either proactively assumed the identity of girls aged 13–14 years of age, taken over the identity of child victims who have reported online grooming offences, or infiltrated Internet forums where online sex offenders can 'virtually' meet and share thoughts, ideas, fantasies and indecent images (Ybarra and Mitchell, 2008).

The current methods of policing can be seen as 'policing proactively or reactively as a result of intelligence'. Proactive policing plays an important role; if the police simply react to intelligence then unrepeated crime remains hidden and unsolved. Intelligence-led policing results in reactive or proactive methods of policing, however certain unreported crimes such as online CSA should have their own level of criminal recognition. The identification of such offending can be as a result of other indicators, not just on police crime reports. Indicators would include the increase in the availability of online indecent images of children available, or the ages of child victims on decrease, or even the success that covert Internet policing can have in identifying online sexual abuse. Such indicators, if accepted and recognised, can introduce a new method of policing, 'proactively reactive'. This method is currently being incorrectly described as 'proactive policing'. Any policing that occurs as a result of a report from victim or source cannot and should not be regarded as proactive policing. This inaccurate title gives a false sense of security and success.

However correct proactive policing allows those areas of crime that are under-reported, perhaps as a result of non-disclosure by victims, to be effectively policed. Online CSA is one such crime; research has shown that indecent images of children are on the increase (IWF, 2008), the ages of children are on the decrease (IWF, 2008), and the proactive policing methods of covert Internet policing are effective (Jewkes and Andrews, 2005; Williams, 2004). It is fundamental to recognise and acknowledge that CSA is best policed in a proactive manner.

Figure 6.2 shows the two recognised policing methods of reactive and proactive policing with the new concept of 'proactive reactive' policing. Intelligence-led policing has always been branded as proactive policing; however this research shows that intelligence-led policing should really be categorised as proactive reactive policing. Any policing that results from reports or information from victims, witnesses or other law enforcement agencies should not be regarded as 'proactive'. The term 'proactive policing' should be used to describe a method of policing that is created and designed by police to tackle crime irrespective of allegations or reports. This new concept allows the correct identification of crimes that may not get reported, but are known to occur. Failure to understand the severity of a problem can result in the incorrect identification of policing methods; if a crime is identified 'incorrectly' then this can only mean that it will be policed 'incorrectly'. Conversely, correct identification of policing methods therefore results not only in the correct understanding of the level of the problem, but also the correct policing methods to be employed to combat such a crime. This research has

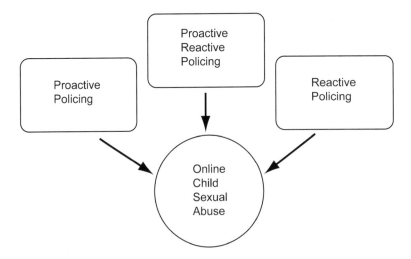

Figure 6.2 Methods of policing Online Child Sexual Abuse

identified that proactive policing, through covert online policing, has identified the problem shown and how correct proactive policing can be successful.

Reactive policing of online CSA

'The primary object of an efficient police is the prevention of crime, the next that of detection and punishment of offenders if a crime is committed,' (Sir Richard Mayne, 1820; cited on Metropolitan Police web page: www.met. police.uk/history/definition.htm). These sentiments are adopted by modern day policing with the implementation of the National Intelligence Model. Police have a duty to investigate allegations of crime; therefore when a victim of online CSA reports the matter to the police it will be investigated like any other reported crime. However there is an anomaly when Government and Police Forces set their key priorities. Child protection does not feature as a key priority, rather as a secondary issue. Police are inevitably target led and policing priorities will mirror the priorities set by the Home Office. Reactive policing is one method that is currently used by most police forces within England and Wales; however as online CSA is underreported there is no need for specialised units to be created to solely investigate online CSA. Policing Authorities appear to discharge their responsibility by ensuring that specialist units deal primarily with reactive interfamilial investigations. However this has the effect that police forces do not train officers sufficiently to either investigate online CSA, or indeed train enough officers in how to deal with the victims of such crime.

Proactive policing of online CSA

Police forces also have the ability to create specialist units to deal with online CSA; here specialised officers are trained to proactively police the Internet through covert methods of policing. Covert Internet Investigators have been trained to police the Internet by either creating profiles as children on Social Networking Sites to interact with online sex offenders, or to assume the identity of victims who have been groomed. CIIs can also assume the identity of arrested sex offenders to identify further offences, further offenders or further victims. Forces within England and Wales have trained 170 officers in total; however currently only 12 such officers work proactively 12 months of the year as CIIs. This is as a result of policing by statistics. The Internet has provided law enforcement unique opportunities to proactively identify those who abuse or have the potential to abuse children, without waiting for the child victims to come forward. This opportunity gives Law Enforcement Agencies the ability to identify some of the 90 per cent of sex offenders who never come to notice (Tanner, 2009). In proactive online cases law enforcement officers are able to pose as children (using the same pretence often used by online sex offenders), something which cannot be achieved offline. CF and SNS allow for the monitoring of sex offender activity, a task impossible offline. And importantly, there is more likely to be online documentary evidence, a factor that makes prosecution difficult in an offline grooming situation. Furthermore, where evidence takes the form of someone's word against another, often a child's against an adult's, covert policing allows young victims to be saved from the trauma of court appearances.

Proactive reactive policing of online CSA

Proactive reactive policing should be the correct term given to agencies and forces who have the ability to proactively react to allegations and reports of specific crimes; an example would be Specialist Detective departments. This would mean agencies with specially trained law enforcement officers or staff specifically trained to work within a field of crime. Within online CSA this would apply to officers or agents who are able to proactively react to reports of online CSA. Whilst these officers/staff do not proactively police the Internet, these agencies have been created to respond proactively to reports from either law enforcement agencies, victims or the general public. These agencies include the Internet Watch Foundation (IWF), the NSPCC, the Child Exploitation Online Protection Service and Law Enforcement Agencies. These agencies specifically deal with online CSA and assist in the awareness and education of online CSA (www.iwf.org.uk; www.nspcc.org.uk; www. ceop.gov.uk) and victim identification. These agencies can also investigate reports of inappropriate websites. They are created to spend all their time responding to such reports, as well as disclosures by victims of online CSA.

The recognition of proactive reactive policing approaches is the first step to understanding the level and type of policing practice that is currently in use. Presently proactive reactive policing is misconstrued as proactive policing; a misconception which stems from the misinformation that current proactive policing is helping to identify sex offenders, helping to disrupt sex offender rings/groups, or has successfully helped to save child victims from sexual abuse. This misidentification of policing methods is misleading and inaccurate. The correct identification of current policing methods employed identifies these methods as a mix of reactive and proactive reactive policing.

Correct identification of policing methods is important as it indicates what policing methods work and which do not. Academics, law enforcement agencies, and government will be able to understand what precise policing methods can be employed for specific areas of crime (for example, online CSA), despite there being no statistics, in the form of crime statistics, being available.

Conclusion

Child exploitation, in the form of online child sexual abuse, has to be accepted as the epidemic crime it has become. Research has shown that 1:4 children are sexually exploited whilst on the Internet, 84 per cent of

12-year-olds have created SNS, and at present the Internet is just not policed. This research has shown that just because child victims of sexual abuse do not disclose, this does not mean it does not occur, and to sit and wait for reports of abuse is just not an option.

Sex offenders from different continents pose as much a danger to children in the UK should they travel to the UK. This has the implication that whilst countries', legislation will or may vary, the methods of policing should remain constant. Failure to investigate may lead to harm of children; interference to the rights of innocent individuals; and financial penalties against law enforcement agencies. This will also have a wider sociological impact both in the medium and long term by breaking the 'cycle of abuse', reducing dysfunctional behaviour, crime and the mental health issues that ensue. The police cannot do this alone. The Government need to address the issue of policing objectives, making child protection a key policing priority, and providing the necessary resources.

The typologies of Online Child Sex Offenders in all parts of the world remain constant, and can be put into the categories of 'reactive', 'active seeker', 'collector', 'engager', 'abuser', and 'promoter' (Tanner, 2009). The 'engager' and 'abuser' representing the online sex offender that targets, grooms, and engages in sexual contact with child victims, corresponding to more than 30 hours of Internet activity a month. This is far more activity than that of the child abuse material viewer or collector (more than 10 hours), thus making the virtual offender far more active and dangerous to children using the Internet.

The Internet has also shown that Finkelhor's four preconditions of child sexual abuse are still important tools in explaining sex offenders' behaviour. However the Internet has speeded up the whole process. The main idea in Finkelhor's theory is that four preconditions must be met before a man sexually abuses a child (Finkelhor, 1984). First, the potential offender must be motivated to sexually abuse a child (that is, he may feel sexually aroused by children, or feel emotionally close to children, or that his sexual needs are 'blocked' and cannot be met elsewhere). Differences between offenders in combinations of these motivators are hypothesised to account for different offence patterns. Furthermore, the potential offender must unleash his motivation to offend by overcoming the internal or moral restraints blocking his offending (for example, through the use of cognitive distortions or substance abuse). The sex offender must also overcome any external restraints blocking his offending (for example, family members who watch over the child). Finally, he must overcome the child's own resistance to the sexual abuse. Sexual abuse of a child will only occur when all of these steps have been played out in a logical sequence. The Internet allows complete anonymity, quick free accessibility, the opportunity to discuss and confirm feelings, easy access to images of young victims, and real interaction with young children (Cooper et al., 2000). This means that the Internet has facilitated the creation of sex offenders that may not have emerged without the Internet, as one of the preconditions may not have been met.

In September 2006, Vernon Coaker MP, the then minister responsible for this area of criminality described the Child Exploitation and Online Protection Centre as 'continuing to spearhead the Government's ongoing work to protect children from sexual abuse while conducting proactive investigations with the police and authorities around the world' (cited on CEOP website). CEOP's work as the lead organisation, as that of other Law Enforcement Agencies, should really be described as proactive reactive policing, which sees these organisations reacting to reports of abuse from victims or intelligence from agencies around the world (Jewkes and Andrews, 2005). This is the harsh reality and now more than ever there is a requirement for all agencies involved in child protection to dispense with the distinction between 'online' and 'offline', 'real' and 'virtual'. Child abuse is a serious crime that violates the dignity, individual autonomy and health of a child. Children have a right to expect protection from society.

Whilst the size of the World Wide Web is such that law enforcement agencies will never 'police their way' out of online CSA (Russ, 2005) correct policing will allow for an increase in the detection and prosecution of offenders and an increase in awareness, education and understanding of the dangers of the Internet. The Internet was built without a way to know who and what you are connecting to. This limits what can be done with Internet investigations and exposes users to the Internet's growing dangers. If we do nothing, we will face rapidly proliferating episodes of online child sexual abuse and child abuse material that will cumulatively erode public trust in the Internet.

Notes

1 Akendiz 2000 PBBS was a bulletin board with at least 500 users in 1985. It was closed down in 1987 following allegations of paedophilia and sex offender material.
2 Boys and girls aged 11–12.
3 Hilary Benn chair: Home Office Task Force for Child Abuse on the Internet (Spindler Ibid).
4 Her Majesty's Inspectorate of Constabulary, 'Safeguarding Children: The Second Joint Chief Inspectors' Report on Arrangements to Safeguard Children, July 2005. Available at www.safeguardingchildren.org.uk/Safeguarding-Children/2005-report.
5 Victoria Adjo Climbié (2 November 1991–25 February 2000) was abused and murdered by her guardians in London, England, in 2000.
6 Victoria Climbié report. Recommendation 106.
7 The research specifically centred on Social Networking Sites (SNS), Instant Messaging Systems (IMS), Email systems (EM) and Chat Facilities (CF).
8 An emoticon is a short sequence of keyboard letters and symbols, usually emulating a facial expression (smiley), that complements a text message or instant message; they can also be moving images, whether cartoon or real life.
9 Social networking sites contact lists can be created and developed by adding other user details.
10 Report on Wilton Park Conference WPS(04/6) Combating Child Abuse on the Internet: An International Response Monday 22–Wednesday 24 March 2004.
11 Seventeen per cent of all men arrested for Internet-related offences will also turn out to be involved in perpetrating sexual abuse.

12 The Metropolitan Police High Tech Crime Unit was established in 2002 to specifically combat online child pornography images.

References

Akendiz, Y. (2000). 'Child Pornography', *The Internet, Law and Society.* Addison Wesley Longman: London, UK.

Alcock, R. (1954). Police Instruction Book 1969. Gaskiya Corp. UK.

BBC News (2002). Fifth of Children 'are Crime Victims'. Monday 16th September 2002.

Benn, H. (2003). 'Home Office Task Force for Child Abuse on the Internet' in Spindler, P. and MacVean, A. *Policing Paedophiles on the Internet,* London: New Police Bookshop.

Bell, J. (1969). *Doing your research project: A guide for first time researchers,* Bucks: OU Press (p27).

Bourke, M.L. and Hernandez, A.E. (2009). The 'Butner Redux': A Report of the Incidence of Hands-on Child Victimization by Child Pornography Offenders. *Journal of Family Violence,* 24, 183–91.

Bryman, A. (2004). *Social Research Methods.* Oxford: Oxford University Press.

Bulmer, M. (1984). *The Chicago School of Sociology. Institutionalisation, Diversity and the Rise of Sociological Research.* University of Chicago Press: Chicago.

Calder, M. (2003). (ed.) *Child Sexual Abuse and the Internet: Tackling the New Frontier.* Russell House Publishing: Dorset.

Carr, J. (2004). *Child Abuse, Child Pornography and The Internet.* NCH: London.

Cooper, A., McLaughlin, I. P. and Campwell, K. M. (2000). Sexuality in Cyberspace. *Cyber Psychology and Behaviour,* 3, 521–36.

Cooper, A. (2002). 'Cybersex: The dark side of the force,' Special Issue of the *Journal of Sexual Addiction & Compulsivity,* 22, 154–163.

Crowe, N. and Bradford, S. (2006). Hanging out in RuneScape: Identity, Work and Play in the Virtual Playground. *Children's Geographies,* 4 (3), 331–46.

Davidson, J. C. (2002). The Context and Practice of Community Treatment Programmes for Child Sexual Abusers in England and Wales. Department of Social Policy. London, London School of Economics and Political Science: 435.

Davidson, J. and Martellozzo, E. (2004). 'Educating Children about Sexual Abuse and Evaluating the Metropolitan Police Safer Surfing Programme'. http://www.saferschoolpartnerships.org/ssp-topics/evaluations/documents/ssfindingsreport.pdf.

Davidson, J. and Martellozzo, E. (2005). 'Policing the Internet, Protecting Children from Sex Offenders on Line', http://www.oii.ox.ac.uk/research/cybersafety/extensions/pdfs/papers. Accessed on 11th November 2008.

Davidson, J. C. (2008). *Child Sexual Abuse: Media Representations and Government Reactions,* Routledge-Cavendish: London.

Davidson, J. (2007). 'Current research and practice into Internet sex offending,' Risk Management Authority Scotland Report. Available at http://www.rmascotland.gov.uk/ViewFile.aspx?id=235

Davidson, Lorenz, Grove-Hills and Martellozo (2009). 'Evaluation of CEOP Think Uknow Internet Safety Programme & Exploration of Young People's Internet Safety Knowledge.' Centre for Abuse and Trauma Studies, Kingston Univertsity. Available at www.cats-rp.org.uk

Demause (1976). The New Psychohistory, New York: Psychohistory Press. ——(2002). The Emotional Life of Nations. New York: Karnac Books.

Durkin, K. (1997). 'Misuse of the Internet by Paedophiles: Implications for Law Enforcement and Probation Practice', *Federal Probation* 61(2), 14–18.

Edwards, S. (2000). 'Prosecuting Child Pornography: possession and taking of Indecent Photographs of Children'. *Journal of Social Welfare and Family Law*, 22(1), 1–21.

Ferrell, J., Hayward, K. *et al.* (2008). *Cultural Criminology – An Invitation*, London, Sage.

Finkelhor, D. (1984) *Child sexual abuse: new thory and research*. Free Press: New York.

Gans, H.J. (1968). '"The Participant–Observer as Human Being': Observations on the Personal Aspects of Field Work", in H.S. Becker (ed.). *Institutions and the Person*: Papers presented to Everett. C. Hughes (Chicago Aldine).

Gillespie, A. A. (2002). Child Protection on the Internet: Challenges for Criminal Law. *Child and Family Law Quarterly*, 14, 411–25.

Gillespie, A. A. (2004). Tackling Grooming. *The Police Journal*, 77, 239.

Gillespie, A.A. (2008). *Child Exploitation and Communication Technologies*. Russell House Publications.

Gillespie, A. (2009). 'Defining Child Pornography: Challenge for the Law,' Global Symposium on Internet Abuse, North Carolina, April, 21–14.

Gillespie, A. and Upton, A. (2004). Child Pornography: Duty to Look? *ChildRight*, 211, 10–11.

Gold, R. L. (1958). 'Roles in Sociological Field Observation'. *Social Forces* 36: 217–23.

Greer, C. (2003). *Crime and Media. A Reader*. Routledge: London.

Grieve (2003) 'Foreword', Spindler, P. and MacVean, A. *Policing Paedophiles on the Internet*, London: New Police Bookshop.

Hammersley, M. and Atkinson, P. (1995) *Ethnography: Principles in practice*, London: Routledge.

Healy, M. (1996). 'Child pornography: an international perspective', paper for the *World Congress against Commercial Sexual Exploitation of Children*, United States Embassy Stockholm, www.usis.usemb.se/children/csec/child_pornography.html

Hernandez, A. (2000). 'Self-Reported Contact Sexual Offenses by Participants in the Federal Bureau of Prisons', Sex Offender Treatment Program: Implications for Internet Sex Offenders. Poster session presented at the 19th Annual Research and Treatment Conference of the Association for the Treatment of Sexual Abusers, San Diego, CA.

Hernandez, A. (2009). Psychological and Behavioural Characteristics of Child Pornography Offenders in Treatment. Global Symposium, University of North Carolina, Chapel Hill.

Home Office (2002). Protecting the Public: Strengthening Protection against Sex Offenders and Reforming the Law on Sexual Offences. Published by the Home Office.

Home Office (2003). Sexual Offences Act. Retrieved from website http://www.opsi.gov.uk/ACTS/acts2003/20030042.htm

Home Office (2006). Consultation on The Draft Code of Practice for the Investigation of Protected Electronic Information. Home Office: London.

Jewkes, Y. and Andrews, C. (2005). Policing the Filth: The Problems of Investigating Online Child Pornography in England and Wales. *Policing and Society* 15 (1), 2005, 42–62.

Martellozzo, E. (forthcoming). Metropolitan Police Practice: Protecting Children Online. Exploring the work of the High Technological Crime Unit. University of Kingston, PhD Thesis.

Miles, M.B. and Huberman, A.M. (1994). *Qualitative Data Analysis, An Expanded Sourcebook*. Thousand Oaks, CA, Sage.

NCH (John Carr). (2003). *Child Abuse, Child Pornography and the Internet*. NCH: London.

O'Connell, R. (2003). A Typology of Child Cybersexploitation and Online Grooming Practices (.pdf 161 KB), Rachel O'Connell, Cyberspace Research Unit, University of Central Lancashire, 17 July 2003, 5, 2, 11.

Ofcom (2009) 'Digital lifestyles: Young adults aged 16–24' May 11–25. Available at http://www.ofcom.org.uk/advice/media_literacy/medlitpub/medlipubrss/digital-young/

Quayle, E. (2003). The Impact of Viewing Offending Behaviour. In Calder, M. (ed.) *Child Sexual Abuse and the Internet*. Russell House Publishing: Dorset.

Quayle, E. and Taylor, M. (2003). Model of Problematic Internet Use in People with a Sexual Interest in Children. *Cyber Psychology & Behaviour*. 6(1), 93–106.

Robson, C. (2002). *Real World Research*. Blackwell Publishing: Oxford.

Russ, B. (2005). ICAC's Approach to Child Exploitation, Crimes Against Children Conference, York, 2005.

Sandberg, G. and Marlatt, G. (1989). Relapse Fantasies. In D. R. Laws (ed.) *Relapse Prevention with Sex Offenders*. Basic Books: New York.

Sanderson, C. (2004). *The Seduction of Children*, Jessica Kingsley: London.

Seto, M. (2009). 'Assessing the risk posed by child pornography offenders', Global Symposium: Examining the relationship between online offenses and preventing the sexual exploitation of children. April 5–7.

Seto, M. C. and Eke, A.W. (2005). 'The future offending of child pornography offenders', *Sexual Abuse: A Journal of Research and Treatment*, 17, 201–210.

Seto, M.C., Castor, J.M. and Blanchard, R. (2006). 'Child pornography offenses are a valid diagnostic indicator of paedophilia,' *Journal of Abnormal Psychology*, 115, 610–615.

Soothill, K. and Walby, S. (1991). *Sex Crime in the News*, Routledge: London.

Sullivan, J. and Beech, A. R. (2003). Are Collectors of Child Abuse Images a Risk to Children? In A. MacVean and P. Spindler (eds), *Policing Paedophiles on the Internet*. The New Police Bookshop: London. pp. 11–20.

Sumner, M. (2006). Ethics. The Sage Dictionary of Social Research Methods. V. Jupp. London, Sage.

Tanner, J. (2009). Inside the Mind of Sex offenders, 21st Crimes Against Children Conference, Dallas, 2009.

Taylor, J. (2009). Grooming in the 21st Century, Crimes Against Children Conference, Dallas, 2009.

The National Intelligence Model – Providing A Model For Policing; By April 2004, all forces in England and Wales were required to officially adopt the model to a set of agreed minimum standards. Codes of Practice came into effect 12th January 2005.

Us Dpt of Justice (1986) 'Report of the Attorney General's Commission on Pornography'.

Van Maanen, J. (1996). Ethnography. In: A. Kuper and J. Kuper (eds) *The Social Science Encyclopaedia*, 2nd edn. Routledge: London. pp. 263–65

Webster, S., Davidson, J., Bifulco, A., Pham, T. and Careffi, V. (2009) 'European Online Grooming Project: Progress Report Covering Period: 1 June 2009–31 December 2009' (7/2010 forthcoming at http://www.natcen.ac.uk/study/european-online-grooming-research).

Williams, K. (2004). 'Child Pornography Law: Does it Protect children?' *Journal of Social Welfare and Famly Law*, 26(3).

Wolak, J., Finkelhor, D. and Mitchell, K.J. (2005). Child-Pornography Possessors Arrested in Internet-Related Crimes: Findings from the National Juvenile Online Victimization Study. National Centre for Missing and Exploited Children. Alexandria, VA.

Wyre, R. (1996). 'The Mind of the Paedophile'. In P. Bibby (ed.) *Organised Abuse: The Current Debate.* Basingstoke Arena.

Ybarra, M. and Mitchell, K. (2008). How Risky Are Social Networking Sites? A Comparison of Places Online Where Youth Sexual Solicitation and Harassment Occurs. *Paediatrics* 121(2), 350–57.

Young, K. (2008). 'Understanding Sexually Deviant Online Behaviour from an Addiction Perspective'. *International Journal of Cyber Criminology,* 2, 298–307.

Internet Sites:

http://www.nspcc.org.uk/Inform/factsandfigures/topics/definition_of_a_child_wda59396.html

http://news.bbc.co.uk/1/hi/business/4502550.stm Social Networking

http://police.homeoffice.gov.uk/operational-policing/crime-disorder/child-protection-task force (accessed on 12th June 2009)

www.aic.gov.au (accessed on 12th Jan 2009)

http://www.statistics.gov.uk/CCI/nugget.asp?ID=8 (accessed on 9th Sept 2009)

http://www.direct.gov.uk/en/Nl1/Newsroom/DG_073380 (accessed on 10th Dec 2008)

R v *Toby Studamaker.* (http://www.dailymail.co.uk/news/article-300465/Marine-jailed-grooming-girl.html0

Home Office. http://www.opsi.gov.uk/ACTS/acts2003/20030042.htm

NSPCC. http://www.nspcc.org.uk

http://www.raywyre.com

http://www.saferschoolpartnerships.org/ssp-

Action for Children. http://www.actionforchildren.org.uk

http://www.direct.gov.uk/en/Nl1/Newsroom/DG_073380

http://www.statistics.gov.uk/CCI/nugget.asp?ID=8

http://www.ofcom.org.uk/advice/media_literacy/medlitpub/medlitpubrss/socialnetworking/report.pdf

http://police.homeoffice.gov.uk/operational-policing/crime-disorder/child-protection-task force

http://news.bbc.co.uk/1/hi/business/4502550.stm

http://www.oii.ox.ac.uk/research/cybersafety/extensions/pdfs/papers

http://newsvote.bbc.co.uk/mpapps/pagetools/print/news.bbc.co.uk/1/hi/programmes/click_online/6897121.stm

http://schools.becta.org.uk/#ofcom

http://news.zdnet.co.uk/news/2001/8/ns-21279.html

http://news.zdnet.co.uk/emergingtech/0,1000000183,2086096,00.htm

http://www.childnet-int.org/downloads/online-grooming.pdf

http://www.ceop.gov.uk/mediacentre/pressreleases/2006/ceop_24042006.asp)

http://www.childnet-int.org/downloads/online-grooming.pdf

http://www.ceop.gov.uk/mediacentre/pressreleases/2007/ceop-20062007.asp

Chapter 7

Assessment and treatment approaches with online sexual offenders

Matt O'Brien and Stephen Webster

Introduction

Given the dramatic increase in the accessibility of the Internet, especially during the last decade, mental health professionals have had to begin to face the challenge of assessing and treating sexual offenders who have used the Internet to facilitate or commit their sexual offences. Child abuse images and sexual abuse are not, of course, new problems, but the increasingly sophisticated computing technology and the advent of the Internet have both eased the production and hastened the distribution of child abuse images, while also facilitating communication between perpetrators and potential victims (Klain, Davies, and Hicks, 2001; Quayle and Taylor, 2002; Wortley and Smallbone, 2006). Despite this, as Seto and Eke (2005) and Armstrong (2009) concede, relatively little is known about the characteristics, and hence treatment needs, of individuals who commit such offences. As Laulik, Allam, and Sheridan (2007) reason, many of the existing studies of online offenders have tended to focus on their behavioural characteristics (Taylor, Quayle, and Holland, 2001) and motivational typologies (Sullivan and Beech, 2004), rather than the psychological functioning of this population, and hence are somewhat limited in the extent to which they can inform robust assessment models and treatment design.

This chapter comprises two discrete sections that describe methods that contribute to the comprehensive assessment and treatment of online sexual offenders. It begins by describing key ethical considerations when conducting assessments within a relatively new area of practice, before setting out the advantages of a collaborative model of assessor and offender working. The chapter will then set out ways in which a robust assessment of risk and need may be conducted, by triangulating information sources from static and dynamic risk instruments alongside psychometric information. The assessment section concludes by outlining future directions and key assessment questions for the field. The second half of the chapter then turns its focus toward treatment responses.

Online sexual offending is a term that can be applied to a diverse range of different attitiudes and behaviours. In keeping with earlier chapters, our definition of online sexual offending encompasses not only the viewing, production and/or distribution of indecent images of children, but also 'online grooming'. As discussed by Davidson in Chapter 1, online grooming involves the process of socialisation during which an offender interacts with a child in order to prepare him/her for sexual abuse (Sexual Offences Act 2003 – Article 15).

It is important to point out that the majority of literature to date has focused on men who access indecent images of children. However, recent research (Webster, Davidson, Bifulco, Gottschalk, Caretti, Pham, and Grove-Hills, 2010) indicates that indecent image use and online grooming are not mutually exclusive behaviours. Therefore, whilst acknowledging the dearth of evidence regarding men who use the Internet to contact and groom children, we feel that a comprehensive review of assessment and treatment processes for online sexual offenders should also encompass those who groom.

Chapters within this volume (that is, Gottschalk; Martellozzo; Taylor) have described the range of cognitions and behaviours associated with online sexual offenders. In this chapter we outline comprehensive assessment and treatment responses. Although presented separately for conceptual clarity, it is important to note that assessment and treatment are not mutually exclusive concepts in practice. Rather information drawn from initial assessments should underpin treatment approaches, with subsequent information gathered from treatment interventions used to update early dynamic assessments.

Assessing online sexual offenders: ethical challenges

Since the early 1970s researchers and clinicians have developed a comprehensive body of knowledge regarding contact sexual offending (Laws and Marshall, 2003a; Laws and Marshall 2003b). Consequently, a *what works* evidence base has developed that allows practitioners to conduct robust and ethical assessments of contact sexual offenders with confidence. This is in sharp contrast to the position with online sexual offenders. Our work (O'Brien and Webster, 2007) alongside that of authors within this volume and law enforcement agencies demonstrates that individuals and groups have quickly identified the Internet as a medium to exploit in order to conduct sexual offences. As such, there is acute pressure from policy makers, practitioners, parents and young people to develop robust assessment responses to the challenges presented by online sexual offenders.

We would argue that although understandable, this demand for assessment developments presents significant ethical challenges and dilemmas for researchers, and treatment providers. Clearly, the vast number of indecent images of children on the Internet, alongside the amount of young people that report risky behaviours after receiving online contact from strangers, makes a compelling case for immediate assessment action. For example, the National Society for the Prevention of Cruelty to Children (NSPCC) estimate that approximately 20,000 indecent images of children are placed on the Internet each week (NSPCC, 2005). In addition, Davidson, Lorenz, Grove-Hills and Martellozzo (2009) conducted an online survey of 11–16-year-olds and report that following online contact from a stranger, 37 per cent had shared an email address; 34 per cent provided information about the school they attended; 23 per cent provided a mobile number; and 26 per cent a personal photograph.

However, despite this acute need for assessment tools to be valid, reliable and defendable, they must be developed according to best practice principles (APA, 2009). This means that items within instruments need to be piloted, refined, re-tested and cross-validated on a range of samples. Developing assessment instruments this way can take a number of years and herein lays the ethical dilemma with regard to the assessment of online sexual offenders. That is, the clamour for any information means that policy makers and those working with sexual offenders do not feel that they have the necessary time to wait for reliable and valid assessments to be developed. Consequently, with the best intentions, researchers and practitioners have adjusted or directly mapped assessments developed and validated on contact or offline sexual offenders to those offending online. Although understandable in the context of the risk presented by online offenders, we believe that this practice is unethical in that practitioners may be making judgements about behaviours for which the tool was not developed. In turn, using assessments not validated on the population of interest means that judgements and subsequent actions may not be legally defensible (Wilkerson and Lang, 2003). Finally, the cornerstone of engaging individuals in the assessment process is a collaborative process using credible methods. Assessments that have not been validated or are seen not to reflect the individual's offending circumstances may lack credibility in the eyes of the online offender and may cause resentment regarding actions or sanctions taken. In turn this may disengage the individual from treatment interventions. Therefore, the risk of future harm to children and young people may in fact be raised by using inappropriate assessment methods.

Researchers and clinicians have a scientific and public safety responsibility to adhere to best practice assessment with online sexual offenders. Therefore, this chapter only discusses instruments that have an evidence base within online environments. Before turning to the range of instruments and tools available, the next section of this chapter describes the foundation of effective assessment process – collaboration.

Collaborative assessments and readiness

Conducting a collaborative assessment means to *work with* the online offender to explore their context, risk and needs, not the offender and assessor working against each other. The emphasis and impact of collaborative approaches to the assessment of sexual offenders is well documented in the literature (Beech and Hamilton-Giachritsis, 2005; Marshall, Ward, Mann, Moulden, Fernandez, Serran, and Marshall, 2005; Shingler and Mann, 2006) where aggressive and confrontational styles of questioning are no longer viewed as effective.

In the previous section we have argued for the use of methods with an online evidence base. The work of Martellozzo described in an earlier chapter indicates that her sample of online groomers had low self-esteem and a general lack of self-efficacy. In addition, our earlier work (O'Brien and Webster, 2007) has shown that indecent image users had unhelpful self-management styles that involved 'feeling good when looking at indecent images of children' and that 'my life is better when I view indecent images on the Internet'. Despite the denial of offence that may prevail in some online offenders' assessment presentation, they can be in little doubt that society finds their behaviours abhorrent. Therefore, taking the negative social view of online offending together with an unhelpful social functioning style, it is not unreasonable to think that like other sexual offenders, online offenders will not respond well to aggressive assessment. Instead, collaborative assessment provides the online offender with the opportunity to engage with the assessment process and therefore begin the process of ownership of their actions and a responsibility to change. Collaborative assessment also removes from online sexual offenders' reasons to be defensive, a trait that was discussed by police officers when discussing offender interviews in ongoing research exploring the process of online grooming (Webster *et al.*, 2009).

Alongside using assessment tools that have an evidence base, practitioners also have a responsibility to assess online offenders using the most effective methods. Collaborative approaches that use open, Socratic questioning techniques help gather the most comprehensive picture of an individual's attitudes and behaviours. This not only assists public protection services but may also set the offender toward recognition that they can lead a *good life* (Ward and Stewart, 2003).

In addition to a collaborative process, practitioners should also be mindful of the timing of assessment and the bearing that this can have on information disclosure. For example, when online offenders are assessed soon after initial arrest they may be at their most defensive and anxious, mindful that decisions regarding their ongoing management will be associated with the nature and extent of their disclosure. Consequently, the information provided at these early assessments may contrast sharply with the account given by an online offender in a treatment context. Here, these offenders have had longer to come to terms with their situation and be open and honest about their attitudes and behaviours. Effective assessment therefore is not a static process but rather one that should be updated throughout the offender's contact with professionals, as the individual becomes more (or sometimes less) open and honest about their lifestyle.

Having described the ethical and practice considerations associated with online offender assessment the next section of this chapter shall outline the instruments available to practitioners.

Assessment methods

Evidence presented in this book, as well as our previous work (O'Brien and Webster, 2007), indicates that online sexual offending is complex and multi-dimensional. This position is further validated by our current work exploring the process of online grooming (Webster *et al.*, 2009). On the basis of this work we are proposing a model of online grooming that has been developed from the interview accounts of practitioners and professionals working with online groomers. Unlike the model proposed by Gottschalk in Chapter 4 it is important to note that movement through different stages of this model of online grooming is neither unitary nor linear, but rather, cyclical, involving a pattern of adoption, maintenance, relapse, and re-adoption over time. Additionally, the actual process of online grooming may take minutes, hours, days or months. As such, online groomers remain at different phases of the model for various lengths of time according to a dynamic inter-relationship between their goals and needs and the style or reactions of the young person. Dashed lines within the model indicate associations that are uncertain, whereas strong lines show relationships that stakeholders felt were evident on the basis of their experience of working with online groomers or young people.

It is clear therefore that the complexity of the online sexual offence process indicates that one assessment method will not capture all aspects of the behaviour and the features underpinning it. Therefore, for assessments to be effective, it is important for professionals to triangulate material drawn from a number of instruments and methods, an approach that has been described as effective in the assessment of contact sexual offending (Webster and Marshall, 2004).

In the sections below we set out assessment tools that will help provide a comprehensive understanding of an individual's needs. These encompass: social history, psychological and sexual functioning; static and dynamic risk; classification of images; cognitive distortions and online offence behaviours; and physiological assessments.

Social history and psychological functioning

A key aspect of the assessment process requires the assessor to look beyond the circumstances of the individual's offending and explore the broader context of their life. This helps the individual start to discuss and identify patterns to their behaviour and provides the assessor with key information to feed into the treatment process. Social history assessments should therefore explore family and childhood history, abuse/trauma history, sexual history, educational/occupational history and social/relational history.

In addition to social history data, psychiatric/psychological functioning should also be explored. Psychiatric illness is prevalent with all offending populations including online sexual offenders (Webb *et al.*, 2007). In a study comparing the characteristics of 210 online offenders with child offenders in the UK, Webb and colleagues reported that a significantly higher number of online offenders had been in contact with mental health services as adults. Consequently, assessors should consider utilising standardised semi-structured interviews for psychiatric illness and personality disorder such as the *Structured Clinical Interview for DSM-IV personality disorders*. Psychopathy is particularly prevalent in some offender groups and this can also have a negative bearing on sexual offenders' treatment process (Webster, 2005). In the comparison of online offenders and contact sexual offenders, Webb *et al.* (2007) reported the Internet offender groups scoring higher on some items on the *Psychopathy Checklist-Revised* (PCL-R; Hare, 1991). Assessors should therefore consider complementing psychiatric assessments with the PCL-R. This semi-structured interview instrument has impressive psychometric properties and has been cross-validated on sexual offender populations (Hanson and Morton-Bourgon, 2005). It is important to note that each of these instruments have stringent user qualifications.

Given the amount of time online sexual offenders disclose spending on the Internet and the bearing that this can have on their life (O'Brien and Webster, 2007) we suggest that assessors should also focus on problematic Internet use. However, there are few relevant instruments that have undergone any form of psychometric evaluation. One exception to this is the Internet Sex Screening Test (ISST; Delmonico, 1999). The ISST contains 34 items split into eight sub-scales: online sexual compulsivity, online sexual behaviour – social; online sexual behaviour – isolated; online sexual spending; interest in online sexual behaviour; non-home use of the computer; illegal sexual use of the computer; and online sexual compulsivity. Although Delmonico and Miller (2003) report only moderate internal consistency for these factors, Delmonico and Griffin (2008) are currently developing a revised ISST that is currently undergoing thorough psychometric evaluation.

Indecent image content

The sheer range and number of abusive images of children on the Internet makes it important for assessors to adopt a standardised classification system as advocated by Carr and Hilton in Chapter 3. For example, we (O'Brien and Webster, 2007) reported an average of 5,000 images seized from the computers of our sample of online offenders. In a seminal paper, Taylor, Holland and Quayle (2001) presented the COPINE scale, a ten level classification system. Level 1 images represent non-erotic pictures of children in their underwear, with Level 10 images depicting sadism or bestiality acts against children. Quayle (2008) reports that the COPINE scale has since been collapsed by sentencing authorities to five levels and is likely to be revised further in the near future.

Static and dynamic risk

The literature concerning sexual and violent offenders' risk has expanded its focus from static risk prediction (historical factors shown to be statistically predictive of future sexual and violent offending) to the nature of dynamic risk factors (Thornton, 2002). In a recent paper, Hanson et al. (2007) classify dynamic risk factors as either Stable (learned behaviours and personal skills/ self-management problems) or Acute (factors than last only hours or days) and are shown to be predictive of imminent sexual offending. There are three benefits of adopting the Hanson et al. (2007) Stable/Acute classification of dynamic risk factors. First, they can help identify targets for intervention that, if changed, will have the effect of reducing the likelihood of recidivism; second, they can help identify whether a sexual offender is making mean- ingful progress against set treatment targets; and third they help supervising officers monitor the risk presented by sexual offenders in the community.

Due to the relatively new nature of online sexual offending, there are only a few studies that have attempted to validate static or dynamic instruments developed for contact sexual offenders with online offender populations. These studies have shown that statistically, online offenders do not appear to have high rates of recidivism either for online, or offline, offences (Seto and Eke, 2005).

Taking static risk prediction instruments first, Middleton et al. (2006) suggest that Risk Matrix 2000 (Thornton et al., 2003) may be a useful measure of risk in online offenders in the UK even though this type of offender was not represented in the original validation 2-year and 19-year follow-up sam- ples. In the original scoring of RM2000, being a non-contact offender is an 'aggravating factor' item in this schedule. Another 'aggravating factor' is whether victims are strangers (which, by definition, most of the people in the images that this type of offender looks at are). In the scoring of RM2000 the presence of two aggravating factors puts the individual up by one risk level (that is from low to medium level). Osborn and Beech (2006) report a revised version of RM2000 where these two items were omitted, this provided a more realistic level of risk for repeat offending in this group. Osborn and Beech also observe that only a small number of those offenders who were considered high-risk on the RM2000/S collected images in the highest severity category (Level 5: Sentencing Advisory Panel [SAP], 2002). This result suggests that the severity of images viewed does not appear to relate to risk of re-offending; a very pertinent finding as the severity of image is often considered a primary factor in sentencing decisions (for example, SAP, 2002). Given the dearth of evidence supporting the use of static prediction tools with online offenders, the need for further validations with existing instruments, or the development of new tools, is pressing.

Regarding tools to explore dynamic factors, the instrument that has shown the most promise is the Stable and Acute 07 (hereafter S & A) (Hanson *et al.*, 2007). The S & A provides a structured method for identifying and measuring dynamic risk factors that are predictive of sexual and violent recidivism. Comprised of two separate but related scales, S & A consists of an initial assessment of Stable items and subsequent follow-up assessment of Acute items. The Stable consists of 13 items. Each Stable item is rated as either zero, one or two where zero is low and two is high risk, to give a total score out of 26 for offenders with child victims or 24 for offenders with adult victims. The Acute consists of four items that provide a score for *Sex/violence* and three items that are scored and added to the S*ex/violence* score to provide an overall risk of recidivism. Each item can be scored between 0 and 2 as above. Despite some evidence that S & A is predictive of both sexual and violent recidivism and that trained supervising officers can reliably use the instrument (Hanson *et al.*, 2007; Fernandez, 2008), supporting studies have been developed using contact sexual offenders. However, in a recent paper, McNaughton-Nicholls and colleagues (2009) evaluated implementation of the S & A pilot across Police forces and Probation areas in England and Wales. McNaughton-Nicholls and colleagues report that when frontline officers considered the efficacy of S & A with online offenders it was felt that the risk factors explored using the S & A had clear relevance for this group. It is important to note, however, that this research did not evaluate the efficacy of the tool with online offenders and so, as with static assessments, the need for outcome evaluations of dynamic tools is urgent.

Cognitive and behavioural functioning

The use of cognitive distortions by contact sexual offenders to justify their behaviour to themselves and others is well documented in the literature (Marshall, Anderson & Fernandez, 1999). Consequently, there are a range of well-validated instruments to assess the nature and extent of distortions amongst both child molesters and rapists (Bumby, 1996; Arkowitz and Vess, 2003; Nicholls and Molinder, 1984). Regarding the position with online offenders, interestingly Middleton *et al.* (2006) did not report high levels of cognitive distortions or emotional congruence with children amongst their sample. This, however, may be a function of the assessment instruments used and in some way speaks to our ethical challenges argument presented earlier in the chapter. That is, Middleton and colleagues evaluated the presence of distortions amongst online offenders using psychometric tools with items developed for and validated on contact sexual offenders. It is perhaps unsurprising then that the Middleton *et al.* results do not support the existence of distortions that are clearly evident in work described throughout this volume.

However, when instruments are used that had items that were developed for and tested on online offenders, the position is very different. For example, in 2005, we (O'Brien and Webster, 2007) developed and validated the Internet Behaviours and Attitudes Questionnaire (IBAQ). The IBAQ was developed and piloted on a prison and community sample of 163 men convicted of the collection, distribution and/or development of indecent images of children. It contains 42 items about offenders' online behaviours and 34 items that measure online offenders' attitudes. Behaviour items are scored on a dichotomous yes/no scale whereas the attitude items are scored on a 5-point Likert scale (response anchors were: 5 = strongly agree; 4 = agree; 3 = neither agree nor disagree; 2 = disagree; and 1 = strongly disagree).

The 34 attitude items are organised into two factors. The first factor contains 16 items that measure distorted thinking (for example, 'The child was often smiling in the child pornography I have looked at, and so I believe that the child is not being harmed'). The second factor contains 18 items and measures online offenders' self-management (for example, 'I feel more confident on the Internet than I do talking to people in real life'). The internal consistency of the 34-item IBAQ was 0.93, with alphas of 0.92 and 0.89 for the Distorted Thinking and Self-Management factors respectively. These results therefore indicate an excellent level of internal consistency for the IBAQ (Nunnaly, 1978).

Alongside the reliability of the measure, its validity was also assessed. First concurrent validity (the degree to which the scores on the IBAQ are related to the scores on another, already established, test administered at the same time) was explored. Here the *Paulhus Deception Scales: Balanced Inventory of Desirable Responding (BIDR)* (Paulhus, 1984) was administered alongside the IBAQ. The BIDR is a 40-item self-report questionnaire that measures the tendency to give socially desirable responses. The BIDR was key to the validation of the IBAQ, as self-report assessment increases the chances of online offenders second-guessing test items and 'faking good' by answering in a more socially acceptable manner (Hammond, 2004). Reassuringly, the IBAQ factors and total score were not influenced by socially desirable responding.

In addition, the criterion validity (how well the IBAQ predicts an outcome based on information from other variables or information sources) was assessed. Here scores on the IBAQ were correlated with participants' previous convictions, and showed that a number of significant positive correlations existed between the two data sources.

Finally, discriminate validity (the extent that IBAQ scores distinguish between different groups of online offenders) was assessed. To this end, participants were assigned to one of two groups based on the number of 'Internet behaviours' they disclosed in the first 42 questions of the IBAQ. The rationale here was to explore the difference in Internet offending attitudes according to the number of actual behaviours disclosed. Encouragingly, the

IBAQ demonstrated strong discriminate validity, whereby those participants who disclosed the greater number of 'Internet behaviours' had significantly higher scores on the Distorted Attitudes and Self Management scales.

We argue that these encouraging preliminary data demonstrate the potential of the IBAQ to assess the attitudes and behaviours of online offenders. The instrument can be used free of charge and is currently being administered by professionals working with online offenders in countries such as the United Kingdom, the Netherlands, the United States, Canada, Australia and New Zealand. However, to further increase confidence in the tool, additional validations are required, such as the ability of the IBAQ to predict re-offending.

The final two behavioural assessments that have shown to have utility in the assessment of online offenders are the penile plethysmograph (PPG) and the polygraph. Turning to the PPG first, research by Seto *et al.* (2006) has suggested that indecent images of children offences are a powerful diagnostic indicator for deviant sexual interest in men. That is, indecent image offenders were almost three times more likely to be identified as having a paedophilic phallometric pattern of sexual arousal than contact child molesters.

Regarding the polygraph, recent research by Robilotta and colleagues (2008) and Buschman and colleagues (2009) indicates that the polygraph does provide additional data from online offenders convicted of possessing indecent images. Therefore both these research groups advocate the use of the polygraph to contribute to a holistic risk and treatment assessment. However, the evidence regarding the reliability and validity of the polygraph is far from robust (Iacono and Lykken, 1997). In addition, at the beginning of this chapter we advocate a collaborative assessment model for online sexual offenders. We suggest that a polygraph examination can have an unhelpful bearing on collaborative assessment and the subsequent therapeutic relationship. In addition there is evidence that the elicitation of a full offence disclosure need not be a necessary treatment target given that providing such a disclosure is unrelated to recidivism (Hanson and Harris, 2001).

Future directions

The first section of the chapter has set out various assessment methods that may be used effectively with online sexual offenders. However, there is much still to be done to enhance the body of knowledge. Specifically, little is known about the potential crossover between offline and online sexual offending but it seems sensible to suggest that the hypothesis should not be dismissed. This then will present further challenges for professionals in order to construct ethical and credible assessment models.

The remainder of the chapter will now focus on treatment approaches with online offenders. Here, we first review current understanding of the treatment needs of online offenders, and then discuss the current psychological treatment strategies, both tailor-made and adapted. The chapter concludes with a brief review of online support for online offenders, preventative strategies, and the consideration of strategies which are being used to address more general problematic Internet usage. It will be seen that the field is progressing from the time when Buttell and Carney (2001) stated that there was little information on whether treatment programmes were addressing the issue of online offenders.

Treatment targets for online sexual offenders

An increasing number of studies have sought to consider the possible differences between contact sexual offenders and online offenders with the apparent aim of helping to determine specific treatment targets that might need to be addressed with the latter group. For example, Rooney (2003) explored personality differences between 15 contact and 15 online offenders. He identified subtle personality differences between these groups and found that, in comparison to contact sexual offenders, online offenders were more open to fantasy, focused more on their inner world and emotional life, and demonstrated higher levels of obsessional and compulsive behaviour than contact sexual offenders.

Elliott, Beech, Mandeville-Norden and Hayes (2009) compared a sample of 505 online offenders and 526 contact sexual offenders on a range of psychological measures. These authors found that online offenders could be successfully discriminated from contact sexual offenders on seven out of 15 measures. Contact sexual offenders were found to have significantly more victim empathy distortions and cognitive distortions than online offenders. This was seen as positive and suggested to the authors that online offenders may be unlikely to be persistent offenders who progress to commit future contact sexual offences. Online offenders were found to have increased scores on scales of fantasy, under-assertiveness, and motor impulsivity. Sheldon and Howitt (2007) also reported that online offenders engage in more fantasy than contact sexual offenders. Elliott and colleagues (2009) concluded that in terms of socio-affective measures online offenders did not differ significantly from contact sexual offenders, and that the differences between them appeared to be more in offence-related measures. Their treatment recommendation was that programmes which focus on factors relating to social adequacy and negative mood states may prove particularly successful.

In their study, Bates and Metcalf (2007) found that online offenders scored a higher level of deviancy from the norm than did contact sexual offenders. They found that the Internet group had fewer self-esteem deficits and a much more internal locus of control. Delmonico and Griffin (2009) have suggested that there is a need for practitioners to spend time working to improve the emotional intelligence of online offenders, as this could be a key to why such offenders appear to be unable to deal with negative emotions. Burgess, Mahoney, Visk, and Morgenbesser (2008) hypothesised that the reasons for such offenders engaging in these behaviours include: stress relief, problem distraction, loneliness, paraphilic interest in children, and other mental health issues.

Malesky and Ennis (2004) investigated evidence of distorted cognitions that were supportive of sexually abusive behaviour on a pro-paedophile Internet message board. They found that individuals who posted used a diverse range of distorted cognitions, commonly romanticising their relationships with children and idealising children. Our work (Webster *et al.*, 2009) also provides support for the use of online forms by communities of sexual offenders. Malesky and Ennis suggested that participation in such message boards might give offenders a sense of membership and community that is lacking in other aspects of their lives. As a result they recommended that a goal of treatment for online offenders should be developing and strengthening real-life pro-social adult relationships.

Bowlby (1988) defined attachment as 'any form of behaviour that results in a person attaining or maintaining proximity to some other clearly identified individual who is conceived as better able to cope with the world' (p.27). Armstrong's (2009) study found that online offenders reported significantly less secure attachment than both non-offenders and matched child and adult contact sexual offenders. Both the online offenders, and a group convicted of these offences plus a contact sexual offence, reported having a significantly more fearful attachment style than non-offenders. The online offenders also reported a more negative view of self than the non-offenders and both the matched sexual offender groups. The online offenders reported more social avoidance and distress than non-offenders.

Middleton *et al.* (2006) tested the applicability of Ward and Siegert's (2002) Pathway model of sexual offending on 72 online offenders drawn from a community sample in England and Wales. Of those men who could be assigned to the pathways (and it is worth noting that over half of the sample could not be assigned to any of the five pathways), the majority were in either the emotional dysregulation pathway (33 per cent) or the intimacy deficits pathway (35 per cent). Middleton and colleagues hypothesised that the emotional dysregulation pathway group may experience strong negative mood states that result in a lack of control, which, in conjunction with sexual desire, can lead those individuals to seek contact with children to meet their sexual needs; that is, accessing the images to alleviate negative emotions and to increase pleasurable feelings. The authors concluded that the intimacy deficits pathway group may be attracted to the Internet at times of loneliness and dissatisfaction given their low estimates of how effective they would be in initiating and maintaining intimacy in appropriate adult relationships; that is, accessing the images to avoid the likelihood, as they see it, of failing in potential appropriate relationships. It should again be noted that a high number of the sample could not be assigned in a separate study. In addition, Connolly (2004) actually had difficulty in allocating contact sexual offenders to Ward and Siegert's model.

Support for Middleton *et al.*'s findings comes, however, from Laulik, Allam, and Sheridan (2007), who found that there were significant differences between online offenders and a normative population in both interpersonal functioning and affective difficulties. This study also found higher than usual levels of depression among the sample of online offenders. This finding supports Morahan-Martin and Schumacher's (2000) assertion that viewing indecent images of children may be used as a mechanism to escape, albeit temporarily, from negative mood states. Middleton *et al.* (2006) suggest that the findings of their study indicate that at least some online offenders display psychological deficits similar to those of contact sexual offenders, and suggest that successful programmes for online offenders will be ones which help them to overcome intimacy deficits and help them to acquire skills to deal more appropriately with negative effect.

A recent review paper presented by Shaw and Imhof (2009) set out the following likely necessary treatment considerations for online offenders: deviant sexual arousal/fantasy, offence history, supporting cognitive distortions, empathy deficits, obsessive compulsive disorders, personality disorders, mood disorders, adjustment disorders, low self-esteem, social withdrawal/isolation, specific social skills deficits, and unresolved childhood sexual trauma.

As we have argued earlier in the chapter, caution must be applied to a number of the studies cited, for as Middleton *et al.* (2006) point out, many of the measures used to indicate dysfunctional mechanisms have not actually been tested for validity or reliability with an Internet offender population. It is also important to note that many of the findings can only be described as indicative given that samples are in some cases too small to allow the formation of definitive conclusions. In addition to this, the previously cited study conducted by Bates and Metcalf (2007) found online offenders to have higher impression management tendencies than contact sexual offenders, a consequence of which may be that their responses are less reliable.

As Sheldon and Howitt (2007) discuss, we must be very cautious about making changes to clinical practice based on emerging findings about online offenders. For instance, while it may be that Internet and contact sexual offenders differ in certain regards, similarities remain. What may differ is the degree to which a problem is present, rather than whether it is or is not present. Sheldon and Howitt state: 'what is abundantly clear is that online offenders are psychologically very similar to contact pedophiles' (p.253). Important similarities that Sheldon and Howitt discuss include sexual interests, cognitive distortions, circumstances that preceded offending, and poor coping with stressful situations. According to these authors, both groups of offenders report similar adverse upbringings and have sexualised backgrounds that may result in them developing sexual scripts involving inappropriate partners.

While highlighting some apparent differences, many of the studies cited above identify broadly similar treatment areas for both contact and Internet offender groups. Where differences were found our clinical observations suggest that those issues that have been found to be likely treatment needs for online offenders are also relatively frequent treatment areas for a number of contact sexual offenders. This underscores the need for the individualised assessment and flexible treatment of all offenders.

A number of other studies have also found strong similarities in the likely treatment targets between contact sexual offenders and online offenders. For example, one of the main findings of the study by Webb, Craissati and Keen (2007) were the notable similarities in socio-affective characteristics between 90 online offenders and 120 matched child molesters. According to the authors, the profiles of both online offenders and child molesters suggested that they tended to be individuals who either retreat from adult interpersonal and social situations (sometimes fearing rejection and cutting themselves off emotionally), or individuals who place excessive reliance on their relationships with others in order to cope. Both groups reported high levels of anxiety, while online offenders had more problems with sexual self-regulation. The work of Webb *et al.* (2007) indicated that treatment needs to focus, just as it does for contact sexual offenders, on areas such as: relationship skills, sexual preoccupation, emotion management, assertiveness, fantasy management, and coping with problematic life events. Consistent with this, Taylor and Quayle (2003) concluded that cognitive distortions and fantasy play as important a role in the offending behaviour of online offenders as they do for contact sexual offenders.

In a very interesting recent paper, Malesky, Ennis, and Gress, (2009) discuss Internet offences with reference to the four stable dynamic risk domains for contact sexual offenders established by Hanson and Harris (2001), pointing out the growing empirical support for these domains with this population. These factors are namely: sexual self-regulation, general self-regulation, intimacy deficits/interpersonal functioning, and offence-supportive cognitions. Malesky *et al.* (2009) cite evidence for the possible relevance of each factor to online offenders. For the sexual self-regulation domain they cite Quayle, Vaughan and Taylor (2006), who describe the Internet as a 'perfect vehicle' for avoiding or altering negative mood states through sexual stimulation because it is readily available, immediate and controllable. Malesky *et al.* (2009) consequently recommend that a primary treatment goal should be the acquisition of additional skills to manage stress in life and to nurture healthy relationships. The authors cite the relevance of Cooper's (1998) 'Triple A Engine of the Internet' (that is, anonymity, accessibility and affordability) to problems with self-regulation. These features of the Internet have, Malesky *et al.* observe, created the opportunity for near immediate gratification for anyone with an interest in child abuse images. The authors suggest that the treatment provider can assist the offender in examining how immediate gratification in general, and downloading child abuse images in particular, may inhibit their ability to fulfill their core values. With respect to intimacy deficits they refer to the work of Middleton *et al.* (2006) who found that many in their sample could be placed into the 'Intimacy Deficit pathway' category. Communication and intimacy skills need to be addressed for such offenders. With respect to offence-supportive cognitions they note the work of Quayle and Taylor (2002) who report that some online offenders will justify their sexual behaviour by framing it as an outlet for sexual urges that allows them to refrain from committing contact sexual offences. Because cognitive distortions impede motivation and behaviour change, the authors assert, they need to be identified and challenged early, and remain an ongoing treatment focus throughout therapy. Likely Malesky *et al.* (2009), Elliott and Beech (2009) state that most online offenders display clinically observable deficits in the dynamic risk areas set out by Hanson and Harris (2001).

At the end of the assessment section we argued for consideration of the crossover between offline and online offending. With regard to treatment, a number of authors have highlighted that any similarities in treatment needs between the two supposed categories of offenders might be due to the emerging evidence that there are many offenders who actually have offended using the Internet and in a hands-on manner. For example, Klain *et al.* (2001), in reviewing the criminal records of a group of offenders convicted for the possession of child abuse images found that between 20 per cent and 36 per cent had committed a previous contact sexual offence. Similarly, Seto and Eke (2005) found that 24 per cent of the online offenders in their sample had a prior sexual offence on record. In their study, Bourke and Hernandez (2009) reported that a group of 62 online offenders perpetrated contact sexual crimes against a total of 55 victims. After participation in the treatment programme, these offenders apparently reported perpetrating contact sexual crimes against an additional 1,379 victims. The authors argue that this means that many online offenders may be undetected contact sexual offenders. Consequently they strongly recommend against the formation of new psychological constructs to explain this behaviour, suggesting that existing ones are likely to be applicable also to online offenders. It is noted that this study relied on polygraph testing. However, as discussed earlier, we hold concerns about the likely reliability of such data given that in Federal US prisons release is contingent on satisfying staff views.

Specifically tailored approaches to treatment

In this section certain specifically designed treatment approaches taken with online offenders are presented and discussed.

i-SOTP

In 2001 the National Probation Service of England and Wales began national implementation of community-based sexual offender treatment programmes. While differing offending types were accommodated within these programmes, according to Middleton (2009) a need to move beyond a 'one size fits all' approach soon became apparent, not least in terms of meeting the needs of those with Internet convictions. According to figures provided by the UK Home Office (2006) Internet offences accounted for almost one-third of all sexual offence convictions in that year. Middleton suggests that this led to questions of suitability of the treatment programme content, appropriate treatment dosage and possible 'contamination effects' of exposure to contact child sexual offenders. The *Internet Sex Offender Treatment Programme* (i-SOTP) (Hayes, Archer and Middleton, 2006) was developed in direct response to these issues. As discussed by Davidson (2008) the theoretical basis of the programme draws upon the module developed by Quayle and Taylor (2003) along with the National Society for the Protection of Cruelty to Children (NSPCC) and Greater Manchester Probation Service, as well as with Finkelhor's 'multi-factorial' approach (1984) upon which the original probation programme was based. The programme also has a basis in the 'Good Lives Model' (Ward and Stewart, 2003).

The programme was originally designed to be delivered on an individual basis. In this format the programme lasts for between 20 and 30 sessions each of 90 minutes duration. Following a pilot, and extensive deliverer feedback, the programme was further developed to be delivered in a group format comprising 35 two-hour sessions, broken into the six modules (see Table 7.1). Completion of the programme is achieved between four and nine months depending on the choice of format and rate of delivery. Importantly, as Quayle (2007) points out, in delivering the i-SOTP much emphasis is placed on the style of the therapist given that successful sexual offender treatment outcomes have been found to be associated with particular therapist behaviours, (Marshall *et al.*, 2002; Marshall *et al.*, 2003; Serran, Fernandez, Marshall, and Mann, 2003).

The i-SOTP begins with motivational exercises designed to help the participant to identify values believed to be important and ways in which the offenders' behaviour has conflicted with these values, leading to the generation of future goals. The second module involves conducting a functional analysis of the participant's offence-related behaviour. The third module seeks to develop the participant's level of victim awareness, developing their awareness of the link between the production of images that they viewed and

Table 7.1 Modules of the i-SOTP Programme

Module 1	Motivation to Change
Module 2	Functional Analysis (What needs did offending meet?)
Module 3	Victim Awareness and Taking Responsibility
Module 4	Emotional Self-Regulation, Self-Management and Relationships
Module 5	Community, Collecting and Compulsivity
Module 6	Relapse Prevention and New Life Goals

Source: Hayes, Archer and Middleton (2006) i-SOTP Treatment Manual.

child abuse. Module four involves engaging in skills practice in order for them to develop an increased ability to deal with intimacy and/or emotional self-regulation deficits. Module five deals with the recognition of, and appropriate responses to, potential tendencies towards collecting and compulsive behaviours. This module also provides an opportunity to examine the needs of the participant that are met through joining pseudo-communities online and how these needs may be met more appropriately, as well as identifying and learning to control compulsive child abuse image accessing behaviours. A number of exercises are then undertaken to deal with deviant sexual fantasy. The final module incorporates and integrates the new skills into the offender's 'New Life Plan' (Middleton, 2009).

The stated specific dynamic risk factors targeted by i-SOTP are listed by Hayes *et al.* (2006) as: lack of readiness/motivation for change, intimacy deficits, emotional loneliness, low level of social skills and self-esteem associated with formation of insecure attachments, sexual interest in children, inability to deal with negative effect, sexual preoccupation, lack of victim awareness and lack of empathic response. Interestingly, all of these dynamic risk factors are also the treatment targets in the majority of programmes for contact sexual offenders. The National Probation Service (2005) even accepted that 'the current accredited programmes can be adapted to be relevant for online offenders' (p.2). This paper explains that one of the reasons why there was value in devising the i-SOTP was the ambivalence of some online offenders to work in the same group as rapists and child molesters, providing an initial barrier to treatment engagement. This has not been the experience of the present authors. It is understood that one of the main benefits of the i-SOTP programme, as seen by those who designed it, was to save resources by providing a shorter programme to online offenders, meaning that the higher dosage provision provided by the National Probation Service on their existing sexual offender programmes could be reserved for those who possess higher risk and needs.

Davidson (2008) suggests that some practitioners have even been sceptical themselves about the benefits of developing a tailored programme for online offenders given the current state of knowledge and research in the area. Davidson quotes one such practitioner as stating, 'It seems quite possible that they are more similar than different from the population of contact sexual offenders we already work with' (p.152). Another Probation Officer that Davidson interviewed pointed out that a number of online offenders attending the i-SOTP had previous convictions for contact sexual abuse.

There is however some emerging evidence demonstrating the effectiveness of the i-SOTP programme. Middleton (2009) presents the test results of 264 convicted offenders being supervised across the National Probation Service who attended the programme from 2006 to 2008. The key treatment targets were grouped into two main categories, addressing socio-affective functioning and changing pro-offending attitudes. Offenders were assessed as having changed post-treatment in the desired direction in 11 of the 12 socio-affective functioning measures. Middleton reports that the change in scores on the pro-offending attitude scales contained within the test battery were also in the desired direction. He further states that 53 per cent of the sample was assessed as having achieved a 'treated profile'. Such a profile was assigned if an offender was indistinguishable in the tests from a non-offending normative sample across a number of key measures that relate to both socio-affective functioning and pro-offending attitudes (Mandeville-Norden and Beech, 2004). Middleton suggests that these emerging data appear to be sufficiently encouraging, notwithstanding the limitations of the use of psychological tests with a group on which they were not validated, to justify the continuation of the wide-scale delivery of the treatment programme. Middleton makes the important point that a long-term reconviction study is still required in order to provide a more pertinent assessment of programme effectiveness as it relates to the overall goal of a reduction in recidivism. However, this programme is clearly an impressive and important step in the attempts to treat online offenders given its scale and research base, and as such this study assessing the clinical impact of treatment is an important one.

Other emerging tailored treatment programmes

Davidson (2008) refers to the fact that, other than the i-SOTP, there appear to be relatively few published programmes dedicated specifically to the treatment of online offenders. Davidson comments that those that are being developed are frequently small scale, ad hoc projects largely developed by practitioners. An example that falls into this category is the developmental work that is being conducted in the Netherlands at the Amsterdam Clinic (Davidson, 2008).

The Safe Network Inc. (2009) in New Zealand has developed the 'SAFE' programme for online offenders. According to their website (www.safenz.org), this is a specifically tailored approach for those who have committed online offences. Importantly, all participants must identify at least one family member or support person who is willing to be in contact with the programme and the client throughout the duration of their programme. The expected outcomes of the programme are for the participant to: commit to being offence-free, accept full responsibility for their offending, be accepted as a safe, responsible member of their family, be able to make safe intimate relationships, and to live a safe and healthy lifestyle. No known outcome data are currently available for this approach.

The Lucy Faithfull Foundation is a UK-based child protection charity which in recent years has provided a service called 'Inform Plus' which provides support, advice, and information for self-referred individuals who have been arrested for a child abusive image offence but are yet to receive a sentence, or who have not been provided with access to a sexual offender treatment programme. Groups usually consist of men with two–three facilitators, running over 10 weekly sessions of 2.5 hours. The programme targets Internet-specific factors, such as compulsion, collecting and online fantasy, in addition to victim empathy issues. It also involves planning and implementing effective self-management strategies in order to avoid re-offending. This is clearly an innovative initiative, however, as yet no outcome data have been presented and consequently its effectiveness is unclear. Whether a programme of such relatively short duration, particularly with an apparent absence of the targeting of a number of likely dynamic risk factors, will prove effective with such offenders remains to be seen. It is laudable that the charity offers, in the form of an education course, information and support to the partners, relatives and close friends of people who have been charged in relation to Internet child abuse images.

A cognitive-behavioural programme for online offenders, which also focuses on the psychodynamic aspects of personality development, has been run at the University Hospital in Basel by Graf and colleagues since 2002. This clinic offers both inpatient and outpatient treatment. Over the first four years, 40 men had attended the clinic, of whom 15 were included in treatment, from which a number were considered to meet inclusion criteria for group therapy. It is understood that those who were not deemed suitable for group treatment were more likely to have problems that could be described as 'Problematic Internet Use' rather than with accessing child abuse images. Davis (2001) characterises Problematic Internet Use, P.I.U., as relating to the experience of negative outcomes resulting from one's use of content-specific Internet functions, involving stimuli that are accessed online (for example, viewing sexually explicit materials). This can be distinguished from those who have committed Internet offences by way of the legality of the images, and, frequently, but not exclusively, the amount of time in one's life that accessing the images took up.

Notably, Graf and Dittman (2009) refer to the majority of those who have accessed child abuse images on the Internet as not needing treatment as they are not considered to possess a psychological disturbance or be at risk of committing a contact sexual offence. This view raises serious concerns given that not enough research has yet been conducted on the likelihood of transitioning from viewing images to contact sexual offending to be confident that treatment for this group is not necessary. Regardless of this possible transition, it is highly likely that those who were accessing such images had lives that were characterised by problems with which they were attempting to cope inappropriately. Untreated, these problems are likely to remain. In addition to this, the more one fantasises about, and masturbates to, particular images, the more likely it is that this sexual interest will become more arousing and hence appealing (see Laws and Marshall, 1990).

The Basel group treatment lasts for one year, consisting of weekly sessions of 1.5 hours, and is based upon relapse prevention models adapted for use with online offenders (Graf, 2006, cited in Davidson 2007). Graf suggests that the intention behind providing such a group was to deal with such offenders more efficiently, in a way that was more closely matched to their needs. For example, Graf hypothesises that such offenders are highly likely to have issues with boredom and loneliness, and to have unfulfilled sexual needs. The modules of this approach appear to be broadly similar to others described in this chapter such as the i-SOTP, but with more of an apparent emphasis on avoidance goals (that is, relapse prevention strategies) which as Mann, Webster, Schofield and Marshall (2004) contend, can be de-motivating and hence involve strategies that are more easily dropped than those which derive from the generation of goals which are more 'approach' focused. Positively, the programme is not highly manualised and there is scope within the programme to discuss important day-to-day issues that can aid treatment engagement and be used to make important learning points. Graf (2006, cited in Davidson, 2007) accepts that only very few men have graduated through the programme to date. It is nevertheless encouraging that after one year he was able to report that there had been no dropouts, and no known recidivism or serious risk behaviour. One future direction suggested by Graf was to include excerpts of the pornographic material collected by the offenders for therapeutic use in treatment, rather than to rely only on their verbal descriptions. We consider this to be of questionable utility and dubious long-term benefit.

In addition to more tailor-made programmes for online offenders a number of programmes for contact sexual offenders have been adapted and applied to address the needs of online offenders. According to Delmonico and Griffin (2008) cognitive behavioural programmes effective for contact sexual offenders are also likely to be effective for online offenders, as long as they have the flexibility to take into account any specific needs of such offenders. This is because the overall goals are likely to be the same: healthier cognitions and safe, non-exploitative sexual behaviour. Cooper, Golden and Marshall (2006) take the same view arguing that when an Internet user is accessing child abuse images he should be seen in the same light as a child molester and offered a full comprehensive sexual offender programme.

Burke, Sowerbutts, Blundell and Sherry (2002) report on the adaptations made to their programme (SOTAP–Sexual Offenders Treatment and Assessment Programme) for contact sexual offenders for use with individuals who have accessed child abuse images on the Internet. According to Burke and colleagues all of their online offenders recognise their sexual arousal to children, which, for some, dates back to early adolescence. In common with other programmes in the area of sexual offending behaviour, this programme focuses on early motivation for treatment, cognitive distortions, victim impact and cycles of offending behaviour. However, as Burke et al. point out, it is the specific content of the material addressed that distinguishes this programme from those delivered to contact sexual offenders.

The approach taken by Burke et al. to motivate these offenders involves assisting them in recognising the existence of victims of their crime and the possibility of progressing to committing a hands-on sexual offence against a child. According to the programme developers, more traditional methods of working with clients around victim impact and distorted thinking issues proved difficult, so they had to be more innovative in helping group members to recognise that a viewed image is a record of actual abuse. The clinical observations of Burke *et al.* were that individuals who access child abuse images are similar to those who commit hands-on offences in that their offending behaviour can be mapped out in a cycle format, and therefore the same concepts could be applied; while the general concepts were common, the specific aspects differed.

Following a pilot of the programme on an individual basis, the SOTAP treatment team developed a 25-week closed group programme for individuals who have accessed child abuse images. Due to low referral numbers this was adapted to an open group format. The authors' early observations were that the programme successfully addressed issues such as motivation to change, offence-supportive beliefs, victim impact, and the cycle of offending behaviour, offering tentative support for the efficacy of making such modifications to programmes for contact sexual offenders.

Results from our study (O'Brien and Webster, 2007) indicated that some of the online offenders had similar psychological problems to contact sexual offenders. It was concluded that elements of the cognitive behavioural treatment model currently in use for contact sexual offenders could have some relevance for online offenders. As discussed in detail earlier, the O'Brien and Webster study described the construction and preliminary validation of a measure of the attitudes and behaviours of men convicted of accessing Internet child abuse images. The two factors that emerged as deficit areas in this sample were distorted thinking and poor self-management, both of which are well-established treatment needs for contact sexual offenders. The main implication was that existing group work programmes, which are designed to address the empirically determined needs for contact sexual offenders in the areas of distorted thinking and self-management, may have some suitability for those men who have been convicted of Internet-related sexual offences. That is, provided that the programme is flexible enough in design and delivery to take account of the more specific distorted thought and self-management issues that may subsequently arise.

The Rockwood Programme for sexual offenders (Marshall, Marshall, Serran and Fernandez, 2006) is operated in the Canadian federal correctional system, and is the current programme of choice for those online offenders currently incarcerated in HMPS prisons (Adam Carter, Personal Communication, November 25th, 2009). The programme, as Marshall, Marshall, Serran and O'Brien (in press) explain is 'rolling' (or open-ended) in nature, which means that there is no fixed start or end point, with group members graduating when they have completed their own individualised treatment plan. This lends itself to the type of flexibility which has been indicated as necessary in order to address the wide range of presentational

Table 7.2 Phases of treatment in the Rockwood Programme for sexual offenders

Phase 1: Engagement	Phase 2: Modifying Treatment	Phase 3: Life-enhancement and Self-management
Outline of treatment	Criminogenic targets:	Modified Good Lives Model
Confidentiality	Attitudes & Cognitions	Limited set of Avoidance strategies
Enhancement of Self-Esteem/Reduction of Shame	Self-regulation issues	Generation of Support Groups
Improving Coping and Mood Management	Relationship problems	Release/discharge plans
Broaden Empathy	Sexual issues	

Source: Marshall et al. (in press)

issues, including those which relate to Internet offending which group members bring to treatment. The programme is conceptualised as a three-phase approach, as outlined in Table 7.2. The goal of Phase 1 is to effectively engage the client in the treatment process. The targets specifically introduced in Phase 2 are those that have been shown to predict recidivism in sexual offenders. The final phase of the programme aims at integrating what has been learned so far into plans for release and for the continued development of a more fulfilling life. The first step in this process involves identifying the goals and plans to achieve these targets within the framework of our conceptualisation of the 'Good Lives Model' (GLM).

As O'Brien, Marshall and Marshall (2008) note, the observed sexual recidivism rate for this programme among 534 sexual offenders treated and released for a mean of 5.4 years, is just 3.2 per cent, which is a marked decrease from the expected recidivism rate of 16.8 per cent (based on STATIC-99 scores). An increasing number of men who attend this programme are incarcerated for Internet offences. It is our experience that these online offenders present as having treated a profile as contact sexual offenders by the time they leave the programme. A more systematic evaluation is currently underway.

Delmonico and Griffin (2008) suggest that the problem with many existing sexual offender treatment programmes is that they have failed both to acknowledge the relevance of the Internet in the treatment of sexual offenders, and to meet these unique challenges. One of the key advantages of employing such a flexible approach as the one outlined above, is the opportunity to meet these challenges in a manner where existing over-manualised and highly structured programmes struggle. What such rigid programmes often also overlook is the need to address deficits in the upbringings of offenders (Sheldon and Howitt, 2007). The Rockwood Programme specifically attempts to address this concern. Delmonico and Griffin go on to suggest that for treatment to be effective it must address the underlying issues of intimacy, attachment, shame, sexuality, and emotional dysregulation, all of which are key treatment components in the Rockwood Programme.

This approach is exemplified by each group member completing an individual functional analysis that explores the context of their behaviour and the needs that were being met by this behaviour. As Middleton (2009) points out, this is likely to be necessary. The important element is, as Elliott and Beech (2009) note, ensuring that the online offenders are treated for the same criminogenic needs (dynamic risk factors) as are contact sexual offenders. In addition to more specific treatment tailored to the problems linked to these offenders' use of online technologies, The Rockwood Programme is able to address such additional targets as compulsivity, community engagement, online relationships, and collecting behaviours in addition to the more standard dynamic risk factors. We conclude that the more flexible existing approaches for treating contact sexual offenders can also be applied relatively straightforwardly for those with Internet offences.

Other (non-group based) approaches

There are a number of other, non-group based, approaches to addressing the problems of online offenders and they are briefly reviewed below.

Delmonico and Griffin (2008) make the point that online offenders should continue to have access to the Internet, not least to assist them in learning healthy ways to use it. Quayle (2005) suggested that while Internet interventions will not replace face-to-face care they are likely to grow in importance as a powerful component of psychological treatment over time. One such Internet treatment intervention can be found at www.croga.org. It is a free and anonymous service and is based on research sponsored by the Daphne Programme using funds from the European Commission. The website is designed to provide education about abusive images and the law, self-exploration including checklists and scales, and self-help based on cognitive-behavioural approaches to those who are worried about downloading child abuse images. The self-help exercises include: understanding how the illegal images are used, dealing with fantasy, dealing with negative emotions, the problems of online relationships and problematic collecting behaviour.

Another online initiative can be found at www.stopitnow.org. According to Quayle (2007), while the majority of people who are offered help for child abuse images related offences are within the criminal justice system, data from Stop-It-Now indicates that there are many people who identify themselves as having problems who are not convicted. The aim of the website is to stop child sexual abuse by encouraging abusers and potential abusers to seek help. Visitors to the site are asked several basic questions about their concerns. The answers lead to a customised selection of information and resources, and they are not required to reveal any personally identifiable information.

A number of authors, most notably Delmonico and Griffin (2008, 2009), have discussed, in addition to psychological treatment methods designed to help change the behaviour of those who have accessed Internet child abuse images, the utility of other more preventative methods of helping online offenders to manage their offence-related Internet usage. This is important, for as Beech, Elliott, Birgden, and Findlater (2008) suggest it is key for the policy response to Internet child abuse images to involve preventative as well as therapeutic approaches. Clearly, an important element of this is effective case management. Delmonico and Griffin (2009) suggest there are three such distinct strategies that could be considered by community case managers. The first is 'basic Internet management', which involves offenders creating an 'Internet Health Plan' covering future computer use. This may include making such changes as moving their computer to a high traffic area where the monitor is visible to others. The second strategy is 'electronic management', which involves Internet usage being monitored, filtered or blocked through the use of specialist software either monitored from the offender's home, or remotely. The third recommended strategy is 'medication management', which Delmonico and Griffin suggest may be an important treatment adjunct especially for those with mental health issues such as depression, anxiety, and attention deficits. Nelson, Soutullo, DelBello, and McElroy (2002) refer to the important role that the selective serotonin reuptake inhibitors have had for people suffering with hypersexuality, reducing obsessional thinking to the point that clients have much more of a sense of control over their thoughts and behaviours. Anti-androgenic medications have also been demonstrated to lower the sexual appetite of those with paraphilias (Galbreath, Berlin and Sawyer, 2002) and so may also be helpful for some online offenders.

An interesting preventative management proposition discussed by Williams (2005) is to have Internet Service Providers attach legal warnings to websites that may contain certain forms of pornography. However, Williams (2005) questions whether such warnings are likely to dissuade anyone from viewing child abuse images or whether they are in fact just as likely to elicit a 'forbidden fruit' response in potential viewers. Williams advocates for further research into this proposal.

Finally, an increasing number of treatment programmes for contact sexual offenders utilise the polygraph (McGrath, Cumming, and Burchard, 2003). Some research indicates that using this technology with such offenders leads them to disclose a substantially larger number of victims and more paraphilic behaviours (Ahlmeyer, Heil, McKee, and English, 2000; Wilcox and Sosnowski, 2005). According to Robilotta, Mercado and DeGue (2008), preliminary evidence suggests that the polygraph may also be of use in the assessment and treatment of online offenders, given that they may have extensive histories of contact, attempted contact, and non-contact offences prior to coming to the attention of authorities. However, as we have argued earlier, this, in our opinion, incorrectly assumes that the polygraph has established scientific merit, and that obtaining such full information about an individual's offending is crucial for the delivery of effective treatment.

Strategies employed to address problematic Internet use

A conclusion made by Armstrong (2009) is that the research on PIU may provide some treatment guidelines for those attempting to design treatment programmes for those convicted of Internet offences. Elliott and Beech (2009) also highlight the need to take into account the 'criminological situational factors, specific to the online environment' (p.191) that may be important to the understanding of online offenders. They point out that such factors frequently appear to have been overlooked in the Internet offender literature, noting the important roles that PIU and habituation to sexual stimuli may have in Internet offending. It is noted by Morahan-Martin and Schumacher (2000) and Weiss (2004) that those who present with PIU are also likely to possess many of the same treatment needs as those with child abusive image offences including: anxiety, depression, isolation, social deficits, shame, loneliness and poor intimacy.

According to Young (2008), information provided by Internet Porn Statistics showed that there were, at that time, about 4.2 million pornographic websites on the Internet, constituting 12 per cent of the total websites accessible. With this multitude of websites and abundance of sexually explicit material online, it is not surprising that some have referred to online pornography as the 'crack cocaine of the Internet' (Cooper, 1997, p.5), and a tempting new outlet to engage in sexually addictive behaviour (Carnes, 2001).

The PIU treatment literature will only be briefly mentioned given the main focus of this chapter (for a fuller review see Cooper *et al.*, 2006). Treatment strategies attempted with PIU include: online resources (Putnam, 2000; Cooper, 2002), pharmacological treatments (Kafka, 1997; Stein, Black, Shapira, and Spitzer, 2001), group treatment (Osborne, 2004) support groups (Carnes, 1989), functionally analysing the target behaviour (Southern, 2008), cognitive behavioural therapy (Young, 2008), motivational interviewing (Miller and Rollnick, 2002), dialectical behaviour therapy (Linehan, 1993), and family therapy (Recupero, 2008), as well as creating a Sexual Recovery Plan (Schneider and Weiss, 2001).

An interesting emerging psychological treatment approach, which has been applied recently to PIU is *Acceptance and Commitment Therapy* (ACT) (Hayes, Strosahl, and Wilson, 1999). ACT is a form of cognitive behavioural treatment that targets inner experiences (thoughts, feelings, bodily sensations) and utilises behaviour change strategies, targets problems as they are presently occurring, and has an empirical focus. ACT generally aims to decrease the effect of certain inner experiences on overt behaviour (for example, in this case the urges to view pornography), and increase the effects of other inner experiences (for example, the values underpinning engagement in more meaningful activities). Ultimately, the aim is for the client to move in a meaningful direction without particular regard for any inner experience (Twohig and Crosby, in press).

In the first published controlled treatment study of PIU, Twohig and Crosby (in press) report on six adult males who reported negative effects on quality of life from viewing Internet pornography. These clients were treated in eight 1.5 hour sessions. The authors report that treatment resulted in an 85 per cent reduction in viewing pornography on the Internet at post-treatment with results being maintained at three-month follow-up. Large increases were seen on measures of quality of life, and notable reductions were seen on measures of obsessive-compulsive behaviours. While this is seen as encouraging, the sample size is clearly small. In fact, as Cooper (2002) and Recupero (2008) both point out, as yet there is relatively little currently available, systematic, large-scale empirical research to support any particular treatment recommendations for PIU.

Conclusion

As Davidson (2008) points out much treatment practice with online offenders is new and innovative and the effectiveness of these different approaches, tailor-made and adapted, will not be apparent until the work has progressed sufficiently to allow for the collection of data and evaluation for online offenders. The key challenge, recognised by Wolak, Finkelhor, Mitchell, and Ybarra (2008) is to ensure that treatment approaches correspond to the needs of the offenders, accepting that many of the targets of existing programmes for contact sexual offenders are likely to also be applicable to online offenders. It is our view, as Elliott and Beech (2009) suggest, that wholesale change to treatment programmes for contact sexual offenders is not likely to be required, and that with a small number of specific theoretical additions, current treatment for online offenders based on sexual offender theory is likely to be appropriate and effective given the research studies conducted into their treatment needs. The most successful approaches are likely to be those that can flexibly address the needs of all offenders, irrespective of their particular offence, but based upon an individualised functional analysis of the problematic behaviour.

References

Ahlmeyer, S., Heil, P., McKee, B. and English, K. (2000). 'The Impact of Polygraphy on Admissions and Offenses in Adult Sex Offenders'. *Sexual Abuse: A Journal of Research and Treatment*, 12, 123–38.

American Psychiatric Association (1984). The Diagnostic and Statistical Manual of Mental Disorders, Fourth Edition (DSM-IV).

American Psychological Association (2009). The Standards for Educational and Psychological Testing. Copyright APA. Retrieved 25th November 2009 from: http://www.apa.org/science/standards.html

Arkowitz, S. and Vess, J. (2003). 'An evaluation of the Bumby RAPE and MOLEST Scales as Measures of Cognitive Distortions with Civilly Committed Sexual Offenders'. *Sexual Abuse: A Journal of Research and Treatment*, 15, 237–49.

Armstrong, J.A.E. (2009). Internet Child Pornography: An Examination of Attachment and Intimacy Deficits. Doctoral dissertation, Deakin University.

Bates, A. and Metcalf, C. (2007). 'Psychometric comparison of Internet and non-Internet sex offenders'. *Journal of Sexual Aggression*, 13, 11–20.

Beech, A.R., Elliott, I.A., Birgden, A. and Findlater, D. (2008). 'The Internet and Child Sexual Offending: A Criminological Review'. *Aggression and Violent Behaviour*, 13, 216–28.

Beech, A.R. and Hamilton-Giachritsis, C.E. (2005). 'Relationship between Therapeutic Climate and Treatment Outcome in Group-based Sexual Offender Treatment Programs'. *Sexual Abuse: A Journal of Research and Treatment*, 17, 127–40.

Bourke, M.L. and Hernandez, A.E. (2009). 'The "Butner Study" redux: A Report of the Incidence of Hands-on Child Victimization by Child Pornography Offenders'. *Journal of Family Violence*, 24, 183–91.

Bowlby, J. (1988). *A Secure Base*. New York: Basic Books.

Bumby, K.M. (1996). 'Assessing the Cognitive Distortions of Child Molesters and rapists: Development and Validation of the MOLEST and RAPE scales'. *Sexual Abuse: A Journal of Research and Treatment*, 8, 37–54.

Burgess, A.W., Mahoney, M., Visk, J. and Morgenbesser, L. (2008). 'Cyber Child Sexual Exploitation'. *Journal of Psychosocial Nursing and Mental Health Services*, 46, 38–45.

Burke, A., Sowerbutts, S., Blundell, B. and Sherry, M. (2002). 'Child Pornography and the Internet: Policing and Treatment Issues'. *Psychiatry, Psychology and Law*, 9, 79–84.

Buschman, J., Bogaerts, S., Foulger, S., Wilcox, D., Sosnowski, D. and Cushman, B. (2009). Sexual History Disclosure Polygraph Examinations With Cybercrime Offences. International Journal of Offender Therapy and Comparative Criminology. Retrieved November 25th 2009 from: http://ijo.sagepub.com/cgi/rapidpdf/0306624 X09334942v1

Buttell, F. and Carney, M.M. (2001). 'Treatment Provider Awareness of the Possible Impact of the Internet on the Treatment of Sex Offenders: An Alert to a Problem'. *Journal of Child Sexual Abuse: A Journal of Research and Treatment*, 10, 117–25.

Calkins, C., Mercado, S., DeGue, A. and Robilotta, S. (2008). 'Application of the Polygraph Examination in the Assessment and Treatment of Internet Sex Offenders'. *Journal of Forensic Psychology Practice*, 8, 383–393.

Carnes, P. (1989). *Contrary to Love: Helping the Sexual Addict*. Minneapolis, MN: CompCare.

Carnes, P. (2001). 'Cybersex, Courtship, and Escalating Arousal: Factors in Addictive Sexual Desire'. *Sexual Addiction and Compulsivity: Journal of Treatment and Prevention*, 8, 45–78.

Carter, A. (2009) 'Comment on Canadian Federal Correctional System', unpublished personal communication, 25th November.

Connolly, M. (2004). 'Developmental Trajectories and Sexual Offending: An Analysis of the Pathways Model'. *Qualitative Social Work*, 3, 39–59.

Cooper, A. (1997). 'The Internet and Sexuality: Into the Next Millennium'. *Journal of Sex Education and Therapy*, 22, 5–6.

Cooper, A. (1998). 'Sexuality and the Internet: Surfing into the New Millennium'. *CyberPsychology and Behavior*, 1, 187–93.

Cooper, A. (2002). *Sex & the Internet: A Guidebook for Clinicians*. New York: Brunner-Routledge.

Cooper, A., Golden, G. and Marshall, W.L. (2006). 'Online Sexuality and Online Sexual Problems: Skating on Thin Ice'. In W.L. Marshall, Y.M. Fernandez, L.E. Marshall and G.A. Serran (eds), *Sexual Offender Treatment: Controversial Issues*. West Sussex: John Wiley & Sons. pp. 79–91.

Davidson, J. (2007) Current Practice and Research into Internet Sex Offending, Risk Management Authority (Scotland), http://www.rmascotland.gov.uk/ViewFile.aspx?id=235

Davidson, J.C. (2008). *Child Sexual Abuse: Media Representations and Government Reactions*. New York: Routledge-Cavendish.

Davidson, J.L., Grove-Hills, J. and Martellozo, E. (2009). Evaluation of CEOP ThinkUknow Internet Safety Programme & Exploration of Young People's Internet Safety Knowledge. Centre for Abuse and Trauma Studies and Kingston University.

Davis, R.A. (2001). 'A Cognitive-Behavioural Model of Pathological Internet use'. *Computers in Human Behaviour*, 17, 187–95.

Delmonico, D.L. (1999). The Internet Sex Screening Test. Retrieved November 25th 2009 from www.Internetbehavior.com/sexualdeviance.

Delmonico, D.L. and Griffin, E.J. (2008). 'Online Sex Offending: Assessment and Treatment'. In D.R. Laws and W.T. O'Donohue (eds), *Sexual Deviance: Theory, assessment, and treatment*. (2nd ed.). New York, NY: Guilford Press. pp. 459–85.

Delmonico, D. and Griffin, E. (2009). Tech, Sex & Exploitation: Working with Online Sex Offenders. Paper presented at the 28th Annual Research and Treatment Conference of the Association for the Treatment of Sexual Abusers, Dallas.

Delmonico, D. L., and Miller, J. A. (2003). 'The Internet Sex Screening Test: A Comparison of Sexual Compulsives Versus Non-Sexual Compulsives'. *Sexual and Relationship Therapy*, 18, 261–76.

Elliott, I.A., Beech, A.R., Mandeville-Norden, R. and Hayes, E. (2009). 'Psychological Profiles of Internet Sexual Offenders'. *Sexual Abuse: A Journal of Research and Treatment*, 21, 76–92.

Elliott, I.A. and Beech, A.R. (2009). 'Understanding Online Child Pornography Use: Applying Sexual Offence Theory to Online Offenders'. *Aggression and Violent Behaviour*, 14, 180–93.

Ennis, L. (2009). Internet Sex Offending Through three Theoretical Lenses. Paper presented at the 28th Annual Research and Treatment Conference of the Association for the Treatment of Sexual Abusers, Dallas.

Fernandez, Y. (2008). An Examination of the Inter-rater Reliability of the STATIC-99 and STABLE 2007. Paper presented at the 27th Annual Conference of the Association for the Treatment of Sexual Abusers.

Finkelhor, D. (1984). *Child Sexual Abuse: New Theory and Research*. New York: Free Press.

Galbreath, N.W., Berlin, F.S. and Sawyer, D. (2002). Paraphilias and the Internet. In A. Cooper (ed.), *Sex and the Internet: A Guidebook for Clinicians*. New York: Brunner-Routledge. pp. 187–205.

Graf, M., Weisert, A. and Dittman, V. (2006). Preliminary Findings from a Cognitive-behavioral Group Therapy with Internet Sexual Offenders. Paper presented at the 9th International Conference of the International Association for the Treatment of Sexual Offenders, Hamburg.

Graf, M. and Dittman, V. (2009). Konsumenten illegaler Internet-Pornographie – psychische Auffälligkeiten und Risiken der Straffälligkeit, translates as 'Users of

Illegal Internet Pornography-Mental health problems and risks of delinquency. *Forens Psychiatr Psychol Kriminol*, 3, 99–106.

Hammond, S. (2004). In Calder, M. (Ed) *Child Sexual Abuse and the Internet: Tackling the New Frontier*. Russell House Publishing, Dorset.

Hare, R. D. (1991). *The Hare Psychopathy Checklist – Revised*. Toronto, Ontario: Multi-Health Systems.

Hanson. R.K. and Harris, A.J.R. (2001). 'A Structured Approach to Evaluating Change among Sexual Offenders'. *Sexual Abuse: A Journal of Research and Treatment*, 13, 105–22.

Hanson, R.K., Harris, A.J.R., Scott, T.L. and Helmus, L. (2007). Assessing the Risk of Sexual Offenders on Community Supervision: The Dynamic Supervision Project. Public Safety Canada 2007–05.

Hanson, R.K., and Morton-Bourgon, K. (2005). 'The Characteristics of Persistent Sexual Offenders: A Meta-analysis of Recidivism Studies'. *Journal of Consulting and Clinical Psychology*, 73, 1154–63.

Hayes, S.C., Strosahl, K.D. and Wilson, K.G. (1999). *Acceptance and Commitment Therapy: An Experiential Approach to Behaviour Change*. New York: Guilford Press.

Hayes, E., Archer, D. and Middleton, D. (2006). Internet Sexual Offending Treatment Programme (i-SOTP) Theory Manual.

Iacono, W. and Lykken, D. T. (1997). The Scientific Status of Research on the Polygraph Techniques: The Case against Polygraph Tests. In D. L. Faigman, D. H. Kaye, M. J. Saks, and J. Sanders (eds), *Modern Scientific Evidence: The Law and Science of Expert Testimony*. St Paul, MN: West. pp. 582–618.

Kafka, M.P. (1997). Hypersexual Desire in Males: An Operational Definition and Clinical Implications for Men with Paraphilias and Paraphilia-related Disorders. *Archives of Sexual Behavior*, 26, 505–26.

Klain, E. J., Davies, H. J. and Hicks, M. A. (2001). Child Pornography: The Criminal Justice-system Response. Retrieved September 1, 2007, from http://www.missingkids.com/en_US/publications/NC81.pdf.

Laulik, S., Allam, J. and Sheridan, L. (2007). An Investigation into Maladaptive Personality Functioning in Internet Sex Offenders. *Psychology, Crime and Law*, 3, 523–35.

Laws, D.R. and Marshall, W.L. (1990). A Conditioning Theory of the Etiology and Maintenance of Deviant Sexual Preference and behavior. In W.L. Marshall, D.R.Laws and H.E. Barbaree (eds), *Handbook of Sexual Assault: Issues, Theories and treatment of the offender*. New York: Plenum Press. pp. 209–29.

Laws, D.R., and Marshall, W.L. (2003a). A Brief History of Behavioral and Cognitive Behavioral Approaches to Sexual Offenders: Part 1. Early Developments. *Sexual Abuse: A Journal of Research and Treatment*, 15, 75–92.

Laws, D.R. and Marshall, W.L. (2003b). A Brief History of Behavioral and Cognitive Behavioral Approaches to Sexual Offender Treatment: Part 2. The Modern Era. *Sexual Abuse: A Journal of Research and Treatment*, 15, 93–120.

Linehan, M.M. (1993). *Cognitive Behavioral Treatment of Borderline Personality Disorder*. New York, NY: Guilford Press.

Lucy Faithfull Foundation (2009). Information retrieved November 27 2009 from http://lucyfaithfull.org/working-with-Internet-abuse/inform – inform-plus.aspx.

Malesky, L.A. and Ennis, L. (2004). Supportive distortions: An Analysis of Posts on a Pedophile Internet Message Board. *Journal of Addictions & Offender Counseling*, 24, 92–100.

Malesky, L.A., Ennis, L. and Gress, C.L.Z (2009). 'Child pornography and the Internet'. In F.M. Saleh, A.J. Grudzinskas, J.M. Bradford and D.J. Brodsky (eds) *Sex Offenders: Identification, Risk Assessment, Treatment, and Legal Issues.* New York: Oxford University Press. pp. 185–92.

Mandeville-Norden, R. and Beech, A. R. (2004). 'Community Based Treatment of Sex Offenders'. *Journal of Sexual Aggression*, 10, 193–214.

Mann, R.E., Webster, S.D., Schofield, C. and Marshall, W.L. (2004). 'Approach vs. Avoidance Goals in Relapse Prevention with Sexual Offenders'. *Sexual Abuse: A Journal of Research and Treatment*, 16, 65–75.

Marshall, W.L., Anderson, D. and Fernandez, Y.M. (1999). *Cognitive Behavioural Treatment of Sexual Offenders.* New York: Wiley.

Marshall, W.L., Fernandez, Y.M., Serran, G.A., Mulloy, R., Thornton, D., Mann, R.E. and Anderson, D. (2003). Process Variables in the Treatment of Sexual Offenders: A Review of the Relevant Literature. *Aggression and Violent Behaviour: A Review Journal*, 8, 205–34.

Marshall, W. L., Ward, T., Mann, R. E., Moulden, H., Fernandez, Y. M., Serran, G., and Marshall, L. E. (2005). 'Working positively with sexual offenders: Maximizing the effectiveness of treatment'. *Journal of Interpersonal Violence.* 20, 1096–1114.

Marshall, W.L., Marshall, L.E., Serran, G.A. and Fernandez, Y.M. (2006). *Treating Sexual Offenders: An Integrated Approach.* New York: Routledge.

Marshall, W.L., Marshall, L.E., Serran, G.A. and O'Brien, M.D. (in press). *Treatment of Sexual Offenders: A Positive Approach.* Washington, D.C.: American Psychological Association.

Marshall, W.L., Serran, G.A., Moulden, H., Mulloy, R., Fernandez, Y.M., Mann, R.E. and Thornton, D. (2002). 'Therapist Features in Sexual Offender Treatment: Their Reliable Identification and Influence on Behaviour Change'. *Clinical Psychology and Psychotherapy*, 9, 395–405.

McGrath, R. J., Cumming, G. and Burchard, B. L. (2003). *Current Practices and Trends in Sexual Abuser Management: The Safer Society 2002 Nationwide Survey.* Brandon, VT: Safer Society Press.

Middleton, D., Elliott, I.A., Mandeville-Norden, R. and Beech, A.R. (2006). 'An Investigation into the Applicability of the Ward and Siegert Pathways Model of Child Sexual Abuse with Internet Offenders'. *Psychology, Crime and Law*, 12, 589–603.

Middleton, D. (2009). 'Does Treatment Work with Internet Sex Offenders? Emerging Findings from the Internet Sex Offender Treatment Programme (i-SOTP)'. *Journal of Sexual Aggression*, 15, 5–19.

Miller, W. R. and Rollnick, S. (2002). *Motivational Interviewing: Preparing People for Change.* New York: Guilford Press.

Morahan-Martin, J. and Schumacher, P. (2000). 'Incidence and Correlates of Pathological Internet use Among College Students'. *Computers in Human Behaviour*, 16, 13–29.

McNaughton-Nicholls, C., Callanan, M., Legard, R., Tomaszewski, W., Purdon, S. and Webster, S.D. (2009) Examining Implementation of the Stable and Acute Dynamic Risk Assessment Tool Pilot in England and Wales. Home Office.

National Probation Service (2005). Probation Circular 92 – Launch of New Internet Sex Offender Treatment Programme (i-SOTP). Retrieved November 27 2009 from http://www.probation2000.com/pit/circulars/PC92%202005.pdf.

Nelson, E.B., Soutullo, C.A., DelBello, M.P. and McElroy, S.L. (2002). 'The Psychopharmacological Treatment of Sexual Offenders'. In B.Schwartz (ed.), *The Sex*

Offender: Current Treatment Modalities and System Issues, vol. IV. Kingston, NJ: Civic Research Institute. pp. 13.1–13.30.

Nicholls, H.R. and Molinder, I. (1984). *The Multiphasic Sex Inventory*. Washington: Nichols and Molinder Assessments.

NSPCC (2005). 'Policy Summary: Child Abuse Images', available at http://www.nspcc.org.uk./Inform/PolicyandPublicaffairs/Policysummaries/childabuseimages

Nunnaly, J. (1978). *Psychometric Theory*. New York: McGraw-Hill.

Office of Public Sector Information (2003). Sexual Offences Act 2003. Crown copyright. Retrieved, November 25, 2009 from www.opsi.gov.uk/Acts/acts2003/ukpga_20030042_en_1.

O'Brien, M.D. and Webster, S.D. (2007). The Construction and Preliminary Validation of the Internet Behaviours and Attitudes Questionnaire (IBAQ). *Sexual Abuse: A Journal of Research and Treatment*, 19, 237–56.

O'Brien, M.D., Marshall, L.E. and Marshall, W.L. (2008). 'Sexual Addiction'. In D.L. Rowland and L. Incrocci (eds), *Handbook of Sexual and Gender Identity Disorders*. New Jersey: John Wiley and Sons. pp. 587–602.

Osborn, J. and Beech, A.R. (2006). The Suitability of Risk Matrix 2000 for use with Internet Sex Offenders. Unpublished Masters Thesis, University of Birmingham, U.K.

Osborne, C.S. (2004). 'A Group Model for the Treatment of Problematic Internet Related Sexual Behaviours'. *Sexual and Relationship Therapy*, 19, 87–99.

Paulhus, D.L. (1984). 'Two Component Models of Socially Desirable Responding'. *Journal of Personality and Social Psychology*, 46 (3), 598–609.

Paulhus, D.L. (1998). Manual for the Balanced Inventory of Desirable Responding: Version 7. Toronto/Buffalo: Multi-Health Systems.

Putnam, D.E. (2000). 'Initiation and Maintenance of Online Sexual Compulsivity: Implications for Assessment and Treatment'. *CyberPsychology and Behaviour*, 3, 553–63.

Putnam, D.E. and Maheu, M.M. (2000). 'Online Sexual Addiction and Compulsivity: Integrating Web Resources and Behavioural Telehealth in Treatment'. *Sexual Addiction and Compulsivity: Journal of Treatment and Prevention*, 7, 91–112.

Quayle, E. (2007). Intervention with Internet offenders. Paper presented at the Conference of the Australia New Zealand Association for the Treatment of Sexual Abuse.

Quayle, E. (2008). 'Online Sexual Offending: Psychopathology and Theory'. In D.R. Laws and W.T. O'Donohue (eds). *Sexual Deviance: Theory, Assessment and Treatment* (2nd Ed.). New York: Guildford Press.

Quayle, E. and Taylor, M. (2002). 'Child Pornography and the Internet: Perpetuating a cycle of abuse'. *Deviant Behavior: An Interdisciplinary Journal*, 23, 331–61.

Quayle, E. and Taylor, M. (2003). Model of Problematic Internet use in People with a Sexual Interest in Children. *Cyber Psychology and Behavior*, 6, 93–106.

Quayle, E. (2005). 'The Internet as a Therapeutic Medium'. In E.Quayle and M. Taylor (eds), *Viewing Child Pornography on the Internet: Understanding the offence, Managing the Offender, and Helping the Victims*. Lyme Regis, UK: Russell House. pp. 127–44.

Quayle, E., Vaughan, M. and Taylor, M. (2006). 'Sex Offenders, Internet Child Abuse Images and Emotional Avoidance: The Importance of Values'. *Aggression and Violent Behavior*, 11, 1–11.

Recupero, P.R. (2008). 'Forensic Evaluation of Problematic Internet use'. *Journal of the American Academy of Psychiatry and the Law*, 36, 505–14.

Robilotta, S.A., Mercado, C.C. and DeGue, S. (2008). 'Application of the Polygraph Examination in the Assessment and Treatment of Internet Sex Offenders'. *Journal of Forensic Psychology Practice*, 8, 383–93.

Rooney, F. (2003). The Internet and Child Sexual Abuse Personality Indicators of Abusive Behaviour. (Masters dissertation, University of Dublin, 2003).

Safe Network Inc. (2009). Information retrieved November 27 2009 from http://www. safenz.org/Internet.htm.

Schneider, J.P. and Weiss, R. (2001). *Cybersex Exposed*. Center City, MN: Hazelden Publishing and Educational Services.

Sentencing Advisory Panel (2002). The Panel's advice to the Court of Appeal on Offenses Involving Child Pornography. Crown copyright. Retrieved, November 25, 2009 from http://www.sentencing-guidelines.gov.uk.

Serran, G.A., Fernandez, Y.M., Marshall, W.L. and Mann, R.E. (2003). 'Process Issues in Treatment: Application to Sexual Offender Programs'. *Professional Psychology: Research and Practice*, 34, 368–74.

Seto, M. C., and Eke, A. W. (2005). 'The Criminal Histories and Later Offending of Child Pornography Offenders'. *Sexual Abuse: A Journal of Research and Treatment*, 17, 201–10.

Seto, M. C., Cantor, J. M. and Blanchard, R. (2006). 'Child Pornography Offences are a Valid Diagnostic Indicator of Pedophilia'. *Journal of Abnormal Psychology*, 115, 610–15.

Seto, M. (2009). 'A Picture is Worth a Thousand Words': What do we Know about Child Pornography Offenders? Paper presented at the 28th Annual Research and Treatment Conference of the Association for the Treatment of Sexual Abusers, Dallas.

Shaw, E. and Imhof, E.A. (2009, October). Internet Child Pornography Offenders: Evaluation, Treatment and Management. Paper presented at the 28th Annual Research and Treatment Conference of the Association for the Treatment of Sexual Abusers, Dallas.

Sheldon, K. and Howitt, D. (2007). *Sex Offenders and the Internet*. West Sussex: John Wiley and Sons.

Shingler, J. and Mann, R.E. (2006). 'Collaboration in Clinical Work with Sexual Offenders: Treatment and Risk Assessment'. In: W.L. Marshall (ed). *Sexual Offender Treatment: Controversial Issues*. Chichester: John Wiley.

Southern, S. (2008). 'Treatment of Compulsive Cybersex Behaviour'. *Psychiatric Clinics of North America,* 31, 697–712.

Stein, D.J., Black, D.W., Shapira, N.A. and Spitzer, R.L. (2001). 'Hypersexual Disorder and Preoccupation with Internet Pornography'. *The American Journal of Psychiatry*, 158, 1590–94.

Sullivan, J. and Beech, A. (2004). 'Assessing Internet Sex Offenders'. In M. Calder (ed), *Child Sexual Abuse and the Internet: Tackling the New Frontier*. Lyme Regis, Dorset: Russell House Publishing. pp. 69–83.

Taylor, M., Quayle, E. and Holland, G. (2001). Child Pornography, the Internet and Offending. *Canadian Journal of Policy Research*, 2, 94–100.

Taylor, M. and Quayle, E. (2003). *Child Pornography: An Internet Crime*. New York: Brunner-Routledge.

Taylor, M., Holland, G. and Quayle, E. (2001). 'Typology of Peadophile Picture Collections'. *The Police Journal,* 7, 97–107.

Thornton, D. (2002). 'Constructing and Testing a Framework for Dynamic Risk Assessment'. *Sexual Abuse: A Journal of Research and Treatment*. 14 (2), 139–53.

Thronton, D., Mann, R., Webster, S., Blud, L., Travers, R., Friendship, C. and Erikson, M. (2003). 'Distinguishing and combining risks for sexual and violent recidivism'. In R. Prentky, E. Janus, M. Seto and A.W. Burgess (eds.). *Understanding and Managing Sexually Coercive Behaviour.* Annals of the New York Academy of Science, 989: 225–35.

Twohig, M. P. and Crosby, J. M. (in press). 'Acceptance and Commitment Therapy as a Treatment for Problematic Internet Pornography Viewing'. *Behaviour Therapy.*

U.K. Home Office (2006). Criminal Statistics. Home Office Statistical Bulletin (19/06). RDS Office for Criminal Justice Reform. p. 51.

Ward, T. and Siegert, R.J. (2002). 'Toward a Comprehensive Theory of Child Sexual Abuse: A theory knitting perspective'. *Psychology, Crime, and Law*, 8, 319–51.

Ward, T. and Stewart, C. (2003). 'Criminogenic Needs and Human Needs: A Theoretical Model'. *Psychology, Crime and Law*, 9, 125–43.

Webb, L., Craissati, J. and Keen, S. (2007). 'Characteristics of Internet Child Pornography Offenders: A Comparison with Child Molesters.' *Sexual Abuse: A Journal of Research and Treatment*, 19, 449–65.

Webster, S.D. (2005). 'Pathways to sexual offence recidivism following treatment: An evaluation of the Ward and Hudson self-regulation model of relapse'. *The Journal of Interpersonal Violence*, 20, 1175–1196.

Webster, S.D. and Marshall, W.L. (2004). 'Generating Data with Sexual Offenders using Qualitative Material: A paradigm to Complement not Compete with Quantitative methodology'. *Journal of Sexual Aggression*, 10, 117–22.

Webster, S., Davidson, J., Bifulco, A., Pham, T. and Casetti, V. (2009). 'European Online Grooming Project: Progress Report Covering period: 1 June 2009–31 December 2009' (7/10 forthcoming at http://www.natcen.ac.uk/study/european-online-grooming-research)

Webster, S., Davidson, J., Bifulco, A., Gottschalk, P., Caretti, V., Pham T., and Grove-Hills, J. (2010). *The European Online Grooming Project: Scoping Report.* European Commission Safer Internet Plus Programme. Luxembourg.

Weiss, R. (2004). Sex addiction. In Coombs, R.H. (ed.) *Handbook of Addictive Disorders.* New Jersey: John Wiley and Sons. pp. 233–72.

Wilcox, D. T. and Sosnowski, D. E. (2005). 'Polygraph examination of British Sexual Offenders: A Pilot Study on Sexual Disclosure Testing'. *Journal of Sexual Aggression*, 11, 3–25.

Wilkerson, J.R. and Lang, S.W. (2003). Portfolios, the Pied Piper of Teacher certification Assessments: Legal and Psychometric Issues. Education Policy Analysis Achieves, 11 No. 45. Retrieved on 25th November 2009.

Williams, K.S. (2005). 'Facilitating Safer Choices: Use of Warnings to Dissuade Viewing of Pornography on the Internet'. *Child Abuse Review*, 14, 415–29.

Wolak, J., Finkelhor, D., Mitchell, K.J. and Ybarra, M.L. (2008). Online 'Predators' and Their Victims. *American Psychologist*, 63, 111–28.

Wortley, R. and Smallbone, S. (2006). Child pornography on the Internet. Washington, DC: Office of Community Oriented Policing Services, U.S. Department of Justice.

Young, K.S. (2008). 'Internet Sex Addiction Risk Factors, Stages of Development, and Treatment'. *American Behavioural Scientist*, 52, 21–37.

Conclusion

Julia Davidson and Petter Gottschalk

This book has explored the dangers the Internet poses to children, the way in which sex offenders use the Internet to perpetrate sexual abuse, measures to both protect young people and to treat offenders. Recent research (Davidson *et al.*, 2009; Livingstone, 2009) has played a key role in raising awareness about children's use of the Internet and online risks as have organisations such as the Virtual Global Taskforce (VGT). However, early research suggested that the routine education of children about Internet sexual abuse in the context of formal education is an important aspect in raising awareness about Internet safety amongst young people, parents and teachers (Davidson and Martellozzo, 2005, 2008). Internet safety is becoming an integral element of formal education in many countries, and organisations such as the European Commission have funded programmes to set up safety nodes throughout Europe; the nodes act as a focal point for the dissemination of Internet safety information via schools across Europe. The Commission has also funded a research programme to inform practice. It is clear that much good work has been undertaken on behalf of children in this area. However, the issue is really much wider than teaching online safety; teachers participating in research conducted by Davidson and Martellozzo in 2005 suggested that it seems pointless to warn children about the dangers they may encounter in cyberspace unless this information is imparted in the context of wider education about sexual abuse and appropriate sexual behaviour. Schools should play an active role in educating children about sexual abuse and safety strategies in the context of the national curriculum (as is the case in some American states and as is planned for the UK during 2010). In order to do this effectively, training and guidance should be provided for teachers and such work should routinely involve parents and carers. A further challenge in terms of effective Internet safety education is that of engaging effectively with teenagers who may not believe that providing personal information to strangers or 'virtual friends' on SNS is anything other than acceptable behaviour. As adults we simply do not know enough about online teenage behaviour and norms to be able to create effective, meaningful educational programmes.

The challenge of working with offenders is rarely discussed in the same context as preventative work with children, but effective educational awareness should be based upon good research exploring offender online behaviour, use of new technology and victim-targeting practices. We need to be prepared to work with offenders in order to understand their behaviour in order to better protect children in the virtual world. One such study is currently ongoing; the European Online Grooming Project (Webster *et.al.*, 2009) is funded by the European Commission safer Internet programme. The European Online Grooming Project has three separate but interlinked phases. The first is a scooping project, the second and third phases include interviews with convicted online groomers across Europe and dissemination activity. The research has the following overarching objectives:

- describe the behaviour of both offenders who groom and young people who are 'groomed' and explore differences within each group and how these differences may have a bearing on offence outcome
- describe how information, communication technology is used to facilitate the process of online grooming
- further the current low knowledge base about the way in which young people are selected and prepared for abuse online
- make a significant contribution to the development of educational awareness and preventative initiatives aimed at parents and young people.

The research will be completed in 2011.

The risk assessment, sentencing and treatment of Internet sex offenders also presents new challenges and practice should be based upon good empirical evidence. The difficulty is that research is in its infancy and there is a danger in proceeding on the basis of current policing, assessment and treatment practice with sex offenders which may or may not be relevant in work with Internet abusers. In the UK, Multi Agency Protection Panel Arrangements potentially provide a good structure in which to locate some of this work but practitioners have suggested that inadequate resourcing results in a lack of monitoring of Internet sexual abusers and interagency communication remains problematic in some areas (Davidson, 2007).

In describing the attempts made by law enforcement agencies to reduce the problem of online abuse, this book has shown that despite moves on the part of agencies, governments, the IT industry and organisations such as the Virtual Global Taskforce to control online abuse, many offenders continue to utilise the Internet to perpetrate abuse. It is suggested that governments are failing to make both the continuing trade in indecent images of children and the online grooming of children a high enough, properly resourced, political priority. The hidden nature of the offending and lack of public awareness makes this possible. Internet abuse presents new challenges to law enforcement agencies accustomed to working within specific geographical boundaries. The Internet transcends such boundaries and facilitates the formation of global offending networks. Consequently, centralised, international efforts are required to both understand and address this form of offending behaviour, alongside national initiatives. The International Corporation for Assigned Names and Numbers (ICANN) is currently the most powerful force in global Internet governance. ICANN regularly makes policies fundamental to any potential for protecting children online. ICANN has the opportunity to influence policies affecting the development of the Internet. Carr and Hilton (Chapter 3) have suggested that fundamental areas of concern and guidance for the adoption of legislation include:

1. clear and shared definition of a 'child' in accordance with the UN Convention of the Rights of the Child
2. defining 'child abuse images' to include specific computer and Internet terminology
3. creating criminal penalties for parents or guardians who agree to or who facilitate their child's participation in child abuse images
4. creating penalties for those who make known to others where to find child abuse images
5. enhancing penalties for repeat offenders, organised crime members and other aggravated factors to be considered upon sentencing
6. ensuring that children have access to justice, are protected through the criminal justice process and that their needs and welfare remains a core concern and that they have access to rehabilitation and welfare.

Carr (2006) advocates a global initiative. He is correct in suggesting that the key issue is one of effective leadership, and that a 'global leadership mechanism' (2006, p1) should be developed. This mechanism, it is suggested, should take the form of a new non-governmental organisation (NGO) or a network that draws upon existing NGOs. This central body would act to scrutinise and advise governments, law enforcement agencies and the industry. It would also provide a hitherto absent degree of IT industry public accountability. This is undeniably an essential move as, at present, attempts to protect children online are ad hoc and some police forces have only just begun to recognise the scale of the problem. The difficulty will be in agreeing upon and establishing a central mechanism that is really able to scrutinise international approaches to the problem and that will have the legal power to intervene effectively where there is inaction or indifference.

References

Carr, J. (2006) 'Out of Sight, out of Mind: Tackling Child Sexual Abuse Images on the Internet – a Global Challenge', NCH, The Children's Charity.

Davidson, J. and Martellozzo, E. (2005) 'Policing The Internet And Protecting Children From Sex Offenders Online: When Strangers Become 'Virtual Friends',

http://www.oii.ox.ac.uk/research/cybersafety/extensions.pdfs/papers/julis_davidson.
pdf.

Davidson, J. (2007) 'Current Practice and Research into Internet Sex Offending',
Report prepared on behalf of the Risk Management Authority (Scotland). http://
www.rmascotland.gov.uk/currentprojects.aspx.

Davidson, J. and Martellozzo, E. (2008) 'Protecting Vulnerable Young People in
Cyberspace from Sexual Abuse: Raising Awareness and Responding Globally',
Police Practice & Research An International Journal. ISSN 1561–4263.

Davidson, J., Lorenz,M., Martellozzo, E. and Grove-Hills, J. (2009) 'Evaluation of
CEOP ThinkUKnow Internet Safety Programme and Exploration of Young
People's Internet Safety Knowledge'. Centre for Abuse and Trauma Studies,
Publication (Kingston University, London). Available at: http://www.cats-rp.org.uk/
media_and_news.htm

Livingstone, S. (2009) 'EU kids Online Report', Conference, June, LSE, London.

Webster, S., Davidson, J., Bifulco, A., Gottschalk, P., Caretti., Pham, T. (2009)
'European Online Grooming Project Progress Report'. Available at http://www.
natcen.ac.uk/study/european-online-grooming-research/details (from 1/5/2010).

Index